NARRATIVE MODE AND THEOLOGICAL CLAIM IN JOHANNINE LITERATURE

BIBLICAL SCHOLARSHIP IN NORTH AMERICA

Number 30

NARRATIVE MODE AND THEOLOGICAL CLAIM IN JOHANNINE LITERATURE

Essays in Honor of Gail R. O'Day

Edited by

Lynn R. Huber, Susan E. Hylen, and William M. Wright IV

SBL PRESS
Atlanta

Copyright © 2021 by SBL Press

All rights reserved. No part of this work may be reproduced or transmitted in any form or by any means, electronic or mechanical, including photocopying and recording, or by means of any information storage or retrieval system, except as may be expressly permitted by the 1976 Copyright Act or in writing from the publisher. Requests for permission should be addressed in writing to the Rights and Permissions Office, SBL Press, 825 Houston Mill Road, Atlanta, GA 30329 USA.

Library of Congress Control Number: 2021944615

Contents

Abbreviations vii

Introduction: The Role of History in Narrative Studies 1
    Susan E. Hylen

Part 1

Unfolding Story and Theology in the Raising of Lazarus
in John 11–12 19
    Vernon K. Robbins

Why Is Pilate So Afraid in John 19:8? Pilate's Fear and the
Dynamics of Power in John 18:28–19:16 39
    Gilberto A. Ruiz

The Resurrection Message and the Literary Shape of
John 20–21 65
    Yoshimi Azuma

A Note on Ambiguity in the Book of Revelation 83
    Patrick Gray

Revealing Christ in Revelation 95
    Lynn R. Huber

Part 2

Nicodemus, Misunderstanding, and the Pedagogy of the
Incarnation in Chrysostom's *Homilies on John* 111
    William M. Wright IV

A Gospel Homiletic 129
    Karoline M. Lewis

Learning How to Tell Time 141
    Thomas G. Long

Stop Waiting, It's Time for an Attitude Adjustment 147
    Teresa Fry Brown

Disciple, Will You Let Me Wash Your Feet? 163
    Veronice Miles

The Time of Revelation 169
    Ted A. Smith

Bibliography 175

Contributors 187

Scripture Index 189
Modern Authors Index 194
Subject Index 196

Abbreviations

AB	Anchor Bible
ABRL	Anchor Bible Reference Library
A.J.	Josephus, *Antiquitates judaicae*
Anom.	Chrysostom, *Contra Anomoeos*
ANTC	Abingdon New Testament Commentaries
Apoc. Mos.	Apocalypse of Moses
AYB	Anchor Yale Bible
BETL	Bibliotheca Ephemeridum Theologicarum Lovaniensium
Bib	*Biblica*
BibInt	*Biblical Interpretation*
BibInt	Biblical Interpretation Series
B.J.	Josephus, *Bellum judaicum*
BZNW	Beihefte zur Zeitschrift für die neutestamentliche Wissenschaft
CBQ	*Catholic Biblical Quarterly*
CBQMS	Catholic Biblical Quarterly Monograph Series
Civ.	Augustine, *De civitate Dei*
ECF	Early Christian Fathers
Ep. Tra.	Pliny, *Epistulae ad Trajanum*
ESEC	Emory Studies in Early Christianity
EstBib	*Estudios biblicos*
ETL	*Ephemerides Theologicae Lovanienses*
FC	Fathers of the Church
Hesperia	*Hesperia: The Journal of the American School of Classical Studies at Athens*
Hist. eccl.	Eusebius, *Historia ecclesiastica*
Hom. Gen.	Chrysostom, *Homiliae in Genesim*
Hom. Jer.	Origen, *Homiliae in Jeremiam*

Hom. Jo.	Chrysostom, *Homiliae in Joannem*
Hom. Matt. 26:39	Chrysostom, *In illud: Pater, si possibile est, transeat*
IBC	Interpretation: A Bible Commentary for Teaching and Preaching
ICC	International Critical Commentary
Inc.	Athanasius, *De incarnatione*
Inst.	Quintillian, *Institutio oratoria*
Int	*Interpretation*
ITQ	*Irish Theological Quarterly*
JBL	*Journal of Biblical Literature*
JFSR	*Journal of Feminist Studies in Religion*
JTS	*Journal of Theological Studies*
LCL	Loeb Classical Library
Legat.	Philo, *Legatio ad Gaium*
LNTS	The Library of New Testament Studies
LSJ	Liddell, Henry George, Robert Scott, Henry Stuart Jones. *A Greek-English Lexicon*. 9th ed. with revised supplement. Oxford: Clarendon, 1996.
NCB	New Century Bible
NCBC	New Cambridge Bible Commentary
NIB	*The New Interpreter's Bible*
NIGTC	New International Greek Testament Commentary
NovT	*Novum Testamentum*
NPNF	*A Select Library of Nicene and Post-Nicene Fathers of the Christian Church*. Edited by Philip Schaff and Henry Wace. 28 vols. in 2 series. 1886–1889.
NTL	New Testament Library
PG	Patrologia Graeca
RB	*Revue biblique*
RBS	Resources for Biblical Studies
SBLDS	Society of Biblical Literature Dissertation Series
SJT	*Scottish Journal of Theology*
SNTSMS	Society for New Testament Studies Monograph Series
SP	Sacra Pagina
StBibLit	Studies in Biblical Literature
SymS	Symposium Series
VC	*Vigiliae Christianae*
Vit. Apoll.	Apollonius, *Vita Apollonii*
WBC	Word Biblical Commentary

WUNT   Wissenschaftliche Untersuchungen zum Neuen Testament

Introduction: The Role of History in Narrative Studies

Susan E. Hylen

Attention to biblical texts as literature emerged in the 1970s and 1980s as a field of study. Although earlier historical-critical scholars also discussed literary elements of the text, they used these details to clarify the historical context in which the text was produced. By contrast, newer studies engaged a wider variety of literary techniques, such as irony, metaphor, and plot, toward a different goal of describing the meaning produced by these elements.

Gail O'Day's early work was part of this shift in method. In her revised dissertation, *Revelation in the Fourth Gospel: Narrative Mode and Theological Claim*, she argued that a fuller understanding of the gospel's perspective must include attention to its literary style. "The substantive claims of revelation and the mode of disclosure are intrinsically related to each other."[1] O'Day sought to intervene in an ongoing argument in Johannine studies over "whether revelation lies in the bare fact of Jesus as revealer or in the content of his revelation."[2] In his well-known work, Rudolf Bultmann had emphasized *das Dass* ("the bare fact") of revelation: the gospel reveals Jesus as the revealer. In conversation with Bultmann, Ernst Käsemann argued for the importance of the content (*was*) of that revelation—in particular, Jesus's relationship to God the Father.[3]

Against this background, O'Day argued for attention to the *wie*, the "how" of revelation. *Revelation in the Fourth Gospel* asserted that

---

1. Gail R. O'Day, *Revelation in the Fourth Gospel: Narrative Mode and Theological Claim* (Philadelphia: Fortress, 1986), 2.
2. O'Day, *Revelation in the Fourth Gospel*, 44.
3. Rudolf Bultmann, *Theology of the New Testament*, 2 vols. (New York: Scribner, 1955), 66; Ernst Käsemann, *The Testament of Jesus: A Study of the Gospel of John in the Light of Chapter 17* (London: SCM, 1968), 24–25.

the content of the revelation of Jesus cannot be understood independently from the narrative of the gospel. "The Fourth Evangelist shapes and communicates revelation through the particular literary characteristics of the Johannine narrative."[4] Therefore, study of the literary modes of communication would further understanding of the message of John's Gospel.

Revelation in the Fourth Gospel addressed irony as a literary device that conveys the gospel's meaning. O'Day pointed to a number of places in John 4 where readers perceive a double layer of meaning. For example, O'Day argued that the Samaritan woman perceives her conversation with Jesus on a literal level, while the reader understands Jesus to be speaking on a figurative level. "The ironic 'double exposure' of Jesus' statements and the woman's responses allows for reader participation in the revelation process in a way that declarative statements could not."[5] The *wie* of the narrative points to the gospel's function as a revealer to its readers. In perceiving this added meaning, the reader experiences the revelation of Jesus that is at the heart of the gospel's message.

In emphasizing the *how* of revelation, O'Day and other scholars shifted away from a number of the specific methodological approaches that were conventional at the time. For example, interpreters of John 4 had commonly divided the story into multiple sources, seeing significant breaks at verses 8 and 27.[6] O'Day saw the passage as a literary whole, and because of this, she could make observations about the text as literature that were invisible to historical critics. For example, reading John 4:27–30 as connected to the previous story rather than a separate source tradition, O'Day noticed how the questions the disciples refrain from asking Jesus in verse 27 ("no one said, 'What do you want?' or 'Why are you speaking with her?'"[7]) are questions readers can already answer. They have seen these ideas already in John 4:7, 10. Thus, "for the moment, the reader is more involved with Jesus' revela-

---

4. O'Day, *Revelation in the Fourth Gospel*, 45–46.
5. O'Day, *Revelation in the Fourth Gospel*, 73.
6. O'Day, *Revelation in the Fourth Gospel*, 50. See also Robert T. Fortna, *The Gospel of Signs: A Reconstruction of the Narrative Source Underlying the Fourth Gospel*, SNTSMS 11 (Cambridge: Cambridge University Press, 1970), 189–90. Fortna and other interpreters saw the core of the story in John 4 as part of the signs source, to which the evangelist added dialogue.
7. All biblical quotations are from the NRSV.

tion than his disciples are."[8] The perception of irony engages the reader and affects the interpretation of the conversations Jesus is having in the narrative.

Another distinctive contribution of O'Day's literary approach was her argument that readers of the gospel need not choose between two apparent meanings in the story. For example, interpreters have argued about whether the indication that Jesus "had to go through Samaria" (John 4:4) pointed to a practical or theological necessity. Rudolf Bultmann suggested it was merely the shortest route, while others argued for a divine impetus.[9] O'Day suggested that the discussion with the disciples in 4:27–38 clarifies that *both* literal and theological necessity were in view. The exchange between Jesus and his disciples underscores that "geographical and theological necessity are inseparable—the necessity to pass through Samaria is part of doing God's will."[10] Again, this kind of insight arises from treating the passage as a whole rather than unrelated component parts.

These methodological shifts met some criticism by scholars who suggest that the search for literary meaning is insufficiently historical. For example, when Jörg Frey outlined various methodological approaches, he criticized literary readings of John because "the historical dimension [is] bracketed out."[11] Here Frey narrowly defined "the historical dimension" in terms of the classical historical-critical questions of the prehistory of the text or the identification of the situation in which the gospel was composed. Without these elements, Frey argued, literary interpretation "draws near again to the approach of the

---

8. O'Day, *Revelation in the Fourth Gospel*, 75.

9. Bultmann and others agreed that this was practical necessity: Rudolf Bultmann, *The Gospel of John: A Commentary*, trans. G. R. Beasley-Murray, R. W. N. Hoare, and J. K. Riches (Philadelphia: Westminster, 1971), 176. See also Edwyn Clement Hoskyns, *The Fourth Gospel*, ed. F. N. Davey (London: Faber & Faber, 1947), 232; C. K. Barrett, *The Gospel according to St. John: An Introduction with Commentary and Notes on the Greek Text*, 2nd ed. (Philadelphia: Westminster, 1978), 193. Others argued for divine necessity. See, e.g., Raymond E. Brown, *The Gospel according to John*, 2 vols., AB 29–29A (New York: Doubleday, 1966–1970), 1:169; and Francis J. Moloney, *The Gospel of John*, SP 4 (Collegeville, MN: Liturgical Press, 1988), 116.

10. O'Day, *Revelation in the Fourth Gospel*, 80.

11. Jörg Frey, *The Glory of the Crucified One: Christology and Theology in the Gospel of John*, trans. Wayne Coppins and Christoph Heilig (Waco, TX: Baylor University Press, 2018), 22.

theological reading" of premodern interpreters who simply sought the "spiritual sense" of the gospel.[12]

Instead, I argue in this introductory essay that literary methods like O'Day's are historically sound even as they lend themselves to unpacking theological meaning. Literary study that uses historical evidence to explore the variety of ways John's language might have been received by its earliest readers is more rigorous historically than traditional historical-critical methods. And because literary approaches assume that the gospel is literature that conveys theological content, they more easily yield theological insights. This essay is structured in four sections. First, I describe the historical nature of literary research. Second, I argue that the pursuit of the goals of historical criticism often fails, methodologically speaking, to be sufficiently historical. Third, I explain how literary methods lend themselves to theological exploration. And last, I outline how the essays of this book contribute to this argument.

Literary Criticism Is Historical Research

Literary criticism combines perceptive literary observations with historical contextualization. In this sense, it shares a good deal in common with its historical-critical predecessors. Indeed, what I am calling *literary criticism* occurs with some regularity even among scholars who do not identify as literary critics. After all, much of New Testament scholarship involves various forms of historical exploration: from philological study to history of religions background to an analysis of cultural expectations that the gospel might evoke for early readers. Many of the features of this exploration are shared by literary critics.

Literary studies often use the same ancient comparative sources as historical critics, but they are used for a different purpose. In the hands of historical critics, the goal was often to situate John in a chronological order with all of these sources to form a smooth historical trajectory or to suggest a direct dependence on a single source or idea as a way of identifying the meaning of a passage in the gospel. For literary critics, however, the same sources are historical data points that can help scholars think about the kinds of cultural cues that readers of John would have been familiar with. Whether the author knew the sources or drew on them directly is impossible to say,

---

12. Frey, *Glory of the Crucified One*, 22; see also 4–5.

but it is also beside the point. Literary sources can inform our understanding of how people of the time made meaning, explained concepts, or employed rhetorical techniques.[13] Understanding how readers of the gospel may have apprehended its language can give a better sense of the range of interpretive options that are historically plausible.

Framed as a literary task, interpreters can compare features of the New Testament to other ancient literature. *Revelation in the Fourth Gospel* discussed irony as a historical topic in ancient philosophy. Many other examples could be named, but since I have cited Frey as a critic of literary approaches, I want also to cite him as a scholar engaging in the work I am calling literary criticism. One recent study by Frey attends to the various forms of dualism in ancient literature. Frey identifies a number of different kinds of dualism found in the historical period. He looks at other literature with dualistic language and compares both the subject matter and the function of the contrasting language in each literary work. As a result, he concludes that John's dualism is unlike other examples of the period and should not be seen as a development from these sources.[14] This is a careful, historical argument. What is more, it seems to advance the conversation about John's Gospel, which has often proceeded as if all dualistic imagery was alike in every way. This kind of research adds depth to the understanding of the ancient sources in order to situate John within that context.

This basic impulse to situate the language of the gospel in its historical context extends to many aspects of the text. Scholars explore the historical context of not only literary devices, like irony and dualism, but also the cultural understanding of time, death, or Roman imperial power. John's unique portrait of the death of Jesus, for example, is conveyed through specific literary cues. The language John uses raises questions about how ancient readers understood death, and should rightly lead to historical investigation of how John's language would have been perceived by readers steeped in the cultural cues of their time.

As literary criticism developed, critics became less interested in the search for the author's intended meaning and instead sought a meaning early readers of the gospel would identify.[15] Although the author's thoughts

---

13. O'Day's treatment of irony explored discussions of the use of irony in Aristotle, Plato, Cicero, and Quintilian; see O'Day, *Revelation in the Fourth Gospel*, 12–18.

14. Frey, *Glory of the Crucified One*, ch. 4.

15. On the use of the phrase *intended meaning* in O'Day's early work, see, e.g., O'Day, *Revelation in the Fourth Gospel*, 136.

and motivations are lost to us, interpreters think historically about the use of the language, theological concepts, allusions to Scripture, and so forth, based on other literary evidence from the period. By situating the gospel in its historical context, modern readers can begin to imagine what early readers of the gospel may have understood or how they made sense of the gospel's various images.

I would take this line of thinking a step further, however, to suggest that the gospel's meaning for its early readers was never singular but was always plural. Scholars should explore not a single meaning but *meanings* early readers were likely to recognize. This decision that the gospel's meaning is plural is both a literary and a historical judgment.

On the literary side, John's language lends itself to multiple meanings. As many scholars have noted, the gospel's many metaphors seem likely to give rise to a variety of possible ways of understanding Jesus.[16] In addition to the number of metaphorical expressions, however, the implicit nature of many of these metaphors suggests that some readers would miss entirely some of the gospel's signals about Jesus. For example, John never explicitly stated an association of Jesus's crucifixion with the Passover, but this connection is implied through time markers and allusions. The nature of John's metaphorical language thus suggests that more than one meaning was always possible.[17]

But historical evidence also reinforces the notion that readers of the gospel always interpreted it a variety of ways. Our earliest interpreters suggest there were different interpretations and disputes over questions of meaning. Origen's commentary took issue with an earlier work by Heracleon and disagreed on a number of points (see, e.g., *Comm. Jo.* 2.100–104). Irenaeus refuted interpretations of John that he attributed to Valentinian readers (*Haer.* 1.8.5). Later Christians also turned to the

---

16. E.g., R. Alan Culpepper, *Anatomy of the Fourth Gospel: A Study in Literary Design* (Philadelphia: Fortress, 1983), 180–99; Craig R. Koester, *Symbolism in the Fourth Gospel: Meaning, Mystery, Community*, 2nd ed. (Minneapolis: Fortress, 2003), 24–32; Susan E. Hylen, *Imperfect Believers: Ambiguous Characters in the Gospel of John* (Louisville: Westminster John Knox, 2009). For a discussion of metaphor in Revelation, see also Lynn R. Huber, *Thinking and Seeing with Women in Revelation* (London: Bloomsbury, 2013), 4–5, 23–33.

17. See the discussion by Hylen, *Imperfect Believers*, 138–48; Karoline M. Lewis, *Rereading the "Shepherd Discourse": Restoring the Integrity of John 9:39–10:21*, ed. Hemchand Gossai, StBibLit 113 (New York: Lang, 2008), 145–57; Culpepper, *Anatomy*, ch. 6. See also the essay by Lynn Huber in this volume.

Gospel of John for evidence to describe the nature of Christ or the Trinity, no matter which of the many sides of those debates they took up. Granted, even these sources are not the very earliest readers of the gospel. Yet the wide variety of ways of being Christian and theological viewpoints in the earliest churches may give us reason to question why interpreters assume that the gospel was written for a community with one viewpoint, facing a single question or problem, and who therefore understood the gospel's language in a unified way. From a historical perspective, this degree of unity seems unlikely.

Historical Criticism Can Be Less Historical

The goals of what I am calling literary criticism differ from classic historical-critical approaches to the New Testament. Literary critics seek to illumine the potential meaning that ancient readers encountered in the biblical texts. Historical criticism seeks to specify the historical location of the author, the author's community, and the sources used in writing. Yet while historical criticism has a goal of telling history, its method is not more historical than literary criticism.

The problems historical criticism addresses are interesting questions, and it is easy to see how they came to be topics of scholarly exploration. It would be useful to know where the gospel came from, who composed it, and so forth. The problem is that the possibility of answering these questions remains limited, because doing so would require sources outside of the gospel itself that could be used to verify historical claims. There is simply not adequate historical evidence to answer these questions. The pursuit of these questions inevitably leads to speculation, because it takes the reader beyond the limits of the evidence available.[18]

Scholars have largely agreed to lay aside some of these traditional topics, like the identification of the gospel's author. There is wide but not unanimous agreement that further pursuit of the gospel's author is not fruitful. On this subject, there is actually some historical evidence to interact with—more than is available, for example, on the question of the gospel's sources. There are a number of early Christian texts that shed light on the question of authorship. The problem is that the evidence does not

---

18. Some historical critics also express skepticism about the possibility of answering the traditional questions. See, e.g., Frey, *Glory of the Crucified One*, 34–35.

agree. Although second-century sources identify the author of the gospel as John, the internal evidence points in quite a different direction. The gospel is anonymous, attributing its writings to a plural "we," which traces its source to an anonymous disciple, the one Jesus loved (e.g., John 21:24). Early commentators noted that there were disputes over the authorship of the gospel, with a variety of claims being made. Because of this discrepancy, it seems a wise historical judgment to say that the author of the gospel is unknown. But at this point, the more responsible thing one can do is to leave the question aside. In the absence of new evidence, continuing to press for a specific answer to the question of authorship is likely to remain speculative.

The same problem holds for the other questions of the gospel's sources and audience. Questions of the gospel's sources and redactors often dominated scholarship of the twentieth century. Take, for example, the question of sources in John 4, mentioned above. Robert Fortna explained that the core of the Samaritan story was from a pre-Johannine tradition, expanded by the gospel writer's insertion of dialogues. John 4:8 was the author's insertion, which prepared the way for the addition of 4:31–38. This kind of analysis attended to the literary nature of the gospel in one sense. Fortna and others perceived that 4:8 was a literary aside, making sense of the disciples' absence: "His disciples had gone to the city to buy food." In addition, this comment by the narrator prepares readers for the return of the disciples in 4:27: "Just then his disciples came." But for these interpreters, the goal of these observations was to identify layers of sources that could be ordered historically. For this task, the interpreter must rely on his own perceptions, creativity, and logic, because there is not an existing manuscript tradition or other ancient source material that can contribute evidence to the question of layers of redaction and sources.

Absence of historical evidence is also an important consideration with the intractable problem of John's relationship to Judaism. The question whether John's community was thrown out of the synagogue is an interesting question that could have consequences for interpretation. It is possible that John's wording (for example, *aposynagōgos* in John 9:22), came about because his community was cast out of their local synagogue. However, other possibilities also exist. Other New Testament and early Christian writings offer evidence that Christians maintained a variety of relationships to Jewish beliefs and practices. Unfortunately, no historical evidence remains that can be used to verify the specific situation of John's community.

The interpretation of *aposynagōgos* is an example of how historical-critical readers experience a gap in the text and respond by explaining the discrepancy as part of the history of the text's production. In the case of *aposynagōgos*, the gap is a mismatch between the word and its setting as a reference to events during Jesus's ministry. Scholars imagine that expulsion from the synagogue was unlikely during Jesus's lifetime and occurred only later. Thus, they assert that this language in the gospel points to the later context of the author's community.

By contrast, literary scholars instead ask what the gap we perceive in the text means or what possible meanings it might produce for an early reader of the gospel. Acknowledging that there is no historical evidence that directly addresses the issue turns our attention to another question: What meaning(s) was the language likely to create for early readers? This is historical research, because assessing which questions are likely to be answered in a responsibly historical manner is part of the historian's task. In the end, a literary approach can have a stronger historical method than that of its historical-critical forebears.

A downside to historical-critical interpretation can be that it separates aspects of a single literary work into discrete categories. Scholars often note that John's Gospel intertwines the narrative of events that occurred during Jesus's life with references to followers later on, and that it highlights a process of reflecting back on the meaning of events of Jesus's life and death. But for historical-critical readers, the search for the community's identity requires interpreters to tease apart references to the author's historical period and the narrative framework of Jesus's life. To decide how to connect John's language to a particular historical setting, interpreters have to fix the meaning of the text around certain literary details, and in doing so, other aspects slide into the background.

For example, deciding that becoming *aposynagōgos* was a historical feature of John's community is a response to one aspect of the literary shape of the gospel (especially the wording of John 9:22 and 16:2). But reading those features of the gospel in this way comes at the expense of other aspects of John. In this case, one aspect that gets lost is the potential contrast John may be developing between responses of well-meaning humans, which result in people being *aposynagōgos*, and the result of Jesus's death, which is to gather into one, *synagagē eis hen*, the dispersed children of God (11:52). The contrast suggests the possibility of a theological agenda rather than a historical one. John creates an expectation of being separated, and also an expectation of being gathered together. Not surprisingly, the difference in being separated or gathered hinges on one's relationship to Jesus. Explaining *aposynagōgos* as a historical experience of the Johannine community is compelling because it fits with a number of other signals in the gospel. However, it is not the only way the pieces could fit together. In addition, it requires that all Christians had the same experience and would have understood the gospel in one way. Our attempts to determine this lost historical context lead us to narrow the possible options for how early readers encountered the gospel.

The tendency to narrow meaning possibilities is a common problem in historical-critical methods. In order to determine the historical context that gave rise to a passage of Scripture, historical critics specify a single meaning of the text. Many of the elements of historical-critical inquiry either assumed that determining a single meaning was possible or explicitly took this as their primary goal. The idea was that by situating the gospel in time and space, modern interpreters could approach the author's intended meaning. That historically grounded meaning could be used as a basis for situating the text in early Christian history.

Instead, literary critics acknowledge that multiple meanings can exist at the same time. O'Day's early work pointed in this direction. Interpreters of John 4:38 had argued over whom the word *others* referred to: "others have labored, and you have entered into their labor." Some asserted *others* pointed to the Samaritan woman; some suggested the early church. Instead, O'Day argued, "it seems best to accept the indefiniteness of the very expression 'others' as part of its intended meaning."[19] The idea that meaning could be open-ended went against the grain of much of historical criticism, for which pinpointing a single meaning aided the process of identifying the specific historical audience or context.

The emphasis on multiple meanings stems from both literary and historical concerns. Ideally, literary methods convey a sense of the historical variety that was available. Ancient readers had many literary and cultural cues to draw from in interpreting texts. Taken as a whole, the historical-critical research of the twentieth century often points to the variety that was available to readers in piecing together a sense of meaning from John's Gospel. Scholars have provided glimpses of multiple communities and philosophical perspectives that might have shaped ancient readers'

---

19. O'Day, *Revelation in the Fourth Gospel*, 135–36. As I noted above, interpreters (including O'Day) have subsequently moved away from the idea of the "intended meaning."

understandings: Gnosticism, philosophy, Jewish Scripture, and so forth. However, individual scholars often select only a single means of understanding John's language, and in doing so, they set limits on what the text could mean. For example, there were multiple ways of thinking about death for or on behalf of another. Some are expressed in stories of individuals, and others in sacrificial practices, or in interpretations of those practices and the stories associated with them. Modern scholars often focus on only a single means of understanding death to illumine John's Gospel, or they lump many together under one umbrella term, like *atonement*. These practices obscure the variety of options that were available to early readers. Doing so often seems to propel a theological agenda rather than to serve historical inquiry.

Theological Claims

In addition to being a historically rigorous method, literary criticism lends itself to expression of theological meaning of the text. For some interpreters, this is not an advantage. As I quoted above, Frey criticized literary methods for being coopted by theological aims. In this section, I argue instead that literary methods also form a solid foundation for readers whose interests lie in the modern world rather than in ancient history.

The problem Frey identifies has a long history. A primary reason scholars moved toward historical approaches was the need to insulate New Testament study from the concerns of dogmatic theology. In 1787, Johann Gabler set out a program for discerning the religious content of the biblical texts in their own historical context. After that task was complete, Gabler argued that theologians could build a systematic theology on the basis of these historical explorations.[20] Many of the important works of the *religionsgeschichtliche Schule* developed from the trajectory Gabler laid out. Over a century later, William Wrede sought a historical method for New Testament theology, a subject that in Wrede's hands became "the history of early Christian religion and theology."[21] In turning to history, these

---

20. Gabler's essay is translated and printed in John Sandys-Wunsch and Laurence Eldredge, "J. P. Gabler and the Distinction between Biblical and Dogmatic Theology: Translation, Commentary, and Discussion of His Originality," *SJT* 33 (1980): 134–44.

21. William Wrede, "The Task and Methods of 'New Testament Theology,'" in *The Nature of New Testament Theology*, ed. Robert Morgan (London: SCM, 1973), 116.

scholars sought to open up space for inquiry that was not dominated by contemporary theological beliefs.

Over time, however, scholars realized that these ideals had overstated the possibility of bracketing theological or other belief systems from historical research. Recent scholars largely agree that all interpretations are shaped by the social position and beliefs of the interpreter. The interpretation of historical data requires judgment, and the interpreter's perspective will always shape the outcome of that process. Yet, while neutrality is not possible, interpreters can become aware that their readings are shaped by their own views and, through this awareness, understand that other observations and interpretations are also possible. Acknowledging that other readers see different elements of a passage and make sense of them in different ways can help scholars to acknowledge that more than one reading of a text is possible, and to step back from communicating that there is only one meaning.

In light of this history, literary methods provide a better link to the theological meanings of New Testament texts than historical-critical methods have. The interpreter's job is not to find the single historically correct meaning in order to piece together a dogmatic theology. Instead, the interpreter considers how the biblical text may have communicated its message to readers steeped in that culture. The narrative modes of a text give readers a number of starting points to think about its theological meanings.

Such literary exploration lends itself to elaborating theological content. For example, Jesus's words in John 14:31 have been a perennial question for historical-critical interpreters. Many saw the Greek words, Ἐγείρεσθε ἄγωμεν ἐντεῦθεν, "Rise, let us be on our way," as a break in the text, because Jesus and the group he speaks to do not seem to move until three chapters later (John 18:1). For many historical critics, 14:31 marked the original ending of the discourse after the Lord's Supper, and chapters 15–17 were added at another layer of composition or redaction. In contrast, O'Day noted the weak historical basis for this argument and went on to ask what the gap perceived by the modern reader might mean on the narrative level. She read the language metaphorically, situating it in its literary and theological context:

> From Jesus' opening words in 14:2, spatial language has doubled for relational language throughout this chapter (see, e.g., 14:6–7). It is consonant, therefore, with the language about place in John 14 to interpret the words "on our way" (ἐντεῦθεν, *enteuthen*) as being about relation-

ship with Jesus at his hour, as much as they are about physical location. The first-person plural pronouns of 14:31d include the disciples in the eschatological moment of Jesus' departure and mark the ushering in of the promise of 14:3—Jesus will take his disciples to himself, and thus to their place and home with God. John 14:31d thus ends this first unit of the discourse on a note of eschatological triumph quite in keeping with the rest of vv. 30–31. The impotence of the ruler of this world is a reality; the disciples' home and full relationship with God beckons. Indeed, this note of eschatological triumph provides the theological foundation for the continuation of the discourse in John 15–16.[22]

Instead of focusing on the source history of this verse, O'Day connected the meaning of the words to the language of the chapter and the trajectory of the Farewell Discourse. The words and their meaning are expressed as part of the theological message unfolding in this part of the gospel. Considering the literary function of the passage leads to an expression of meaning, which in John's case is likely to be theological.

For O'Day, these theological meanings were important both as historical artifacts and as meanings that contemporary Christians could contemplate. O'Day was a professor and scholar of both New Testament and homiletics, and she understood exegetical skills as necessary to both subjects. When literary criticism is undertaken as a historically grounded task, it is a method that also offers preachers a way to proclaim a message of good news in the present. Preachers/exegetes do not discover ancient doctrine that can somehow endure over time and space. Instead, their literary study can connect listeners to the revelatory message of the biblical text. The message preachers experience as revealed through the literary modes of Scripture becomes a message they communicate to others in preaching.

The Organization of This Book

The essays in part 1 of this book are examples of the fruitfulness of literary approaches for Johannine literature. Each of the essays involves both historical contextualization and literary analysis. The identification of rhetorical features of the text becomes more compelling when they are aspects ancient readers might also have apprehended. The essays offer new insight

---

22. Gail R. O'Day, "The Gospel of John: Introduction, Commentary, and Reflections," *NIB* 9:753.

into potential meanings (and varieties of meanings) that ancient readers may have encountered.

Vernon K. Robbins's exploration of characters in John 11 focuses in part on the ironic character of "the Judeans." Although John's language creates some expectation that the Judeans will reject Jesus, Robbins brings out the positive nature—and thus the irony—of the Judeans' character. These positive elements of the text are often ignored or downplayed by other scholars. Reading John in this way creates opportunities to see how Christians of the period—whether Jewish or not—may have understood aspects of John's Gospel.

Gilberto Ruiz takes up the difficult question of Pilate's fear following the Jews' assertion that Jesus claimed to be the Son of God (John 19:8). Ruiz argues that Pilate's fear does not render him less of a tyrant, and that readers of the time would likely have expected Pilate to be portrayed in a negative light. Instead, Ruiz asserts that Pilate comes to be less concerned that Jesus seeks political power and more aware that Jesus possesses divine power. Readers who understood Pilate's fear in this way would have understood Jesus's power to surpass that of the Roman Empire.

Yoshimi Azuma reads John 20–21 as a literary unity and in doing so draws attention to the way the gospel conveys meaning regarding Jesus's resurrected life. In contrast to scholars who have focused only on the fact of Jesus's departure as part of the gospel's message, Azuma argues that these concluding chapters of the gospel point to the continuity between Jesus's life and the ongoing life of the church. She argues that the narrative asides of John 20:8–9, 20:30–31, and 21:24–25 point to the revelatory function of the gospel itself.

Patrick Gray draws attention to the connection between the layers of meaning in Rev 14 and the function of the text. The possibilities in meaning cause readers to choose a perspective with which to interpret the text. John used the ambiguity in imagery as a strategy to persuade readers to commit to his point of view.

Lynn R. Huber also writes about the *how* of Revelation's revealing. She describes the shifts in imagery of Christ as instances of irony, because the shifts create disparity between the text and the reader's expectations. She addresses the change in Christ, first from Lion to Lamb in Rev 5 and then from Lamb to warrior in Rev 19. As in the Gospel of John, the irony of Revelation involves the reader in the production of meaning.

In part 2, the essays move toward questions of the use of literary approaches for interpreters, including ancient and modern preachers.

William M. Wright IV's essay on John Chrysostom argues that Chrysostom communicated a message of divine accommodation based in part on his understanding of the literary modes of Scripture. The character of Nicodemus reflects the human need for accommodation, and Jesus's responses to him were a reflection of divine mercy. Like O'Day, Chrysostom drew on literary modes of the narrative to make a theological claim.

Karoline M. Lewis argues that preachers who approach John from a historical-critical angle often have difficulty preaching it. Literary methods, however, can connect an appropriate historical meaning of the gospel with the experience of the preachers' communities. Lewis argues that greater attention should be given to the potential for the function of the sermon to mirror the literary mode of the gospel.

Part 2 closes with a series of sermons, each of which exhibits in its own way how attention to the literary shape of the text can inform preaching. In their attention to the narrative modes of the text, these preachers use the biblical story as a revealer. They capture elements of the literary nature of the text and its message and communicate that message as good news for the listening audience.

Thomas G. Long's sermon, "Learning How to Tell Time," draws attention to the way John's language brings together human chronology and eschatological time. Present, past, and future times overlap at times in the Fourth Gospel. In John 2, it both is and is not already Jesus's hour, and Long builds on this tension by drawing parallels that bring out the same dimension of the listener's own experience.

"Stop Waiting, It's Time for an Attitude Adjustment," by Teresa Fry Brown, follows the narrative shape of John 5:5–9. Fry Brown brings out details of the story by describing them in modern terms. These contemporary comparisons fit the narrative logic of the passage. Fry Brown's sermon has a consistent message yet does not reduce the story to a single point, something O'Day also encouraged in her writing on preaching: "We need to take a close look at the text itself, to linger with the text, to ask not only what the biblical story says but how it says it."[23] Without naming literary devices as such, Fry Brown brings the listener's life experience alongside the biblical story, shaping their perception of reality according to what she

---

23. Gail O'Day, *The Word Disclosed: Preaching the Gospel of John* (St. Louis: Chalice, 2002), 3.

sees in the text. In doing so, the passage of the gospel functions as revealer for the listener.

Veronice Miles's sermon, "Disciple, Will You Let Me Wash Your Feet?," also puts the listener into the biblical story. Miles draws on the literary context of the footwashing story to remind listeners of all that they have witnessed in the gospel story and to place them, like disciples, as those whose feet Jesus washes. Drawing on historical background of footwashing as a slave's chore, she creates tension in Jesus's offer that parallels that of the passage.

"The Time of Revelation," a sermon by Ted A. Smith, relates the verb tenses of Rev 21:1–6 to theological claims about God's action in the past, present, and future. He compares the historical context of Revelation to elements of the context of preaching, in the sense that both are "fearful times." In doing so, Smith prepares listeners to hear the promises of Revelation for their own context.

Conclusion

The essays in part 1 situate literary modes of the gospel historically to suggest meanings that early readers of the gospel could identify. The authors in this section often suggest more than one possible meaning or point to the ways readers with different perspectives may have found different meanings. Attention to the narrative modes of the text as they took shape within their historical context opens up various possibilities for reading.

The essays in part 2 understand that elaborating the theological meaning of the gospel is also situated historically, in the sense that preachers speak to and are shaped by their own contexts. These authors do not understand preachers' task to be to assert doctrinal claims that originate in the gospel or Revelation. Instead, preachers perceive theological meaning in the text of John or Revelation that is relevant for their context. They demonstrate how attention to the narrative modes of the text is useful for making this kind of theological claim.

All of the authors in this collection of essays and sermons dedicate their work to the memory of Gail O'Day. She was variously our friend, colleague, and mentor. She taught and advocated a method of reading Scripture that bears fruit both in academic study and in preaching. We hope that this volume testifies to her academic and pastoral contributions and to the fruitfulness of integrating historical, literary, theological, and homiletic interests.

Part 1

Unfolding Story and Theology in the Raising of Lazarus in John 11-12

Vernon K. Robbins

This paper focuses on the Lazarus episode in the Gospel of John with special attention to Jesus and three groups of people: the sisters of Lazarus who are part of the beloved family of Mary, Martha, and Lazarus;[1] Jesus's disciples; and Judeans. In each instance, when a group emerges through the narrator's voice, the group speaks with a single voice (sisters: 11:3; disciples: 11:8, 12; Judeans: 11:36). Only after initial speech and action by a group do individual members of the group speak, sometimes to other members of the group and sometimes to Jesus. As the paper unfolds, the complex interaction among Judean individuals and subgroups exhibits the deep irony in how belief in Jesus works and spreads in the realm of darkness on earth.

The approach in this essay builds on the focus on narrative in the works of Gail R. O'Day,[2] in whose honor this essay is written. In her book *Revelation in the Fourth Gospel*, O'Day presents a commanding discussion of irony and an exquisite discussion of revelation. Then she presents a detailed analysis and interpretation of the Samaritan woman at the well

---

1. For the beloved family, see Jerome H. Neyrey, S.J., *The Gospel of John*, NCBC (Cambridge: Cambridge University Press, 2007), 201–2, 207–11, 234.
2. Gail R. O'Day, *Revelation in the Fourth Gospel: Narrative Mode and Theological Claim* (Philadelphia: Fortress, 1986); O'Day, "The Gospel of John: Introduction, Commentary, and Reflections," *NIB* 9:811–27; O'Day, "Narrative Mode and Theological Claim: A Study in the Fourth Gospel," *JBL* 105 (1986): 657–68; O'Day, "John 6:15–21: Jesus Walking on Water as Narrative Embodiment of Johannine Christology," in *Critical Readings of John 6*, ed. R. Alan Culpepper, BibInt 22 (Leiden: Brill, 1997), 149–59; O'Day, "'Show Us the Father and We Will Be Satisfied' (John 14:8)," *Semeia* 85 (1999): 11–17; O'Day, "Jesus as Friend in the Gospel of John," *Int* 58 (2004): 144–57.

in John 4:4–42. One of her major reasons for selecting this episode is its presentation of Jesus as revealer in three different contexts, "an encounter with an individual (the Samaritan woman) and with two groups (the disciples and the Samaritan villagers)."[3] Twenty years later (2006), Susan E. Hylen collaborated with O'Day to coauthor the commentary on John in the *Westminster Bible Companion* series.[4] After their collaboration, Hylen expanded O'Day's work by focusing on six individuals (Nicodemus, the Samaritan woman, Martha, Mary, the beloved disciple, and Jesus) and two groups (the disciples and the Jews) as "imperfect believers."[5] Focusing on their action and speech as characters, Hylen proposes that all the characters, including Jesus, are ambiguous, and this ambiguity is productive for the overall story. Hylen uses metaphor rather than irony to explore this ambiguity, especially in relation to Jesus as a character.[6] As she proceeds, she emphasizes the use of multiple metaphors where "each metaphor adds something to the reader's understanding of a complex concept," so that Jesus is presented as "a complex and ambiguous character."[7] In the end, she asserts that "the "metaphorical 'truth' is not one of expressing a preexisting reality but of enabling us to structure our conception of 'reality.'"[8]

The present essay presupposes this rich sequence of discussion, from irony through metaphor to ambiguity, in the context of two currently developing issues. First, a debate has been growing about the Gospel of John in relation to apocalyptic since John Ashton's publications in 1991 and 2014.[9] Second, Troels Engberg-Pedersen has introduced a major *tour de force* into the discussion with an argument that *logos* and *pneuma* in the Fourth Gospel, understood in relation to Stoic philosophy, provide the overarching unity in the Fourth Gospel.[10] These two developments suggest

---

3. O'Day, *Revelation in the Fourth Gospel*, 48.

4. Gail R. O'Day and Susan E. Hylen, *John*, Westminster Bible Companion (Louisville: Westminster John Knox, 2006).

5. Susan E. Hylen, *Imperfect Believers: Ambiguous Characters in the Gospel of John* (Louisville: Westminster John Knox, 2009).

6. Hylen, *Imperfect Believers*, 7–9, 138–43.

7. Hylen, *Imperfect Believers*, 143–50.

8. Hylen, *Imperfect Believers*, 148.

9. John Ashton, *Understanding the Fourth Gospel* (Oxford: Clarendon, 1991); Ashton, *The Gospel of John and Christian Origins* (Minneapolis: Fortress, 2014).

10. Troels Engberg-Pedersen, *John and Philosophy: A New Reading of the Fourth Gospel* (Oxford: Oxford University Press, 2017), 252: "the way in which Jesus 'exegetes' God (1:18) is this: by himself undergoing death and then being resurrected through

the importance of interpreting the Gospel of John as a literary production in the context of conceptual blending of apocalyptic and philosophical systems of belief in emerging Christian discourse during the last half of the first century CE. The challenge is to produce a form of exegesis and interpretation that helps us see the rhetorical force of this blending in the context of a richly textured narrative focused on the earthly adult life of Jesus of Nazareth.

The Overall Boundaries of the Lazarus Episode

The initial issue of importance is the length of the Lazarus episode. Usually interpreters consider the episode to be completed by the end of chapter 11, even though everyone knows that Lazarus is at the Bethany home of the beloved family in the next chapter and Jesus's raising of Lazarus creates the context for the Jerusalem leaders among the Judeans to plan the arrest and death of Jesus. An important part of Engberg-Pedersen's recent philosophical interpretation is detailed argument for the continuation of the Lazarus episode to the end of chapter 12. For him, the final portion in 12:20–50 brings the narrative that started in the prologue to a dramatic conclusion before the events in the context of Passover in Jerusalem that bring the glorification of Jesus in the crucifixion and the return of Logos Jesus to the Father through death, burial, and resurrection.[11]

Our analysis and interpretation follow Engberg-Pedersen's lead for the length of the Lazarus episode. A major difference in our interpretation is a focus on the relation of light to life and death in the episode. Engberg-Pedersen emphasizes the role of *pneuma* in the episode even though it occurs only once (11:33). The result is an interpretation of John 11–12 in a manner close to Paul's pneumatic interpretation of resurrection in 1 Cor 15. Instead of presenting a pneumatic interpretation of the Lazarus

---

the *pneuma* with which he was initially endowed. Once believers understand *that*, they are saved—by themselves having obtained a share in the all-important *pneuma*, which will eventually resurrect them, too, to eternal life.... Initially, they may come to believe in him in some lower form when they respond to the *pneuma* that streams out of his mouth in his *rhēmata*. Later, however, they may also themselves receive the *pneuma*. Then they will possess full belief in the form of access to Jesus' (and God's) full *logos*. And then they will also themselves be able to obtain eternal life. From then on, the *pneuma* will be directly operating in them to bring them there."

11. Engberg-Pedersen, *John and Philosophy*, 224–26, 232, 247–52.

episode that focuses most fully on the relation of *pneuma* to light, which at times allows life (*zōē*) to move into the background, our approach focuses on Jesus as a *zōogenetic* (life-generating) embodiment of Logos-life on earth. To be sure, the spirit is an important epistemological-ontological agency in the Fourth Gospel. But there are three aspects that at times move into the background in Engberg-Pedersen's interpretation:

1. God and Logos are in a realm called "above" at the beginning of the prologue, not in "heaven," which comes into being with the creation of the cosmos through the agency of the Logos;
2. The primary ontological nature of the Logos is life rather than *pneuma*;
3. The epistemological network of belief in the Lazarus episode creates a constellation of topoi that blends life and death with glory and light, rather than a constellation focused primarily on *pneuma*.

Action and Speech of Jesus in the Lazarus Episode

To analyze the story of the raising of Lazarus well using the insights introduced above, it is necessary for us to start with Jesus as a character in the episode. Just prior to this episode, Jesus goes across the Jordan to the place where John had previously been baptizing (10:40). While Jesus is staying there, people come to him, saying that John performed no sign, but everything that John has said about Jesus is true, and the narrator adds that "many believed in him there" (10:41–42).[12] At this point in the story, the narrator describes the illness of Lazarus, introduces Mary and Martha and their village of Bethany, and presents the message sent by the sisters to Jesus telling him that the one he loves is ill (11:1–3). This information in the story line leads to Jesus's first statement in the Lazarus episode, "This illness does not lead to death; rather it is for God's glory, so that the Son of God may be glorified through it" (11:4). To understand the nature of Jesus as a character at this point, it is necessary for us to take a brief detour that can make it possible to understand what Jesus has asserted to those who brought the sisters' message to him.

Throughout the Gospel of John, the narrator creates scenes of interaction among groups and individual people for the purpose of revealing how

---

12. Unless otherwise indicated, all biblical translations are based on the NRSV.

cosmic Logos Jesus comes from outside created heaven and earth to dwell temporarily in the human sensorimotor earthly-heavenly realm, passing through heaven to earth to fully participate in the realm where humans live.[13] Logos Jesus does not simply come from heaven to earth as a traditional apocalyptic messenger, but he comes from a realm called "above," namely, a realm that exists above the created heaven and earth.[14] A major goal of the episodes in the Gospel of John is to juxtapose traditional human ways of thinking about things with a belief that an extraworldly being—a being outside (above) the created realm of both heaven and earth—brought heaven and earth into being and then came down through heaven onto the earth with human nature like he himself created through cosmic creational life that is in him. Logos Jesus, then, does not simply lead humans to eternal life, like a traditional apocalyptic angel/messenger may be perceived to do. He gives them eternal life. He himself is the agency of eternally regenerating cosmic creational life in the heaven and earth that continually happens through him. Thus, the fullness of this regenerating agency is continually present in him as Logos Jesus moves through earthly space and time.[15] No wonder, then, that the things Jesus says in the Fourth Gospel are ambiguous. The major technique the narration uses is to continually run major topoi from the prologue through episodes as they happen in the story line.[16] This means, as Engberg-Pedersen rightly emphasizes, that topoi from the prologue are continually blended into and with other major topoi in the episodes as the narrative unfolds.

---

13. Vernon K. Robbins, "Kinetic Divine Concepts, the Baptist, and the Enfleshed Logos in the Prologue and Precreation Storyline of the Fourth Gospel," in *Seeing the God: Image, Space, Performance, and Vision in the Religion of the Roman Empire*, ed. Marlis Arnhold, Harry O. Maier, and Jörg Rüpke, Culture, Religion, and Politics in the Greco-Roman World (Tübingen: Mohr Siebeck, 2018), 281–99.

14. Benjamin E. Reynolds, "Apocalyptic Revelation in the Gospel of John: Revealed Cosmology, the Vision of God, and Visionary Showing," in *The Jewish Apocalyptic Tradition and the Shaping of New Testament Thought*, ed. Benjamin E. Reynolds and Loren T. Stuckenbruck (Minneapolis: Augsburg Fortress, 2016), 111–13. Reynolds seems not to be fully clear that "above" is above and beyond heaven; thus, Jesus comes to earth from "above all," through heaven to earth.

15. Robbins, "Kinetic Divine Concepts," 287–88.

16. For "running the blend," see Gilles Fauconnier, *Mappings in Thought and Language* (Cambridge: Cambridge University Press, 1997), 150–58; Gilles Fauconnier and Mark Turner, *The Way We Think: Conceptual Blending and the Mind's Hidden Complexities* (New York: Basic Books, 2002), 44–50.

It is understandable, then, that Logos Jesus has a much harder time than any traditional apocalyptic angel or messenger explaining to people who he is, who God is, and the process by which humans may receive eternally regenerating life. Conventional apocalyptic messengers often take righteous humans around the heavens to their outer limits to show them who and what is there. And some righteous humans, like Enoch and Ezra, are given the opportunity even to see God in the highest heaven. In the cosmic creational belief system in the Gospel of John, a journey throughout the heavens surely would not come to a realm where God dwells. In the Fourth Gospel, there is no possibility for any human to see God. God exists in an invisible, extracreation realm called "above," into which only the Logos Son can see. Only the creational Son can see and hear God, and he continually sees the works and communicates with the invisible Father. Humans cannot see these works or hear the voice of God as articulate speech from the heavens, in contrast to the Synoptic Gospels.[17]

In the Fourth Gospel, humans can only see the works of the Logos Son and hear his words on earth. In addition, in the Gospel of John, humans do not have dream-visions of events in heaven, like many humans in traditional apocalyptic literature.[18] Logos Jesus is not an apocalyptic interpreter of dreams or visions in the Fourth Gospel. The only way to

---

17. Engberg-Pederson, *John and Philosophy*, 105 n. 35, about John 12:28–30: "It seems to me of crucial importance that here God is meant to be directly interacting with *Jesus*—and *not* to be understood by all the others. For here God makes the whole content of his 'plan' (*logos*) explicit: 'I have glorified and will glorify'. *Nobody* but Jesus could understand that at the time." Compare John 1:18; 5:19–20, 30, 37; 12:28–30 and contrast with Matt 3:14–17, where John hears the voice from heaven, and Matt 17:5; Mark 9:7; and Luke 9:35–36, where disciples hear the voice from heaven.

18. Contrast the presence of dream-visions in the prophetic-apocalyptic discourse of Matt 1:20–25; 2:12–14, 19–23; 27:19; Luke 1:22; 24:23; Acts 2:17; 9:10–12; 10:3, 17–19; 11:5; 12:9; 16:9; 16:10; 18:9; 26:19. Reynolds, "Apocalyptic Revelation," emphasizes Jesus's promise to Nathaniel that he "will see the heaven opened and the angels of God ascending and descending upon the Son of God" (111: John 1:51) and Isaiah's seeing of "his glory" (116: John 12:41) as apocalyptic in force, but he misinterprets the cosmic view of *above* in the Gospel of John as *heaven* in apocalyptic literature (111–14). Most noticeably, Reynolds misconstrues the relation of the spatial nature of heavenly transcendental reality in apocalyptic literature (110), in which humans can see and hear if they are taken into it, and which can be destroyed or have chaos come into it. In contrast to apocalyptic literature, *above* in the Gospel of John is spatially and temporally cosmic, invisible to humans, and lying beyond the human sensory realm of seeing and hearing in heaven and earth, and impervious to chaos or destruction.

know, understand, and believe is to hear and see what Logos Jesus himself says and does in the human earthly realm. In our terminology, this means that the Gospel of John is *inverted apocalyptic*. John Ashton explains it as follows:

> Throughout the Gospel, whoever is doing the witnessing, whether it is John the Baptist, Moses and the Scriptures, the Paraclete, the disciples, and finally the evangelist himself, the object of the witness, what they are witnessing to, is none other than Jesus himself, not in his preexistence or in his eventual abode in heaven, but in his earthly life, recollected and newly conceived. So the new revelation is the Gospel itself, a story set on earth—which is why it may be called an apocalypse in reverse.[19]

Ashton's description of the focus of the Fourth Gospel on activities of Jesus's life on earth is right on target. What Ashton does not explore and explain is why Jesus's witnessing is ambiguous. In traditional apocalyptic literature, the message of the messenger/revealer is regularly quite clear. The reason for the special ambiguity in the Fourth Gospel lies in the task of communicating the message about God and the world in inverted apocalyptic, because the truth about things is not simply hidden somewhere in heaven. Rather, the truth lies beyond the heavens and the earth in deep cosmic time and space called *above*, which is outside the cosmos of heaven and earth. This means that God's action and speech cannot be seen and heard through direct earthly experiences, through revelations enabled by the heavens opening, or by travel through the heavens enabled by an angel messenger. In the Fourth Gospel, the travel occurs between places on earth, with the enfleshed precreation Logos Son Jesus moving through various spaces and places encountering and being encountered by multiple human beings. During all of this activity, Logos Jesus can see and hear what the Father is saying and doing in the invisible limitless universe above the created cosmos that contains heaven and earth. But no one on earth can see the Father, and if they hear anything, it is not speech from the Father to humans on earth, and the people in the setting cannot recognize the sound as speech by the Father to the Son (John 12:28–30).[20]

As a result of the inverted apocalyptic belief system that informs the narration in the Gospel of John, the narrator often places a statement on the

---

19. Ashton, *Gospel of John*, 118.
20. See n. 17.

lips of Jesus near the beginning of an episode that reintroduces at least one of the key topoi in the prologue that metonymically prompts a remembering of the precreation story line overarching the episodes in the Gospel. In the episode of the raising of Lazarus, Jesus explicitly introduces the topos of glory—using both the noun and the verb *to glorify*—and he implicitly evokes the topos of life when he speaks of death.[21] The words with which Jesus does this are as follows: "This illness does not lead to death; rather it is for God's glory, so that the Son of God may be glorified through it" (11:4). These words rerun the precreation story line through the episode, reintroducing the topoi of life and glory associated with life in the Logos that generated all things that become (1:3–4, 10) and enables humans to see his glory, which is one with the Father (1:14). This seeing became possible when logos became enfleshed Logos Jesus, entering into and dwelling in the human sensorimotor realm that came into being through him.

The second time Jesus speaks in the Lazarus episode, he reconfigures the topos of *light* in relation to his doing his *work* of generating and regenerating life in heaven and earth. This is a primary function of life in Logos Jesus as he enters the limited time and space sphere of heaven and earth. Jesus's statement is elaborated in a diatribe style as Jesus asks a question and answers it: "Are there not twelve hours of daylight? Those who walk during the day do not stumble, because they see the light of this world. But those who walk at night stumble, because the light is not in them" (11:9–10). This statement is a reintroduction of the topos of light in the prologue in a manner that reconfigures it for understanding in the context of the death and revivification of Lazarus, which is Logos Jesus's work of generating and regenerating life in the sensorimotor realm of humans on earth. Jesus does not simply raise Lazarus up. Rather, Logos Jesus regenerates Lazarus's putrid, smelling corpse into a living, walking human being. To understand this, one must return to the function of life in the Logos as stated in the prologue.

While Jesus's speech in the Lazarus episode leads the way, action by Jesus is also extremely important. First, the question is whether Logos Jesus will move through earthly space from his location in the wilderness where John baptized people to the place where Lazarus is ill. We will see below that it is the movement of people from the village of Bethany to Jesus that enacts Jesus's movement from his space in the wilderness to the tomb

---

21. See the topoi of life and glory in the prologue: John 1:4, 14.

of Lazarus. This is important movement (*kinēsis*) of Logos Jesus through various places in earthly space and time that brings the presence of regenerating life in Jesus into the local environments where humans drink wine or water (John 2, 4), eat food (John 6), need healing (John 4–5), and so forth.[22] This movement is the means by which the glory of God is revealed to humans on earth, rather than movement throughout the limits of earth and heaven as in traditional apocalyptic literature. This is the nature of the inversion of apocalyptic where the glory of God and his Son occurs in limited environments on earth, rather than the wide expanses of the heavens, earth, and Sheol.

Just before Logos Jesus brings Lazarus out of the tomb, he says to Martha, "Did I not tell you that if you believed, you would see the glory of God?" (11:40). After they take away the stone, Jesus looks into the above and says, "Father, I thank you for having heard me. I knew that you always hear me, but I have said this for the sake of the crowd standing here, so that they may believe that you sent me" (11:41–42). Then Jesus cries out to Lazarus, he comes out, and Jesus commands the people there to unbind him and let him go. At this point, let us turn to the sisters of Lazarus and their role in the episode.

Action and Speech of the Sisters of Lazarus, Mary and Martha

In the episode of Jesus's raising of Lazarus, initial interaction occurs between the sisters of Lazarus and Logos Jesus. Mary and Martha send a message with their combined voice to Jesus, telling him that the one whom he loves is ill (11:1–3). This leads to interaction between Jesus and his disciples as a group (11:7–16), which takes Jesus and the disciples to Bethany, the village of the beloved family of Mary, Martha, and Lazarus. In Bethany, Judeans emerge in the episode, because they have come as a group to the home of Martha and Mary to console them about the death of their brother Lazarus (11:19). The Judeans who are present in the episode have deep feelings of grief for the family of Mary, Martha, and Lazarus, and this is what eventually leads to a prominent role by women in the episode itself and in subsequent scenes. But Judeans do not begin to play a major role until 11:31, after the disciples and the sisters have played initial roles in the overall episode.

---

22. Robbins, "Kinetic Divine Concepts," 286–88.

As the episode unfolds, the really important thing the sisters do is notify Jesus that the one whom he loves is ill. Jesus interprets this as their having asked him to come and heal Lazarus. In John 16:24, Jesus complains to his disciples that they have never asked him for anything. Jesus assures them, "Very truly, I tell you, if you ask anything of the Father in my name, he will give it to you. Until now you have not asked for anything in my name. Ask and you will receive, so that your joy may be complete" (16:23–24). Indeed, it is symptomatic of the disciples' lack of knowing in the Fourth Gospel that they cannot truly see and understand who Logos Jesus is, so they do not realize what they could and should ask Jesus to do. In contrast, the sisters of Lazarus send a request to Jesus to come and heal Lazarus, and what they ask for they receive. But they receive it in a manner that is both less and more than they ask for. They simply wanted healing. What they receive is regeneration of the deteriorated body of their brother Lazarus, which reveals both the glory of God and the glorification of the Son of God. Jesus promises the sisters at the beginning of the episode (11:4) that both the glory of God and the glorification of the Son of God will be revealed through the severe illness of Lazarus. Then just before the sisters experience Lazarus coming out of the tomb, Jesus tells Martha, "Did I not tell you that if you believed, you would see the glory of God?" (11:40). This is the nature of creational revelation. A person experiences both the glory of God and the glorification of the Son of God before the end of time in episodes that occur while Logos Jesus is on earth.

Still, Mary and Martha do not totally understand what has happened in their sight. In Martha's discussion of death and resurrection with Jesus (11:21–27), Martha only knows the prophetic-apocalyptic process of death and resurrection at the end of time, namely eschatological revelation. Engberg-Pedersen accurately calls this a form of "initial belief." In contrast, Logos Jesus teaches the Johannine creational process of generating life "from above" (3:3, 7).[23] Martha does not understand the creational process

---

23. Martha does not understand what Jesus is saying: Ruben Zimmerman, "The Narrative Hermeneutics of John 11: Learning with Lazarus How to Understand Death, Life, and Resurrection," in *The Resurrection of Jesus in the Gospel of John*, ed. Craig R. Koester and Reimund Bieringer, WUNT 222 (Tübingen: Mohr Siebeck, 2008), 90–93; Engberg-Pedersen, *John and Philosophy*, 236–37: Martha does not understand the last part of John 20:31: "and in order that *believing that* (*pisteuontes*) you may have *life* in or through his *name*.... not understanding the *ultimate* thing about Jesus: that he is about to return to God through his death and resurrection (and that this has crucial

of generating and regenerating life, but she has a significant glimpse into Logos Jesus's relation to the Father. She says, "But even now I know that God will give you whatever you ask of him" (11:22). She seems not to know that Logos Jesus does what he sees the Father doing, that the Father raises the dead and gives them life, and that the Son also gives life to whomever he wishes (5:19, 21). But she and her sister have asked Logos Jesus to heal their brother, and what they have asked he will grant them. The sisters asked, then, and, because they asked, they see the creational process of revelation of the glory of God in Jesus's call to Lazarus that brings him out of the tomb (11:43–44), even though they do not fully understand it.

Action and Speech of Disciples of Jesus, including Thomas

In contrast to the sisters, the disciples do not understand what is happening throughout the entire Lazarus episode. When the disciples recognized that the water had changed to wine at Cana near the beginning of the Gospel of John, they experienced creational revelation of Logos Jesus, saw Jesus's glory, and believed in him (2:1–11). Nevertheless, as the story proceeds, they do not know and understand. In the Lazarus episode, they fear that Jesus will be stoned if they go to Judea again, where the home of Lazarus and his sisters is in Bethany (11:7–8). Jesus tells them how cosmic creation works in the earthly realm, when he says, "Are there not twelve hours of daylight? Those who walk during the day do not stumble, because they see the light of this world. But those who walk at night stumble, because the light is not in them" (11:9). But the disciples cannot understand this. Even though they have seen the glory of Logos Jesus at Cana and believed in him, they do not understand how Logos Jesus works as the light of the world. Because they do not understand, it is clear that the light is not yet in them. They do not understand how Jesus heals people, doing "nothing on his own, but only what he sees the Father doing; for whatever the Father does, the Son does likewise" (5:19). Perhaps the problem is that Jesus had told this to Judeans after he had healed the paralyzed man by the pool of Beth-zatha, but he has never told this directly to the disciples. So, even though the disciples saw Logos Jesus's glory when the water

---

implications for human beings). Seen in that light, it is not enough to believe in Jesus as 'the Christ', 'the Son of God', or 'the one who comes into the world'. In themselves, those titles describe Jesus quite well. But they precisely do not go far enough. They only express what we have earlier called initial belief."

changed to wine, they cannot yet see his glory in relation to the fullness of life in him, which enables him to heal people and raise them from death. Indeed, Logos Jesus will lay down his own life in order to take it up again (10:17). In chapter 10, Jesus tells some Pharisees—who are a group within the larger group of Judeans in the Fourth Gospel (9:40–10:19)—that he will lay down his life and take it up again. But up to this point in the story, Logos Jesus has not told his disciples that he will lay down his life and take it up again.

The inability of the disciples to understand Jesus becomes evident when Jesus tells them he wants to go to Lazarus and awaken him, because Lazarus has fallen asleep (11:11). The disciples, speaking with one voice, say that if Lazarus has fallen asleep, he will be all right,[24] because, as the narrator tells us, they did not understand that Jesus was speaking about Lazarus's death (11:12). So Jesus told them plainly, "Lazarus is dead," and for their sake, he is glad he was not there, so they might believe (11:14–15). At this point, an individual disciple speaks. Thomas tells his fellow disciples, "Let us also go, that we may die with him" (11:16). So, while Logos Jesus talks to his disciples about believing, Thomas talks about dying. It is remarkable how the disciples do not understand creational Logos Jesus in the Gospel of John. Indeed, their role of not being able to understand the actions and speech of creational Logos Jesus in the Fourth Gospel has a fascinating relation to the disciples' inability to understand prophetic-apocalyptic Jesus as "the Son of Man" who must suffer, die, and rise again in the Gospel of Mark. Especially for this reason, it is important for us to look at the role of the Judeans in the Gospel of John.

Action and Speech of Judeans, Pharisees, and Chief Priests, including Caiaphas

Judeans become deeply involved in the Lazarus story after Jesus's initial discussion with his disciples and with Martha (11:7–16, 20–27) and after Martha returns to Bethany and tells her sister Mary that Jesus has arrived and is calling for her (11:28). When Mary gets up quickly and leaves the house (11:29), the Judeans who were consoling her at her home follow her, because they think Mary is going to Lazarus's tomb to weep there (11:31). So the Judeans go along with Mary, and when she comes to Jesus, both she

---

24. Or be saved (*sōthēsetai*). See Hylen, *Imperfect Believers*, 65.

and the Judeans are weeping (11:33). This causes Jesus himself to be deeply moved, and when he asks Mary where they have laid Lazarus and Mary addresses him as Lord and says, "Come and see," Jesus himself begins to weep. This leads the Judeans to remark, "See how he loved him" (11:36), and some of them at this point interrelate Jesus's healing of the blind man in chapter 9 with this episode in chapter 11 by saying, "Could not he who opened the eyes of the blind man have kept this man from dying?" (11:37).

The Judeans in the scene, then, were witnesses to Jesus's healing of the blind man in chapter 9, and they reason that if he could heal a blind man, he probably also could have healed Lazarus of his illness before he died. When the Judeans see Lazarus emerge from the tomb, therefore, many of them "believe in him" (11:45). This stands in contrast to the disciples, who do not bring knowledge of previous healings by Jesus into reasoning about his speech and actions in the Lazarus episode.

In the Lazarus episode, therefore, Judeans actively participate in witnessing and believing as it occurs throughout the Gospel of John. Ironically, the disciples are not participants in the process of witnessing and believing in the Lazarus episode. They became disciples through the witnessing process in the first chapter of the Fourth Gospel, but they will only participate further in it after the story in the Gospel of John ends. To understand the importance of this, it is important for us to review the witnessing process that leads to initial belief.

In the first chapter of the Fourth Gospel, John the Baptist witnesses to Jesus as the Lamb of God, and the two disciples with him, Andrew and an unnamed disciple, follow Jesus (1:36–37).[25] This witnessing procedure continues with Andrew. After hearing John the Baptist give witness to Jesus's identity, Andrew not only follows Jesus, but also he finds his brother Simon, tells him "We have found the Messiah," and brings Simon to Jesus (1:40–42). Later, when Jesus finds Philip and tells him, "Follow me" (1:43), Philip finds Nathaniel, witnesses to him that they have found "him about whom Moses in the law and also the prophets wrote, Jesus son of Joseph from Nazareth," and invites him to "come and see" Jesus (1:45–46). As a result of Nathaniel's dialogue with Jesus, he witnesses aloud to the hearer/reader: "Rabbi, you are the Son of God! You are the King of Israel!" (1:47–49).

After these episodes in the Fourth Gospel, Jesus's disciples no longer witness to other people. Rather, they become people who cannot at the

---

25. Some think the Beloved Disciple is the unnamed disciple.

moment understand the significance of what they see and hear, but they will remember and understand after Logos Jesus returns to the Father. As a result of this, Hylen describes the disciples as an "'eschatological character', shaped in the present by the same promises that God will fulfill on the last day."[26] They do not know and understand cosmic creational revelation when it occurs in the story line of the Gospel of John, but they will perfect their understanding and belief after the events that occur in the story.[27]

The promise that the disciples will remember in the future begins when Jesus creates a disturbance in the temple on his visit to Jerusalem for the Passover in chapter 2. When he tells the Judeans he will destroy the temple and in three days raise it up (2:13-19), the disciples do not understand the significance of what Jesus says, but the narrator tells us that they remembered what Jesus said and did after Jesus was raised from the dead, and then they believed both "the scripture and the word Jesus had spoken" (2:22). In contrast, during the Passover festival itself, many Judeans "believed in his name because they saw the signs he was doing" (2:23). The disciples, then, are delayed knowers and witnesses. They live under a promise, but they do not know and understand what is happening as the Johannine story unfolds. In contrast, many Judeans progressively become believers when they see what Jesus does, and their belief progressively becomes known throughout the group of Judeans as a whole.

As a result of belief that spreads among the Judeans, a Pharisee named Nicodemus, who is not only one of the Judeans but also "a leader of the Judeans," comes to Jesus and says, "Rabbi, we know that you are a teacher who has come from God; for no one can do these signs that you do apart from the presence of God" (3:1-2). But since Nicodemus comes in darkness, he cannot understand the things Jesus says. Therefore, Jesus becomes unhappy with his dialogue with Nicodemus and asserts, "Very truly, I tell you, we speak of what we know and testify to what we have seen; yet you do not receive our testimony" (3:11). As a result of Logos Jesus's conversation with Nicodemus, however, the hearer/reader of the story hears Jesus's testimony about being born "from above" (3:7, 11). Do we make a mistake if we read Jesus's negative comments to Judeans as totally harsh rebukes but read his negative comments to his disciples as only mild rebukes? Should we conclude, rather, that negative remarks by Jesus in the Fourth Gospel

---

26. Hylen, *Imperfect Believers*, 74.
27. Hylen, *Imperfect Believers*, 69–72.

are most of all a result of the difficulty Logos Jesus has communicating his remarkable nonearthly message to humans of any kind or group? Either the narrator or John the Baptist explains this to Judeans at the end of chapter 3 after John reasserts that he is not the messiah but was sent ahead of Jesus (3:28).[28] In this context, either the narrator or John speaks words very similar to those of Jesus in other places in the Fourth Gospel, saying:

> The one who comes from above is above all; the one who is of the earth belongs to the earth and speaks about earthly things. The one who comes from heaven is above all. He testifies to what he has seen and heard, yet no one accepts his testimony. Whoever has accepted his testimony has certified this, that God is true. He whom God has sent speaks the words of God, for he gives the Spirit without measure. The Father loves the Son and has placed all things in his hands. Whoever believes in the Son has eternal life; whoever disobeys the Son will not see life, but must endure God's wrath. (John 3:31–36)

Both Jesus and John the Baptist understand the cosmic creational belief system. Jesus is the Logos who was sent by the Father from above heaven and earth to become flesh and dwell in the sensorimotor realm where humans live until the hour when he returns to the Father. John the Baptist was sent to be the precreation witness to Logos Jesus. Both of them know, understand, and believe the cosmic creational story about Logos Jesus. Other humans, be they disciples or some other group, are not able to understand the creational story line fully, even if they benefit from it.

After Jesus talks with Nicodemus (3:1–21) and John the Baptist or the narrator elaborates his witness to Judeans about creational Logos Jesus (3:31–36), Jesus travels through Samaria and talks with a Samaritan woman at Jacob's well. This results in many Samaritans believing in Jesus "because of the woman's testimony" that Jesus had told her everything she had ever done (4:39). When many Samaritans come to Jesus and he stays with them two days, many more believe in him "because of his word" and

---

28. Most commentators presuppose that John 3:31–36 is comment by the narrator, but it could be possible that it is speech by John the Baptist: O'Day and Hylen, *John*, 49; cf. C. K. Barrett, *The Gospel according to St. John: An Introduction with Commentary and Notes on the Greek Text* (London: SPCK, 1962), 182. Also, see the excellent discussions of this passage in Ashton, *Understanding the Fourth Gospel*, 48, 534–36; D. Moody Smith, *John*, ANTC (Nashville: Abingdon, 1999), 102–9; Neyrey, *Gospel of John*, 86–87.

they tell the woman, "It is no longer because of what you said that we believe, for we have heard for ourselves, and we know that this is truly the Savior of the world" (4:42). When many Samaritans believe after we have been informed that many Judeans believe, we are reminded of the process of evangelization in the book of Acts, where belief in Jesus as the Messiah spreads beyond Judeans to Samaritans (Acts 8). But in the Gospel of John, belief is focused on the cosmic creational story line of Logos Jesus rather than the prophetic-apocalyptic story line of Messiah Jesus who will come as the glorious Son of Man in the future in the Synoptic Gospels and Acts. For this reason, belief is a process of moving from initial belief to full cosmic creational belief, and, therefore, the reader cannot be certain where the believer is in the process of belief. The narrator holds the reader in suspense about whether certain people move beyond initial belief into full belief or even decisively toward it. Perhaps the reason is to keep the reader in the process of growth into full belief and to communicate that no human can ever fully understand the generation and regeneration of life and eternal life as God and his Logos Son perform it.

After many Samaritans believe in Logos Jesus, the royal official from Capernaum believes Jesus's word (4:50), his son recovers, and he truly believes along with his whole household (4:53). What is the level of belief of the royal official? He believes the word of Jesus that his son will live (4:50), and when he is told his son is alive, he and his whole household believe (4:53). But does the royal official believe that Jesus was sent to earth from above by the Father to generate and regenerate life from above? Probably not. His belief probably remains at an initial level, but he has at least started on the journey of belief.

After Jesus's encounter with the royal official, he travels to Jerusalem for a festival of the Judeans (5:1). While at the festival, Jesus heals a paralyzed man alongside the pool of Beth-zatha. When the healed man tells the Judeans about being healed, they start persecuting Jesus, because he is healing on the Sabbath (5:16). When Jesus tells them, "My Father is still working, and I also am working" (5:17), the Judeans begin to seek "all the more to kill him," because he is not only breaking the Sabbath but also "calling God his own Father, thereby making himself equal to God" (5:18). Here the story line is similar to the prophetic-apocalyptic story line in the Synoptic Gospels about Jesus's healing of people on the Sabbath, but in the Fourth Gospel, the issue has been reconfigured from an accusation of blasphemy into accusation that Jesus is making himself equal to God by calling him his own Father.

As a result of the accusation in the Fourth Gospel that Jesus is making himself equal to God, Jesus teaches the Judeans with great detail about his relation to the Father, with special emphasis on life and raising the dead:

> As the Father raises the dead and gives them life, so also the Son gives life to whomever he wishes [5:21].... Anyone who hears my word and believes him who sent me has eternal life, and does not come under judgment, but has passed from death to life [5:24].... The hour is coming, and is now here, when the dead will hear the voice of the Son of God, and those who hear will live [5:25].... Just as the Father has life in himself, so he has granted the Son also to have life in himself [5:26].... The hour is coming when all who are in their graves will hear his voice and will come out—those who have done good, to the resurrection of life, and those who have done evil, to the resurrection of condemnation [5:28–29].... I have a testimony greater than John's. The works that the Father has given me to complete, the very works that I am doing, testify on my behalf that the Father has sent me [5:36–37].... You search the scriptures because you think that in them you have eternal life; and it is they that testify on my behalf. Yet you refuse to come to me to have life [5:39–40].... How can you believe when you accept glory from one another and do not seek the glory that comes from the one who alone is God? [5:44]

This long statement by Jesus is a blend of prophetic-apocalyptic and cosmic creational reasoning about giving life and possessing eternal life. As a result of the blending, it contains emergent structure for full belief but leaves ambiguity concerning the nature of life within full earthly belief and the relation of life on earth in full belief to eternal life after death. Can a person be born from above into eternal life while existing in earthly life, or does this happen fully only after death? This seems to be an ambiguity for the narrator and, as a result, for the reader. With full belief on earth, a person receives eternal life. But what exactly is the nature of eternal life for a person living within the earthly sensorimotor realm? Engberg-Pedersen asserts that the answer lies in humans receiving of the Spirit, which provides the energy-force for receiving eternal life, and this may be correct.[29] But in the Fourth Gospel, there is a level of ambiguity about the relation of Spirit-filled life to being born from above that is not present in the prophetic-apocalyptic conceptuality of 1 Corinthians, Galatians,

---

29. Engberg-Pedersen, *John and Philosophy*, 243–47, 252.

and Luke-Acts. Being born from above has an ambiguity that probably no human can ever understand.

In the Lazarus episode, the Judeans apply knowledge they have gained from past episodes with Jesus to the new things that happen, and they continue to tell others what they have seen and believe. Some of the Judeans go and tell the Pharisees how Jesus raised Lazarus, and this results in the chief priests and Pharisees calling a meeting of the council to consider what should be done, since "This man is performing many signs," and if they let him go on like this, "Everyone will believe in him, and the Romans will come and destroy" their holy place (Jerusalem) and their nation (11:47–48).

In the Lazarus episode, Judeans first act and speak as a group; then as the episode continues, Pharisees and chief priests begin to act and speak as subgroups. After the chief priests emerge as a special subgroup of Judeans, the high priest Caiaphas speaks individually, much like Thomas emerges as an individual speaker among the disciples earlier in the episode (11:16). When the high priest Caiaphas speaks, he tells the other Judeans that they know "nothing at all," because they do not understand that it is better for them "to have one man die for the people than to have the whole nation destroyed" (11:50). The narrator then tells us that Caiaphas "did not say this on his own," but since he was the high priest that year, "he prophesied that Jesus was about to die for the nation, and not for the nation only, but to gather into one the dispersed children of God" (11:51–52). Caiaphas, then, speaks in a prophetic-apocalyptic mode of belief and understanding related to the Synoptic Gospels and Acts. At this point, Judean officials make a plan to put Jesus to death. Judeans who believe in Jesus function as a major agency for collusion between the Judean Pharisees, chief priests, high priest, and council to kill Jesus. The irony is that their agency is not based on a misunderstanding of who Jesus is but on quite a robust form of belief about Jesus.

Further action by Judeans then occurs during the next Passover, when the Judean chief priests and Pharisees give orders that anyone who knows the whereabouts of Jesus should let them know so "they might arrest him" (11:57). When Jesus comes to the Passover, he goes to Bethany and has dinner with Martha, Lazarus, and Mary six days before the festival (12:1–2). When Lazarus is at the table with Jesus, Mary anoints Jesus's feet with costly perfume and wipes his feet with her hair, and Martha serves (12:2–4). After Judas Iscariot asks why Mary has wasted this perfume rather than selling it and giving the money to the poor, Jesus rebukes him for his remark, telling him that she bought it for the day of his burial (12:4–7). When the Judeans learn that Jesus is in the house, they come to see both Jesus and Lazarus, and the Judean chief priests plan to put both Jesus and Lazarus to death, because so many Judeans are "deserting and believing in Jesus" (12:11).

When Jesus goes to Jerusalem the next day, the great crowd coming to the festival hears that Jesus is coming to Jerusalem, and they go out to meet him with branches of palm trees, crying out, blessing him as "the one who comes in the name of the Lord" (12:13). Jesus's disciples did not understand what was happening, "but when Jesus was glorified, then they remembered that these things had been written of him and had been done to him" (12:16). But the crowd who had been with Jesus when he called Lazarus out of the tomb and raised him from the dead "continued to testify" (12:17). And the narrator explains that it was because Jesus had performed the sign of the raising of Lazarus that they went out to meet him (12:18). Then the Judean Pharisees said to one another, "You see, you can do nothing. Look, the world has gone after him!" (12:19).

Conclusion

In the context of the extreme difficulties of communicating cosmic creational belief so that any human other than John the Baptist can see, hear, know, understand, and believe it, the Gospel of John shows multiple groups struggling *in their own way* to understand it. The disciples cannot understand it as the story unfolds, even though they have strong initial belief, but they will perfect their understanding after the story ends, except that they experience division among themselves, with the sharpest division between the eleven and Judas, into whom Satan enters. Samaritans experience belief through the witness of the Samaritan woman at the well. As a result of her witness, they come to Jesus, spend two days with him, and then tell the woman, "It is no longer because of what you said that we believe, for we have heard for ourselves, and we know that this is truly the Savior of the world" (4:42). Judeans have the hardest time understanding Logos Jesus. One of the reasons is that they have so much information from biblical history. The disciples do not show significant memory of biblical history, in contrast to the Judeans. So they do not show significant progress in their understanding. As the Judeans work through biblical history with Logos Jesus, significant conflict and divisions occur. But in the process, Jesus tells the Judeans more about himself and God than he tells anyone else. In the end, a large number of Judeans come to believe in Jesus and want to make him king of Israel, with even many of the authorities believing in him (12:42; cf. 18:39; 19:19–22).

The Lazarus episode is especially interesting, because only the Judeans are able to relate Jesus's previous healing of the blind man to his potential for healing Lazarus. When the Judeans see Jesus regenerate Lazarus's deteriorated body into a living human being, they grow in their belief, tell others in their group about the amazing things he is doing, and the people to whom they *testify* understand quite clearly the implications! The Judeans, then, who exhibit the greatest growth in belief about Jesus, become the primary agency for revealing his glory by his laying down of his life, raising it up, and returning to the Father. But those Judeans who reject Jesus are judged by the words of God that Logos Jesus has spoken to them. As Jesus says:

> The one who rejects me and does not receive my words [*ta rhēmata*] has his judgment; on the last day the word [*ho logos*] that I have spoken will judge him, for I have not spoken on my own, but the Father who sent me has himself given a commandment about what to say and what to speak. And I know that this commandment is eternal life. What I speak, therefore, I speak just as the Father has told me. (12:48–50)

Since God the Father is invisible to humans, living in the *above* realm rather than the sensorimotor realm of heaven and earth, Logos Jesus is the agent and agency for humans seeing and hearing the works of God. Each group of humans in the Gospel of John functions in a distinctive way, helping the hearer/reader explore multiple ways to begin to experience the glory of Logos Jesus through seeing and hearing Jesus's deeds and words in contexts of belief, questioning, conflict, division, and death. All of these *events* in the lives of humans work metaphorically toward full belief in the movement of regenerating life from the realm *above* downward through the cosmos of heaven and earth to specific places where people hear the words of God and see the amazing things God is continually doing through enfleshed Logos Jesus. Hearing the words Logos Jesus speaks and seeing the works he performs are the media of communication that give earthly humans the possibility of moving into full cosmic creational belief, which enables them to become children of God "born from above."

Why Is Pilate So Afraid in John 19:8? Pilate's Fear and the Dynamics of Power in John 18:28–19:16

Gilberto A. Ruiz

In the conclusion of *Revelation in the Fourth Gospel*, Gail R. O'Day connects Jesus's trial before Pilate in John 18:28–19:16 to her analysis of John's use of irony as a tool for engaging his reader's participation in the narrative.[1] Rather than presenting a straightforward report, this "masterpiece of Johannine narrative technique" depicts Jesus's trial in a manner that invites readers to participate in the revelation experience and to recognize Pilate's powerlessness before Jesus.

> In this trial, Pilate attempts to exercise his power and authority over Jesus, but what the reader senses from the workings of the narrative is that Pilate never achieves mastery. Instead, Pilate's power and authority diminish as the narrative progresses. His questions and responses to Jesus underscore his distance from any true command of power, authority, and knowledge. Yet the Fourth Evangelist does not *tell* the reader that Pilate is ineffectual, that Pilate is powerless and without authority. Instead, he allows the narrative to draw the reader in so that the reader can form his or her own conclusions.[2]

According to O'Day, the narrative presents Pilate as "a ruler with all the accoutrements of power, with the authority to take away life, who stands

---

1. Gail R. O'Day, *Revelation in the Fourth Gospel: Narrative Mode and Theological Claim* (Philadelphia: Fortress, 1986), 112–13. I would like to thank Lynn R. Huber, Susan E. Hylen, and William R. Wright IV for their invitation to contribute to this volume honoring Gail and to Lynn and Susan for their helpful comments on an earlier draft of this essay. I miss Gail dearly, and I am ever grateful for her friendship and exemplary mentorship both during and after my years as her doctoral student. May her joy now be complete (John 16:24).

2. O'Day, *Revelation in the Fourth Gospel*, 112, emphasis original.

powerless in the face of true power, authority, and life."[3] This remark captures the central theological claim made by John's narration of the Roman trial of Jesus: true power, authority, and life lie in Jesus, not in Rome and its agents.[4]

Pilate's powerlessness before Jesus becomes especially apparent in 19:7–8 when he becomes afraid after being told that Jesus made himself the Son of God. Yet neither John's characterization of Pilate as a strong character nor what we know about the power Roman governors wielded when hearing cases would lead readers to expect Pilate to become so fearful, making 19:7–8 a key point in John's narration of the trial. This dissonance elicits the reader's participation to make sense of the passage's claims about both Jesus and Pilate. In this essay, I argue that a close narrative analysis of John's trial scene shows that Pilate's fear in 19:8 functions as a signal to the reader that Pilate recognizes his powerlessness before the Johannine Jesus. Interpreting Pilate's fear in this way contributes to John's characterization of Pilate as a strong Roman ruler and shows that Pilate's fear confirms for John's readers the theological claim that other elements of the narration have already suggested: Jesus is more powerful than Rome.

This essay thus supports the newer reading of Pilate, initially proposed by David Rensberger and adopted by O'Day in her commentary on John, as a strong, shrewd character who seizes Jesus's trial as an opportunity to assert Rome's sovereignty.[5] Although this reading represents a significant advance beyond the view of the Johannine Pilate as a weak, indecisive

---

3. O'Day, *Revelation in the Fourth Gospel*, 112.

4. Analyses of the Fourth Gospel that foreground its Roman imperial context have paid special attention to Jesus's trial in 18:28–19:16, seeing Pontius Pilate as "the face of Rome" in John's Gospel. David Rensberger, for example, writes that, while it is an interpretive mistake to read Pilate in John as representing "the state" as an abstract philosophical concept, Pilate "may well represent the *Roman* state" (*Johannine Faith and Liberating Community* [Philadelphia: Westminster, 1988], 90, emphasis original). Lance Byron Richey also considers Pilate to be "the representative of Rome" in the Gospel (*Roman Imperial Ideology and the Gospel of John*, CBQMS 43 [Washington, DC: Catholic Biblical Association of America, 2007], 174), and Stephen D. Moore calls Pilate "the face of Rome in John" (*Empire and Apocalypse: Postcolonialism and the New Testament*, Bible in the Modern World 12 [Sheffield: Sheffield Phoenix, 2006], 52).

5. David Rensberger, "The Politics of John: The Trial of Jesus in the Fourth Gospel," *JBL* 103 (1984): 395–411; Rensberger, *Johannine Faith*, 87–106; cf. Gail R. O'Day, "The Gospel of John: Introduction, Commentary, and Reflections," *NIB* 9:811–27, esp. the excursus on John's portrayal of Pilate on 815.

ruler, it fails to explain why Pilate becomes afraid in 19:8 when told of Jesus's claim to be the Son of God. A ruthless Roman governor should not fear a beaten and accused provincial like Jesus. Tom Thatcher's claim that Pilate's fear is "the most unusual—and most significant—feature of John's trial story" thus merits serious consideration.[6]

To do so, I begin by considering the problem that Pilate's fear poses for reading Pilate as a strong character in John. I then examine the verbs of motion in John's trial scene to illustrate how the narration reinforces the Johannine perspective of Jesus as ultimately holding the power in John's trial scene. I then propose 19:8 as John's indication to the reader that Pilate realizes, even if only momentarily, the inferior nature of his power before Jesus. An analysis of the two dialogues between Jesus and Pilate during the trial (18:33-38a; 19:9-11) demonstrates that Jesus's power comes from his connection to the world "above," that is, from his access to divine power. Jesus's access to divine power causes Pilate's fear. Finally, I discuss how this understanding of Pilate's fear supports John's characterization of Pilate as a strong, imposing tyrant and assures John's readers that they have placed their faith in a divine power stronger than Rome and its agents.

The Problem of Pilate's Fear

Scholarship is divided on whether to read Pilate in John as a strong or weak character.[7] Many of the great commentaries on John view the Pilate of 18:28-19:16 as a weak, indecisive ruler earnestly seeking to give Jesus a fair hearing, and this reading persists in more recent commentaries as well.[8]

---

6. Tom Thatcher, *Greater Than Caesar: Christology and Empire in the Fourth Gospel* (Minneapolis: Fortress, 2009), 71; see also 84-85.

7. See D. Francois Tolmie, "Pontius Pilate: Failing in More Ways Than One," in *Character Studies in the Fourth Gospel: Narrative Approaches to Seventy Figures in John*, ed. Steven A. Hunt, D. Francois Tolmie, and Ruben Zimmerman, WUNT 314 (Tübingen, Mohr Siebeck, 2013; repr. Grand Rapids: Eerdmans, 2016), 578-97.

8. E.g., C. K. Barrett, *The Gospel according to St. John: An Introduction with Commentary and Notes on the Greek Text*, 2nd ed. (Philadelphia: Westminster, 1978), 531-46; Raymond E. Brown, *The Gospel according to John*, 2 vols., AB 29-29A (New York: Doubleday, 1966-1970), 2:863-64, 872, 885-96; Rudolf Bultmann, *The Gospel of John: A Commentary*, trans. G. R. Beasley-Murray, R. W. N. Hoare, and J. K. Riches (Philadelphia: Westminster, 1971), 655-65; Ernst Haenchen, *John*, ed. Robert W. Funk and Ulrich Busse, trans. Robert W. Funk, 2 vols., Hermeneia (Philadelphia: Fortress, 1984), 2:175-88; Rudolf Schnackenburg, *The Gospel according to St. John*, trans. Kevin

According to this view, the Jews persuade Pilate to crucify Jesus despite his misgivings.[9] The staging of the scene, which features Pilate going back and forth between Jesus inside the praetorium and the Jews outside, such commentaries say reinforces the appearance of Pilate's inability to decide Jesus's fate, portraying Pilate "as caught between the truth of Jesus and the relentless pressure of his Jewish adversaries."[10] Interpreters who hold this view take at face value Pilate's repeated claims to find no case against Jesus (18:38; 19:4, 6) and his attempts to secure Jesus's release (18:39, 19:12). Pilate deems Jesus innocent before Roman law and sincerely "seeks to save him right up to the last minute."[11] While the scourging in 19:1 poses a problem for this view (why would Pilate scourge Jesus if he considers him

---

Smyth et al., 3 vols. (New York: Seabury/Crossroad, 1968–1982), 3:241–67. More recent commentaries that adopt this reading include Herman N. Ridderbos, *The Gospel of John: A Theological Commentary*, trans. John Vriend (Grand Rapids: Eerdmans, 1997), 585–607; D. Moody Smith, *John*, ANTC (Nashville: Abingdon, 1999), 338–51; and Johannes Beutler, *A Commentary on the Gospel of John*, trans. Michael Tait (Grand Rapids: Eerdmans, 2017), 464–79. On this tradition of interpretation, see Helen K. Bond, *Pontius Pilate in History and Interpretation*, SNTSMS 100 (Cambridge: Cambridge University Press, 1998), 174; Rensberger, *Johannine Faith*, 92; Christopher M. Tuckett, "Pilate in John 18–19: A Narrative Critical Approach," in *Narrativity in Biblical and Related Texts*, ed. G. J. Brook and J.-D. Kaestli, BETL 149 (Leuven: Leuven University Press, 2000), 131–32.

9. The author of the Fourth Gospel regularly, though not exclusively, uses οἱ Ἰουδαῖοι to refer to opponents of Jesus (5:16, 18; 7:1; 8:57–59; 10:31; 11:8) and his followers (7:13, 9:22, 20:19) (Marianne Meye Thompson, *John: A Commentary*, NTL [Louisville: Westminster John Knox, 2015], 200). This usage results in a largely negative characterization of "the Jews." In John 18:28–19:16, for example, they clamor for Jesus's crucifixion (19:6–7) to the point of denying God's kingship over them (19:15). Though I will avoid using quotation marks to distinguish this character group from the historical Jewish people, this distinction is critical. Without it, John's use of οἱ Ἰουδαῖοι too easily leads to inaccurate, problematic conceptualizations of earliest Christian history (e.g., as a conflict between "Christians" and all "the Jews"), fosters anti-Semitism, and—as has happened historically, with tragic results—provides fodder to justify anti-Semitic violence by Christians.

10. Smith, *John*, 339. See also Brown, *John*, 2:858, 864; Sherri Brown, "What Is Truth? Jesus, Pilate, and the Staging of the Dialogue of the Cross in John 18:28–19:16a," *CBQ* 77 (2015): 69–86; Mark W. G. Stibbe, *John as Storyteller: Narrative Criticism and the Fourth Gospel*, SNTSMS 73 (Cambridge: Cambridge University Press, 1992), 105–6.

11. Schnackenburg, *John*, 3:263. Similarly, according to Beutler, Pilate "is always trying to set Jesus free" (*John*, 476).

innocent?), Raymond Brown, for example, explains this as Pilate's attempt to pacify the Jews' desire to punish Jesus.[12] More recently, Johannes Beutler sees the scourging as Pilate's attempt to elicit pity and clemency for Jesus on the part of the Jews.[13] Ultimately, Pilate, who as the scene progresses becomes "like a fish in a net, which desperately wants to be free and feels that its free space grows ever smaller," succumbs to their clamor for Jesus to be crucified (19:15–16), as the Jews remind him that his own status before the emperor is at stake (19:12).[14] Forced to decide between Jesus and his own associations with the imperial powers of the world, Pilate chooses the world.

Against this reading, Rensberger showed that John portrays Pilate as a strong, shrewd character who senses that the Jews' urgent desire to have Jesus executed gives him an opportunity to use Jesus to remind the Jews of their subjugation to Rome.[15] According to Rensberger, Pilate's disingenuous recommendations that the Jews carry out Jesus's execution themselves (19:6; cf. 18:31) shows that, rather than provide a fair trial for Jesus or genuinely seek his release, Pilate seizes this moment as a power play to assert Rome's sovereignty over the Jews.[16] He scourges Jesus before the trial's end not to pacify the Jews' desire for Jesus to be punished but rather to present Jesus as a bruised and beaten "King of the Jews" and thereby "make a ridiculous example of Jewish nationalism."[17] Pilate's actions toward Jesus undermine all his claims of finding no case against Jesus (18:38; 19:4, 6), making all his references to Jesus's innocence and to Jesus as "King of the Jews" (18:39) and "your king" (19:14, 15) ironic taunts intended to rile the Jews and elicit from them the striking confession, "We have no king except Caesar" (19:15).[18] Once the Jews profess allegiance to the Roman emperor, Pilate is finished with Jesus and sends him out for crucifixion without further ado (19:16).[19]

---

12. Brown, *John*, 2:886–89.
13. Beutler, *John*, 471–72.
14. Haenchen, *John*, 2:186–87.
15. Rensberger, "Politics of John," 395–411; *Johannine Faith*, 87–106.
16. Rensberger, *Johannine Faith*, 92–95.
17. Rensberger, *Johannine Faith*, 94.
18. Rensberger, *Johannine Faith*, 93–95. Unless otherwise indicated, all biblical translations are mine.
19. Rensberger, *Johannine Faith*, 95. Readings that modify and expand upon Rensberger's basic line of interpretation include Bond, *Pontius Pilate*, 163–93; Warren Carter, *John and Empire: Initial Explorations* (New York: T&T Clark, 2008), 289–314;

John's portrayal of Pilate as a conniving Roman governor with a penchant for stoking the passions of the Jews under his control coheres well with the depiction of Pilate in Philo (*Legat.* 299–305) and Josephus (*B.J.* 2.169–177; *A.J.* 18.55–62; see also 18.85–89).[20] Whereas the Synoptics appear to rehabilitate Pilate's character in order to emphasize the Jewish leaders' guilt in Jesus's execution, John's Gospel follows the convention in ancient Jewish literature of depicting Pilate as a cruel ruler, insensitive and even outright hostile to his Jewish subordinates.[21] The image of Roman governors as excessively cruel that we observe from Philo, Josephus, and John's depiction of Pilate is tempered somewhat by Pliny's famous letter seeking the emperor Trajan's instruction on trying accused Christians (*Ep. Tra.* 10.96).[22] Nonetheless, Pliny's letter confirms that, if it came down to it, torturing those brought to trial was a real option for governors to deploy during an interrogation. Pliny informs Trajan of an instance when he found it "all the more necessary to extract the truth by torture" in order to determine whether two Christian women violated Trajan's edict banning political societies by convening Christians for wor-

---

Moore, *Empire and Apocalypse*, 45–74; Thatcher, *Greater Than Caesar*, 63–85; Tuckett, "Pilate in John 18–19," 131–40. O'Day's commentary is one of the few that accepts and builds on Rensberger's reading ("Gospel of John," *NIB* 9:811–27; see n. 8 above).

20. On Pilate in Philo and Josephus, see Bond, *Pontius Pilate*, 24–93; Brian C. McGing, "Pontius Pilate and the Sources," *CBQ* 53 (1991): 416–38.

21. The degree to which the testimonies of Philo and Josephus reflect the historical Pilate must be carefully assessed in light of their respective theological and political agendas, as Bond's analysis especially shows (*Pontius Pilate*, 24–93; also, Warren Carter, *Pontius Pilate: Portraits of a Roman Governor*, Interfaces [Collegeville, MN: Liturgical Press, 2003], 1–20). What matters for our purposes is that Philo and Josephus illustrate the convention of depicting Pilate as a malevolent figure, and that John's depiction follows suit (Cornelis Bennema, *Encountering Jesus: Character Studies in the Gospel of John*, 2nd ed. [Minneapolis: Fortress, 2014], 326–27; O'Day, "Gospel of John," *NIB* 9:815). For an argument that, likewise, John's use of οἱ Ἰουδαῖοι corresponds to how Philo, Josephus, and other ancient Jewish literature use the term, see Thompson, *John*, 199–204.

22. Even as he flaunts his power by warning them of "the punishment awaiting them" (*Ep. Tra.* 10.96.3), Pliny will not carry out punishment until completing an interrogation that includes several opportunities for the accused to answer his questions in a manner that may avoid punishment, or at least reduce its severity. Punishment is reserved for those who persist in calling themselves Christian (10.96.3–4). Translations of Pliny follow that of Pliny, *Letters: Books VIII–X; Panegyricus*, trans. Betty Radice, LCL (Cambridge: Harvard University Press, 1969).

ship (10.96.8). The Johannine Pilate's actions of scourging Jesus in the middle of the trial (19:1) rather than at the end thus poses no problems for John's readers in terms of whether a Roman governor would act this way. John's readers need not suspend their disbelief to accept John's depiction of Pilate as torturer.[23]

But one event in the Johannine account of Jesus's trial not only gives us pause in terms of the image we get of Pilate from Philo and Josephus and in terms of the expectations early Christians had of Roman governors, it also threatens to undermine our reading Pilate as a strong character in John. That one event is the narrator's statement in 19:8 that Pilate becomes afraid when in 19:7 the Jews tell him that Jesus made himself out to be the Son of God. Neither John's characterization of Pilate up to this point nor what we know about the power that Roman governors wielded when hearing cases would lead any reader to expect that Pilate could become so fearful.[24] This surprising turn of events demands a response from the reader, who must decide what this fear says about Pilate, and thus marks another instance of John's narrative strategy, so clearly presented in O'Day's *Revelation in the Fourth Gospel*, of soliciting the reader's engagement and participation in his version of the Jesus story.

Pilate's fear arises upon hearing from the Jews that they want Jesus put to death "because he made himself the Son of God" (ὅτι υἱὸν θεοῦ ἑαυτὸν ἐποίησεν, 19:7; cf. 5:18; 10:33). His fear poses no problem for readings that interpret Pilate as weak, including readings maintaining this view even as they foreground the gospel's Roman imperial context. Thus, for Richard J. Cassidy, Pilate's fear shows that Pilate becomes nervous about playing a role in the execution of the Son of God.[25] But as discussed above, recent readings have demonstrated that John's Pilate is a strong character, not a weak, indecisive one.

---

23. See Jennifer A. Glancy, "Torture: Flesh, Truth, and the Fourth Gospel," *BibInt* 13 (2005): 107–36; Moore, *Empire and Apocalypse*, 59–63; Thompson, *John*, 382–83. Glancy argues convincingly that the scourging in John is best read as an act of judicial torture intended to extract the truth from Jesus in the process of interrogation, not as a preliminary flogging meant to punish Jesus and pacify his accusers' desire for punishment ("Torture," 121–27).

24. Bennema notices the problem when he states, "It may surprise the reader that the strong Pilate shows fear on one occasion" (*Encountering Jesus*, 326).

25. Richard J. Cassidy, *John's Gospel in New Perspective: Christology and the Realities of Roman Power* (Maryknoll, NY: Orbis Books, 1992), 46.

For the most part, however, such readings attend to 19:8 only in cursory fashion, perhaps because it poses a difficulty for reading Pilate as a ruthless figure. Both Rensberger and Stephen D. Moore consider Pilate's fear to be genuine, even though John depicts Pilate as a strong, cruel ruler. For Rensberger, Pilate's fear is religious in nature. He is truly afraid of Jesus as the Son of God and so only now genuinely seeks to release Jesus.[26] For Moore, Pilate's fear shows that the Fourth Gospel does not concern itself with verisimilitude in its depiction of Roman governors, a reading indicative of how difficult it is to make sense of Pilate's fear when one would expect Roman governors to be fearless.[27]

Warren Carter reads Pilate's fear as an indication "of the seriousness of Jesus's challenge and the need for action."[28] For Carter, the language of "Son of God" in 19:7 catches Pilate's attention because in imperial contexts this phrase was used to promote emperors as having a filial relationship to deceased emperors who had been divinized, thus declaring the living emperor to be a θεοῦ υἱός or *divi filius*, son of a god.[29] This means the Jews accuse Jesus of making himself emperor by proclaiming to be the Son of God, a treasonous claim on Jesus's part that would require a swift response from Pilate.[30]

Thatcher makes the most of Pilate's fear in 19:8. For Thatcher, Pilate's fear is genuine and is in fact the conceptual linchpin of the trial scene.[31] According to Thatcher, the key to understanding why Pilate is afraid has to do with Jesus's identity as the Son of God introduced in 19:7, but not because of its imperial connotations (which would at most amuse Pilate) but because it is the foundational premise of Johannine theology and provides the explicit rationale for composing the gospel (20:30–31). In other words, the remark about Pilate's fear is part of a conversation the Gospel of John has with its readers, who are to believe that, as the Son of God, Jesus is more powerful than Pilate and is able to strike fear even in the represen-

---

26. Rensberger, *Johannine Faith*, 94–95.
27. Moore, *Empire and Apocalypse*, 57–58.
28. Carter, *John and Empire*, 307.
29. Carter, *John and Empire*, 194, 307.
30. Carter, *John and Empire*, 194, 307; cf. Martinus C. de Boer, "The Narrative Function of Pilate in John," in *Narrativity in Biblical and Related Texts*, ed. G. J. Brook and J.-D. Kaestli, BETL 149 (Leuven: Leuven University Press, 2000), 153–54; Beth M. Stovell, *Mapping Metaphorical Discourse in the Fourth Gospel: John's Eternal King*, Linguistic Biblical Studies 5 (Leiden: Brill, 2012), 285.
31. Thatcher, *Greater Than Caesar*, 84–85.

tative of the Roman Empire. As I will show below, the dialogues between Pilate and Jesus during the trial support Thatcher's interpretation.

Pilate's fear arises from a realization that his own power is no match for Jesus. Before turning to the dialogues between Pilate and Jesus, an analysis of the verbs of motion in 18:28–19:16 shows that the question of who holds power and control is an integral element of this scene. The narration deploys these verbs to reinforce the Johannine perspective of Jesus as the one having the power and control to determine the mode and manner of his death, despite Pilate's initial misunderstanding that he holds all the power.

Who's Moving?

Throughout the trial scenes, John crafts the story to communicate the agency of Jesus and to suggest that Pilate only appears to be in control. As I argue in this section, Jesus remains static and poised while Pilate moves about frenetically. As the scene moves toward his crucifixion, John's verb choices suggest that it is Jesus who acts decisively.

The verbs of motion inform the rhetoric of John 18:28–19:16's narration, making it worthwhile to list them here:

18:28	ἄγουσιν	The Jews, a group that includes the chief priests and their attendants (ὑπηρέται) (19:6–7), and the Roman soldiers who had arrested Jesus bring Jesus from Caiaphas to the praetorium.[32]
18:28	(οὐκ) εἰσῆλθον	The Jews do not enter the praetorium.
18:29	ἐξῆλθεν	Pilate goes out to the Jews.
18:33	εἰσῆλθεν	Pilate goes into the praetorium to speak with Jesus.
18:38	ἐξῆλθεν	Pilate goes out to the Jews.
19:1	ἔλαβεν	Pilate takes Jesus to scourge him.
19:3	ἤρχοντο	The soldiers come to Jesus to mock him.
19:4	ἐξῆλθεν	Pilate goes out to the Jews.
19:5	ἐξῆλθεν	Jesus goes out of the praetorium.
19:9	εἰσῆλθεν	Pilate goes into the praetorium.

---

32. I list ἄγω ("lead, bring") (18:28, 19:13), λαμβάνω ("take") (19:1), παραδίδωμι ("hand over") (19:16), and παραλαμβάνω ("take with") (19:16) as verbs of motion in this passage because they signify Jesus being taken and moved from one place to another.

19:13	ἤγαγεν	Pilate brings Jesus out of the praetorium.
19:13	ἐκάθισεν	Pilate either sits Jesus down on the judicial bench or sits on it himself.[33]
19:16	παρέδωκεν	Pilate hands over Jesus to be crucified.
19:16	παρέλαβον	The Roman soldiers (see 19:23) take Jesus to be crucified.
19:17	ἐξῆλθεν	Jesus goes out to be crucified.[34]

The narration of 18:28 does not identify the group that brings Jesus to Pilate. Nor does it specify who brings Jesus into the praetorium and who remains outside. Shortly after Jesus is brought inside, Pilate states that the chief priests handed over Jesus to him (18:35), and 19:6–7 identifies the chief priests and their ὑπηρέται ("attendants") as the group that remains outside the praetorium to avoid ritual defilement on the eve of Passover. This group of Jewish religious authorities thus constitutes the Jews in this pericope.[35] Since the Jews remain outside, it must be the Roman soldiers of 18:12 (or at least some of them) who bring Jesus inside to Pilate. The Fourth Evangelist presupposes the presence of Roman soldiers from the scene of Jesus's arrest here.[36]

Pilate does most of the moving in this passage. Once Jesus is brought into the praetorium, he must stay there until taken outside. Pilate, then, must exit the praetorium to talk to the Jews and reenter to talk to Jesus. Among others, Raymond Brown interprets Pilate's constant moving back and forth as symbolic of his struggle to adjudicate the case.[37] But given the problems with reading Pilate as a docile and indecisive figure, at this point it is prudent to take the verbs of motion more simply as reinforcing

---

33. Ἐκάθισεν ("he sat") can be read transitively (Pilate seats Jesus on the βῆμα) or intransitively (Pilate himself sits on it). For a convincing, classic argument in favor of the transitive reading, see Ignace de La Potterie, "Jésus Roi et Juge d'Après Jn 19,13: Ἐκάθισεν ἐπὶ βήματος," *Bib* 41 (1960): 217–47. For a detailed discussion of this exegetical puzzle that defends the intransitive reading, see Raymond Brown, *The Death of the Messiah: From Gethsemane to the Grave; A Commentary on the Passion Narratives in the Four Gospels*, 2 vols., ABRL (New York: Doubleday, 1994), 2:1388–93.

34. I include 19:17 because it will figure into the discussion below.

35. In his commentary, Brown argues that οἱ Ἰουδαῖοι in John often, but not exclusively, designates Jewish religious authorities, based in Jerusalem, who oppose Jesus (*John*, 1:lxxi).

36. Bultmann, *John*, 651 n. 1.

37. Brown, *John*, 2:858, 864; Brown, *Death of the Messiah*, 1:860.

the narration's interest in Pilate in this pericope. The narration "follows his movements."[38]

In contrast, Jesus does little moving of his own accord. He is mostly led around by his opponents in this sequence and in the scenes leading up to it, beginning with his arrest. Roman military personnel together with the ὑπηρέται of the Jews bring (ἤγαγον) Jesus to Annas in 18:13, who then sends (ἀπέστειλεν) him to Caiaphas in 18:24. In 18:28, the Jewish authorities and the Roman soldiers bring Jesus to Pilate (ἄγουσιν). These verbs are all in the active voice, which emphasizes Jesus's opponents as the doers of these actions. At one level, they control Jesus's movements.

John 19:1–3 maintains the dichotomy the passage establishes between Jesus as the protagonist who either remains in place or is moved by his opponents, and Pilate as the active antagonist of the pericope.[39] In 19:1–3, Pilate takes Jesus, flogs him, and has his soldiers mock him, dress him up as a pseudo-king, and strike him. Adding vividness to these verses is the repeated use of the aorist active tense in 19:1–2 for verbs narrating Pilate's taking Jesus to scourge him and the mockery heaped upon Jesus when the soldiers place the crown of thorns on him and clothe him with the purple robe (ἔλαβεν ... ἐμαστίγωσεν ... ἐπέθηκαν ... περιέβαλον). Moreover, the verbs in 19:3 that narrate the soldiers' actions of coming to Jesus, mocking him, and striking him are in the imperfect tense (ἤρχοντο, ἔλεγον, ἐδίδοσαν), signifying a repeated or continual action. The soldiers keep coming to Jesus to taunt him as "King of the Jews" and to give him multiple ῥαπίσματα ("slaps").

Even with the Roman soldiers taking part, the narration emphasizes Pilate's agency in torturing Jesus by stating outright that "Pilate took

---

38. Carter, *John and Empire*, 300; cf. Ignace de La Potterie, *The Hour of Jesus: The Passion and the Resurrection of Jesus according to John; Text and Spirit*, trans. Dom Gregory Murray (Slough, UK: Saint Paul, 1989), 81.

39. These verses are the centerpiece of the chiasm that structures 18:28–19:16a (Brown, *John*, 2:858–59; Brown, *Death of the Messiah*, 1:758). This structure divides 18:28–19:16a into seven scenes according to whether the action takes place inside or outside the praetorium, a structure initially proposed by B. F. Westcott (*The Gospel according to Saint John: The Authorised Version with Introduction and Notes* [London: John Murray, 1882], 258), developed by A. Janssens de Varebeke ("La Structure des Scènes du Récit de la Passion en Joh., xviii–xix," *ETL* 38 [1962]: 504–22), and now accepted by many Johannine scholars (Francis J. Moloney, *The Gospel of John*, SP 4 [Collegeville, MN: Liturgical Press, 1998], 497–98). For an argument against this structure, see Charles Homer Giblin, "John's Narration of the Hearing before Pilate (John 18,28–19,16a)," *Bib* 67 (1986): 221–24.

[ἔλαβεν] Jesus and flogged [ἐμαστίγωσεν] him" (19:1). Moore argues that we should take literally the aorist active ἐμαστίγωσεν and therefore imagine Pilate himself, lash in hand, whipping Jesus.[40] Moore accepts this is an exaggerated and historically implausible image, but citing the full Roman cohort of six hundred soldiers falling to the ground at Jesus's words in 18:6 and the notice of Pilate's fear in 19:8, he argues it is no more far-fetched than other imagery in John's version of Jesus's arrest and trial.[41] Regardless of whether one reads 19:1 this way, at the least, we can say "the directness of the Greek statement maintains focus on Pilate's agency as Jesus's torturer."[42]

The verbs of motion and the emphasis on Pilate's agency give the impression that Jesus's opponents have control over Jesus in 18:28–19:16. They physically take Jesus wherever they must to achieve their ends. Together with the Roman soldiers, the Jewish authorities take him from Caiaphas to Pilate, seeking a sentence of death. Pilate takes Jesus and orders the soldiers to scourge him, and possibly participates in the scourging himself. These verbs are in the active voice (ἄγουσιν in 18:28; ἔλαβεν in 19:1), a trend that begins with Jesus's arrest in 18:12 and that places an emphasis on Jesus's opponents as being in control of his movements. The Roman soldiers take control over Jesus's physical appearance by scourging him and dressing him with a purple robe and a crown of thorns. Throughout this process, it appears Jesus is led around, beaten, and mocked against his will.

Yet as O'Day's comments quoted at the start of this essay point out, the narrator constructs the scene in a way that makes it impossible for the reader to reach the conclusion that Jesus's opponents, including Pilate, have power and control over him. Pilate's repeated movement in and out of the praetorium contrasts sharply with Jesus's lack of movement. While Pilate is shuttling back and forth, Jesus remains poised, despite having been tortured and abused by the Roman authorities. Though facing execution and having been beaten throughout his trial, Jesus remains able to

---

40. Moore, *Empire and Apocalypse*, 56–59. For Moore, the language of the Johannine text is such that, even if we accept the traditional assumption that the soldiers performed the actual scourging, their agency in the matter is "entirely erased" (*Empire and Apocalypse*, 58).

41. Moore, *Empire and Apocalypse*, 57–58. It is possible that σπεῖρα ("cohort") refers to a maniple of two hundred soldiers, but even if this is the case, John intends to suggest the presence of a substantial number of Roman troops (Bond, *Pontius Pilate*, 166–67).

42. Carter, *John and Empire*, 300; cf. Bond, *Pontius Pilate*, 182; Stovell, *Mapping Metaphorical Discourse*, 285.

hold conversations with Pilate, the face of Roman power in Jerusalem, on such weighty matters as regal authority, identity, truth, and power (18:33–38a; 19:9–11). When Pilate, after the scourging, asks Jesus where he is from, Jesus defies him with silence (19:9). When Pilate tries to impose his authority over Jesus—"Do you not know that I have power to release you and I have power to crucify you?" (19:10)—Jesus bluntly tells Pilate that Pilate would have no power over him had it not been granted from above (19:11). The narration offers the reader contrasting images of a Jesus who has been tortured and yet holds his own against the powers of the world, and of a Pilate unable to elicit the responses he seeks from Jesus. The same torture tactics that normally work for Roman governors during interrogations are not working for Pilate.[43]

So while Pilate might be gaining the upper hand in his interchange with the Jews outside the praetorium, he is not achieving his ends in his interrogation of Jesus inside the praetorium. As discussed above, Rensberger and others have shown that, outside, Pilate deftly provokes the Jews to the point that they affirm allegiance to the emperor (19:15). But any responses that Jesus offers to Pilate while inside the praetorium come on Jesus's own terms, not Pilate's (18:34, 36, 37; 19:11).

We can now observe that Pilate's constant movement in and out of the praetorium reflects his inefficacy, not his indecisiveness. As his actions demonstrate, he knows what he wants to do. Outside, he wants to use Jesus to lord Roman power over the Jews; inside, he seeks to gain information from Jesus. Thus, as O'Day remarks, the inside/outside staging of the scene is among the narrative strategies the Fourth Evangelist uses to depict Pilate as powerless before Jesus: "Pilate's frenetic movement inside and outside of the praetorium during the trial embodies his ineffectualness."[44]

While the narration of 19:1–3 emphasizes the scourging as a moment in which Pilate flexes his authority, in 19:4–5, the narrator subtly indicates the ephemeral nature of Pilate's power. In 19:4, Pilate goes out to speak to the Jews, and continuing the repetitive use of ἐξῆλθεν/εἰσῆλθεν to narrate Pilate's movements, ἐξῆλθεν is used (19:4a). He tells them he will bring Jesus out to them (19:4b). But Pilate's words in 19:4b are immediately contradicted in 19:5a, where the text states ἐξῆλθεν οὖν ὁ Ἰησοῦς ἔξω. The superfluous use of ἔξω makes 19:5a parallel with 19:4a:

---

43. See Glancy, "Torture," 124–27.
44. O'Day, *Revelation in the Fourth Gospel*, 112.

19:4a: Καὶ ἐξῆλθεν πάλιν ἔξω ὁ Πιλᾶτος
19:5a: Ἐξῆλθεν οὖν ὁ Ἰησοῦς ἔξω

The main action—to go outside—is the same, but the agent of the action is different: Pilate goes outside in 19:4a, Jesus in 19:5a. This shift in agent contradicts Pilate's words in 19:4b: Pilate tells the Jews he is bringing Jesus outside (ἴδε ἄγω ὑμῖν αὐτὸν ἔξω), but Jesus is the agent of this particular action, not Pilate. Pilate does not bring Jesus out; Jesus goes outside of his own accord.[45] The narration thus communicates Jesus's power over Pilate by transferring to Jesus the verb associated with Pilate up to this point, ἐξέρχομαι. While Pilate says he will bring Jesus outside, the narration of 19:4–5 shows that Pilate does not have the control over Jesus's movements that he claims to have.[46]

Moreover, despite his suffering abuse, Jesus remains animate. He exits the praetorium right after being flogged and mocked by Pilate and his soldiers. The narration reinforces Jesus's agency in 19:5 by supplying the participle φορῶν to indicate that Jesus bears the crown of thorns and the purple robe. The image of Jesus wearing the crown of thorns and the purple robe had already been supplied in 19:2, and the mention of them here further emphasizes Jesus's ability to withstand and even "take on" the abuse set upon him. In so doing, the narration of 19:4–5 continues to display the illusory nature of Pilate's control over Jesus. Whatever Pilate might say, *Jesus* walks out and wears a ruler's garb.[47]

Finally, 19:16–17 confirms that the verb ἐξέρχομαι now belongs to Jesus in the narration of this sequence. Pilate hands over Jesus for crucifixion in 19:16a, and in 19:16b, the soldiers take Jesus. But 19:17 keeps Jesus as the subject of ἐξέρχομαι to endorse Jesus as going out to be crucified of his own volition. Verse 17 further emphasizes Jesus's agency with the superfluous use of ἑαυτῷ, since the participial phrase βαστάζων ἑαυτῷ τὸν σταυρὸν does not require it to make the agent of βαστάζων clear. The narration stresses that Jesus carries the cross *by himself*.[48] As with φορῶν in 19:5, the narration employs a participial phrase to modify the main verb

---

45. Brown, "What Is Truth?," 79; Paul D. Duke, *Irony in the Fourth Gospel* (Atlanta: John Knox, 1985), 132; Moloney, *John*, 495, 499.
46. Moloney, *John*, 499.
47. Brown, "What Is Truth?," 79; Duke, *Irony*, 132; Moloney, *John*, 499.
48. Cf. Brown, *John*, 2:917; Moloney, *John*, 502, 506.

ἐξέρχομαι (whose subject is Jesus) in order to emphasize Jesus's agency in withstanding an instrument of Roman torture.

The cumulative rhetorical effect of the narration of Jesus's arrest and trial is to reinforce for the reader what other statements in the gospel make explicit: Jesus lays down his life of his own accord (10:18); he and his Father alone determine his "hour" (2:4; 7:30; 8:20; 12:23, 27; 13:1; 17:1). Though Pilate is said to "hand over" Jesus for crucifixion in 19:16 (παρέδωκεν αὐτὸν αὐτοῖς ἵνα σταυρωθῇ), it is Jesus who "hands over" his own spirit (παρέδωκεν τὸ πνεῦμα) to die on the cross (19:30). The narrator constructs the scene of Jesus's trial to reflect Jesus's agency to determine the mode and manner of his death. As is the case throughout John's passion narrative, "Jesus, not the imperial power occupying Jerusalem, is in control."[49]

Pilate's Fear as Recognition of the Illusory Nature of His Power over Jesus

Within this careful narrative construct, the narrator's statement about Pilate's fear in 19:8 indicates to the reader that Pilate recognizes, even if only momentarily, that Jesus—not Pilate—is in charge of his own destiny. Pilate comes to know that he is on the losing side in the conflict between the God revealed by Jesus and the powers of the world. Pilate's fear is John's notice to the reader that "no matter what the world may see, Rome falters in Christ's presence."[50] Pilate recognizes this and becomes afraid.

The dialogues between Pilate and Jesus during the trial support Thatcher's view that the key to understanding Pilate's fear has to do with Jesus's identity as the Son of God, understood not primarily for its imperial connotations but as the christological title designating Jesus's relationship to God.[51] What makes Jesus more powerful than Pilate is that, while Pilate is "of the world," Jesus's power comes "from above" (cf. 19:11).

Pilate has two dialogues with Jesus in 18:28–19:16, one in 18:33–38a before he becomes afraid and another in 19:9–11 that immediately follows his becoming afraid. Nothing in Pilate's first conversation with Jesus, not even Jesus's statement that his followers could fight on his behalf (18:36), indicates that Pilate fears Jesus as a political threat to Rome's power.[52] If

---

49. Glancy, "Torture," 128; cf. Thompson, *John*, 371–72.
50. Thatcher, *Greater Than Caesar*, 71.
51. Thatcher, *Greater Than Caesar*, 84–85.
52. De Boer, "Narrative Function of Pilate," 151–53; Rensberger, *Johannine Faith*, 94, 104 n. 46.

anything, Pilate's responses to Jesus in the first dialogue exhibit dismissiveness toward Jesus and even impatient annoyance at Jesus's replies to his questions.[53] But this is not the same thing as fear.

From the Fourth Evangelist's point of view, Pilate's dismissiveness toward Jesus signifies his rejection of Jesus, since during the first dialogue Jesus reveals his heavenly origins openly to Pilate.[54] When Pilate asks Jesus what he has done in 18:35, Jesus twice says that his kingdom is not from this world (18:36). In the Johannine worldview, Jesus's kingdom—the realm in which he has authority over ὑπηρέται who fight on his behalf—is the world "above" (cf. 19:11), the realm of the God who sent Jesus to the world over which Rome presently rules.

As their first dialogue progresses, Jesus continues revealing himself and his mission to Pilate.[55] Having first asked Jesus in 18:33 whether he is "King of the Jews," Pilate questions Jesus again about whether he is a king in 18:37. Jesus explains the nature of his kingship in a statement brimming with Johannine vocabulary. He comes into the world (κόσμος) in order to testify (μαρτυρέω) to the truth (ἀλήθεια) (18:37), that is, the truth of God's revelation that Jesus himself embodies (14:6). Moreover, belonging to the truth entails responding positively to Jesus's testimony about the truth, or as the gospel puts it here, it entails hearing Jesus's voice (18:37; cf. 10:3, 16, 27).[56]

While the truth may be present in the world (as evidenced by Jesus's own presence in it), ultimately the truth and the world stand in opposition to each other in the Johannine theological framework.[57] Pilate's response to Jesus's testimony about himself in the first dialogue shows that he remains tied to the world. He does not belong to the truth, does not

---

53. Bennema, *Encountering Jesus*, 320; Brown, *John*, 2:869; Colleen M. Conway, *Men and Women in the Fourth Gospel: Gender and Johannine Characterization*, SBLDS 167 (Atlanta: Society of Biblical Literature, 1999), 156–57; Moloney, *John*, 498; Tuckett, "Pilate in John 18–19," 135.

54. Moloney, *John*, 495–96; Schnackenburg, *John*, 3:249–51; Tolmie, "Pontius Pilate," 586–87.

55. Conway, *Men and Women*, 157.

56. Belonging to the truth and listening to Jesus's voice are equivalent to each other, as seen especially in the textual links between 18:37 and the good shepherd discourse (10:3, 16, 27) (Stovell, *Mapping Metaphorical Discourse*, 282–83).

57. John 7:7; 8:23; 12:31; 14:30; 15:18–19; 16:20; and 17:14 all show the stark opposition between "the world" and Jesus and his followers (Bond, *Pontius Pilate*, 172–73).

recognize that the truth stands before him (14:6), and does not hear Jesus's voice.[58] If he did, he would have no need to ask his famous question in 18:38a ("What is truth?"), and he would surely stay for its answer.[59] In the conflict between the truth and the world, Jesus reveals the former to Pilate, but Pilate remains tied to the latter.[60]

Pilate's second conversation with Jesus, in 19:9–11, occurs as a direct consequence of Pilate's sudden fear of Jesus, as indicated by the construction of 19:8–9 as a single sentence.[61] After Pilate had Jesus flogged, dressed as a king, and brought out to the Jews (19:1–5), the Jews reveal that their real problem with Jesus is that he made himself the Son of God (19:7). This disclosure leads Pilate to become afraid and spurs his reentry into the praetorium to question Jesus (19:8–9). While many commentators read μᾶλλον ἐφοβήθη in a comparative sense, so that Pilate was "more afraid" and therefore must have been afraid of Jesus before 19:8, it makes better sense to interpret this phrase as elative or intensive, since the text gives no reason to think Pilate had been afraid at all before 19:8.[62] According to O'Day, reading fear into Pilate's earlier interaction is an interpretive decision that "borders on excessive psychologizing about the character and motives of the Johannine Pilate."[63] Pilate became "very much afraid" or "exceedingly afraid," not "more afraid" than he was previously, and reenters the praetorium to continue interrogating Jesus.[64]

What could cause Pilate to dismiss Jesus at first but now to fear him? The first question Pilate asks Jesus in the second conversation is revealing, "From where are you?" (19:9). In the Fourth Gospel, asking Jesus where he is from is a religious question, not one of geographical provenance. It pertains to Jesus's heavenly origins with the Father (1:1–3, 18; 3:34; 6:33; 7:28–29; 16:27–28). In the first dialogue, Pilate's line of questioning involved the worldly political sphere, a sphere in which, as Pilate saw it, Jesus posed no real threat. But now,

---

58. Beutler, *John*, 469; O'Day, "Gospel of John," *NIB* 9:818; Thompson, *John*, 381.
59. Brown, *John*, 2:869; Conway, *Men and Women*, 157; O'Day, "Gospel of John," *NIB* 9:817–18; Giblin, "John's Narration," 226; Haenchen, *John*, 180; Rensberger, *Johannine Faith*, 93; Schnackenburg, *John*, 3:246–47, 251.
60. Bond, *Pontius Pilate*, 179; Rensberger, *Johannine Faith*, 97.
61. O'Day, "Gospel of John," *NIB* 9:820.
62. Barrett, *John*, 542; Brown, *Death of the Messiah*, 1:830; Conway, *Men and Women*, 159; Barnabas Lindars, *The Gospel of John*, NCB (London: Oliphants, 1972), 567; O'Day, "Gospel of John," *NIB* 9:820; Rensberger, *Johannine Faith*, 94.
63. O'Day, "Gospel of John," *NIB* 9:820.
64. For an argument to the contrary, see Tolmie, "Pontius Pilate," 592.

Pilate's questioning raises the issue of Jesus's origins, "one of the most important christological and theological issues in the Gospel."[65] Whereas in the previous conversation Jesus spoke with Pilate in distinctly Johannine terms (18:37), here Pilate introduces a key Johannine theme.

The parallel to Apollonius of Tyana's interrogation before Ofonius Tigellinus, the prefect of the Praetorian Guard in Nero's Rome, in *Vit. Apoll.* 4.42–44 helps explain why Pilate's fear leads to this religious line of questioning.[66] Upon hearing of Apollonius's ability to predict a lightning bolt that nearly struck Nero, Tigellinus is said to fear Apollonius "as an expert in supernatural matters" (4.43.2).[67] As Apollonius's political superior, Tigellinus has no worldly reason to be afraid of Apollonius. What gives rise to his fear is Apollonius's deep connection to the realm of the supernatural. Access to this realm means the Roman authorities have no real power over Apollonius that they can enforce, and indeed *Vita Apollonii* later includes a sequence in which the chains of imprisonment cannot keep Apollonius shackled in place (7.38.1–2). Tigellinus openly admits his impotence before Apollonius when he says, "Go where you like, for you are too powerful to be ruled by me" (4.44.4).

Similarly, Pilate begins to recognize that the source of Jesus's regal authority has nothing to do with him as a seditionist, as Pilate had assumed in their first conversation. Upon hearing from the Jews that Jesus made himself the Son of God, Pilate fears Jesus as someone with access to divine power, that is, as someone having power and authority not from this world, as Jesus had told him in 18:36. Thus, in their second dialogue, Pilate no longer speaks to Jesus using the language of kingship but rather raises the question of origins in 19:9 and the issue of authority in 19:10 (using ἐξουσία twice, for emphasis). The possibility that his power "to release and to crucify" is no match for the power to which Jesus has access dawns on Pilate and causes him intense trepidation.[68]

---

65. O'Day, "Gospel of John," *NIB* 9:821. Moloney describes Pilate's question as "the fundamental question of Johannine christology" (*John*, 495). See Louis-Marie Dewailly, "'D'où es-tu?' (Jean 19,9)," *RB* 92 (1985): 481–96.

66. See Haenchen, *John*, 2:182; Schnackenburg, *John*, 3:260, 452 n. 79.

67. Ἀκούσας δὲ Τιγελλῖνος τὸν λόγον τοῦτον ἐς δέος ἀφίκετο τοῦ ἀνδρός, ὡς σοφοῦ τὰ δαιμόνια (*Vit. Apoll.* 4.43.2). Translations are from Philostratus, *The Life of Apollonius of Tyana, Books 1–4*, ed. and trans. Christopher P. Jones, LCL (Cambridge: Harvard University Press, 2005).

68. To be sure, interpreting Pilate's fear as fear of an otherworldly power that is greater than the power of Rome would be a Johannine claim that is made without

What the narration has suggested to the reader through its use of verbs of motion—that Jesus has the power and control despite external appearances—now occurs to Pilate and is thus made explicit to the reader. As O'Day points out in her analysis of John 4:4–42, 6:25–35, and 16:25–33 in *Revelation in the Fourth Gospel*, there comes a point in Johannine dialogues at which Jesus makes his identity explicit to his dialogue partner, and by extension, to the reader, often through an ἐγώ εἰμι statement whose force only a reader who has participated in the revelatory process of the narration up to the point that the statement is made can fully appreciate.[69] In other words, as part of John's narrative strategy, the theological claim embedded in the narration of a given pericope is eventually openly revealed in a manner that builds on the narration that precedes this revelation.[70] Something similar happens here. The notice of Pilate's fear baldly presents to the reader what had been implied by the narration of motion in this scene: between Jesus and Pilate, it is Jesus who ultimately has the power, giving this emissary of Rome reason to become suddenly very afraid. The narration presents this theological claim to the reader by depicting Pilate as recognizing his powerlessness.

In the dialogue that follows, Jesus confirms Pilate's suspicion about his powerlessness, especially in 19:11, where he indicates to Pilate that Pilate is something of a marionette, an instrument in God's plan temporarily given earthly power by God, who is the true source of power and authority. Pilate's condition is thus no different from that of the soldiers at the arrest scene who respond to a sudden revelation of Jesus (delivered with an ἐγώ εἰμι statement) by falling to the ground, a surprising—though from the Johannine point of view, appropriate—response that illustrates their ultimate ineffectualness (18:6). Whatever control they have over the events that lead to Jesus's crucifixion is granted to them from a divine, otherworldly power.

---

concern for verisimilitude, since from the point of view of Roman officials, the earthly power of Rome would be seen as a sign of divine favor. But the early Christians did make a distinction between earthly power and cosmic power, and it is for readers who hold this worldview that John constructs his narrative.

69. O'Day, *Revelation in the Fourth Gospel*, 73, 103–4, 108.

70. Cf. the following comments by O'Day on John 16:25–33: "When the Johannine Jesus speaks of revelation *en paroimias* and revelation *parresia* [16:25], he gives a name to the revelatory dynamic that has been inherently present throughout the Gospel narrative" (*Revelation in the Fourth Gospel*, 108).

That Pilate's fear of Jesus emerges from his dialogue with the Jews solidifies for John's reader that Pilate is aligned with the forces of the world, in opposition to the truth.[71] Jesus revealed outright to Pilate his connection to an otherworldly kingdom in 18:36-37, yet it had no influence on Pilate's approach during the interrogation. But when the Jews tell Pilate that Jesus ought to die because he "made himself [ἑαυτὸν ἐποίησεν] the Son of God" (19:7; cf. 5:18; 10:33), he approaches Jesus with fear, a fear that leads to a desperate self-assertion of his authority when Jesus refuses to answer Pilate's question about his origins, that is, when Jesus refuses to offer his voice to Pilate (19:9-10).[72] Pilate heard two testimonies about Jesus—one by Jesus, the other by the Jews—but listens only to the Jews' testimony. In 19:10, he is said to "hear" (ἀκούω) their λόγος about him. He disregards the testimony that comes directly from Jesus, the λόγος himself (1:1), and his questioning of Jesus in the second dialogue "is not any indication of an honest searching or incipient faith, but only the expression of uncertainty and fear."[73] Those who are of the truth "hear" (ἀκούω) Jesus's voice (18:37); Pilate, on the other hand, hears Jesus's enemies.[74]

This need not mean that Pilate interprets Jesus's identity as the "Son of God" in the same manner as the Jews understand it.[75] But when faced with

---

71. Conway, *Men and Women*, 162.

72. The accusation on the part of the Jews that Jesus "made himself" the Son of God contradicts the Johannine narrator's view of the nature of Jesus's identity as God's Son (cf. 10:33-36). According to Johannine Christology, Jesus did not acquire his identity as the Son of God by his own agency; he always held that distinction as part of his being (e.g., 1:1, 14, 18, 34, 49). The Jews' accusation thus contains irony, because in articulating their unbelief in Jesus as God's Son, they correctly identify that the true nature of Jesus's kingship (which is being judged at this trial) is Jesus's divine sonship (Brown, *John*, 2:891; Schnackenburg, *John*, 3:259).

73. Schnackenburg, *John*, 3:260.

74. On a political level, it makes sense that Pilate would give consideration to what the Jewish authorities say about Jesus, since throughout the empire, members of the local urban elite were allied with Roman rulers. Carter suggests that John's readers would actually presume that Pilate and the Jews are in cahoots before the Jews bring Jesus to Pilate in 18:28 (*John and Empire*, 293-94). The Roman cohort's involvement in Jesus's arrest (18:3) supports this point (Bond, *Pontius Pilate*, 167; Brown, *John*, 2:847; Tolmie, "Pontius Pilate," 583). The implication for John 19:7-8 is that, as one allied with the Jewish authorities in Jerusalem, Pilate would pay attention to their concerns about Jesus.

75. O'Day rightly points out that Pilate would not take seriously this accusation against Jesus on the Jews' own terms, for why would the religious sensitivities of the

this term that has both political and religious connotations, it is the religious element—the connection with the supernatural realm—that causes Pilate's fear.[76] From a strictly political standpoint, the claim to be the "Son of God" does not differ substantially from the claim to be "King of the Jews," the claim around which Pilate's first interrogation of Jesus centers (18:33–38a). Both would represent the threat of political insurgency that from Pilate's point of view must be vanquished, yet only the latter claim instills fear in him and leads to a line of questioning centering on Jesus's origins (19:9)—a significant religious question in the Fourth Gospel—not his political aspirations. By linking Pilate's fear to Jesus's identity as the

---

Jews have any bearing on Pilate's own disposition toward Jesus? Accordingly, Pilate views Jesus's claim to divinity according to pagan religious categories (Beutler, *John*, 474; Bond, *Pontius Pilate*, 187; Carter, *John and Empire*, 307; C. H. Dodd, *Historical Tradition in the Fourth Gospel* [Cambridge: Cambridge University Press, 1963], 114; Lindars, *John*, 567–68).

76. Craig S. Keener, *The Gospel of John: A Commentary*, 2 vols. (Peabody, MA: Hendrickson, 2003), 2:1125. John 19:8's history of interpretation has produced two basic ways of understanding Pilate's fear, as outlined by Conway, *Men and Women*, 160. One possibility is that Pilate sees the events of the trial as threatening his political standing (O'Day, "Gospel of John," *NIB* 9:820–21). So by informing Pilate that Jesus is guilty of blasphemy, the Jews remind him that as a competent Roman prefect, he must uphold regional religious practices (Brown, *John*, 2:890–91). Pilate's fear is thus fear for his job, since failure to handle such a serious accusation from the Jews in a manner that keeps peace and order could end Pilate's days as governor of Judea. The second explanation for Pilate's fear, with which my own reading agrees, is memorably described by Schnackenburg as "numinous terror before the divine" and by Conway as "the unavoidable reaction to the notion of Jesus's divine identity" (Schnackenburg, *John*, 3:260; Conway, *Men and Women*, 160; cf. Bennema, *Encountering Jesus*, 322; Duke, *Irony*, 133). Two difficulties arise with this latter interpretation, but they do not present an insurmountable case against it (Conway, *Men and Women*, 160). The first is that such terror does not prevent Pilate from going back inside the praetorium to further interrogate and even threaten Jesus with his power to crucify. The second is O'Day's well-taken point that this understanding of Pilate's fear "assumes that Pilate would honor and respect 'the Jews'' language about God, an assumption that the text does not otherwise support" (O'Day, "Gospel of John," *NIB* 9:820). As Conway notes, Pilate's fear and subsequent return to the interrogation is akin to 18:6, where the soldiers are "momentarily overcome" at hearing Jesus's "I am" statement and yet "proceed to arrest Jesus as if nothing had happened" after getting up from the ground (*Men and Women*, 160). As for O'Day's critique, that Pilate hears from the Jews about Jesus's claim to be the "Son of God" does not necessarily mean that he understands the term in the same way as they do. See n. 75 above.

Son of God understood in the religious sense, John underscores for his readers the conditional nature of Pilate's power. During Jesus's trial, Pilate may have the power to release and to crucify (19:10–11), but ultimately real power lies with the Son of God, who instills fear even in the Roman governor who temporarily has power over him.[77]

Jesus's Power over Rome and Its Agents

The idea that Pilate is a strong character does not contradict John's depiction of Pilate as fearful for recognizing that his power is fleeting before Jesus's own power. For one thing, the parallel in *Vit. Apoll.* 4.42–44 shows that depicting a high-ranking Roman official as fearing an individual of lower status with access to supernatural power lies within the bounds of ancient literary conventions. A similar scenario occurs in *Vit. Apoll.* 1.21. A satrap, frightened by the sight of Apollonius, presumes him to be a supernatural figure, covers his own face as a result, and asks Apollonius about his origins "as if questioning a spirit [δαίμονα]" (1.21.1). In Matthew's Gospel, Herod becomes troubled or frightened (ἐταράχθη) by the magi's news of a star portending the birth of a new king (2:3; cf. 14:26), and Herod Antipas, while not explicitly said to fear Jesus, surmises that Jesus's reputed powers identify him as John the Baptist raised from the dead with a statement that may betray a sense of foreboding on his part (14:1–2), given his culpability for John's death (related immediately afterward in a flashback, 14:3–12). Another example from Matthew's Gospel—one that happens to involve Pilate—is the intervention by Pilate's wife in 27:19. During Pilate's deliberations, she tells him that she has suffered much (πολλὰ γὰρ ἔπαθον) in a dream because of Jesus and warns Pilate not to have anything to do with him. Pilate's fear in John 19:8 lies within this trajectory of portraying powerful governing officials (or, in the case of Matt

---

77. As Thompson explains, Pilate's asking Jesus about his origins in 19:9 "suggests that the identification of Jesus as 'Son of God' triggers the suspicion that Jesus's power has the potential to surpass and even supplant Caesar's" (*John*, 385). Characterizing Pilate's fear as the effect of a perceived religious threat to Pilate's authority as a Roman governor might appear to contradict the Johannine idea, expressed earlier in the trial to Pilate, that Jesus's power is not tied to the world (18:36). However, in his conversations with Pilate, Jesus never claims that the world "above," which is the source of his kingship, has no bearing on this world or the empire that currently rules it (see Rensberger, *Johannine Faith*, 97; Stovell, *Mapping Metaphorical Discourse*, 299–301; Thatcher, *Greater Than Caesar*, 74–75).

27:19, the wife of such an official) expressing a fear, dread, or concern over lower-status provincials that is influenced by belief in supernatural phenomena.

Moreover, Pilate's newfound recognition of the illusory nature of his power relative to Jesus's makes sense in light of the fierceness with which Pilate interacts with the Jews in 19:12–16. Having declined Jesus's call to align himself with the power Jesus represents—offered during their first conversation but not the second one—Pilate reacts by aggressively displaying whatever power he has over the Jews in the context of "the world." Even if we recognize Pilate's attempt to release Jesus in 19:12 as genuine, it does not take long for him to resume manipulating the situation to assert Rome's sovereignty over the Jews.[78]

Reading Pilate's fear as a recognition of his powerlessness before Jesus also makes sense in terms of the emerging view in Johannine scholarship that the imperial context of John's readers contributes to their experience of alienation "as men and women with divided hearts, torn between Christ and Caesar."[79] The Gospel of John implies an audience of members who considered themselves marginalized for their belief in Jesus as God's Messiah.[80] The most influential *Sitz im Leben* proposed for this perspective of the Fourth Gospel, developed by J. Louis Martyn and Raymond Brown, argues that the Gospel's "us-against-them" rhetoric stems from the persecution, and even excommunication, leveled at Jesus followers by those Jews who were not.[81] The prominence of the Martyn-Brown reconstruction of the experiences of the Johannine community has been waning, though, and new explorations of the sources of alienation and persecution that affected John's readers have arisen.[82] While attending

---

78. Conway, *Men and Women*, 161; Rensberger, *Johannine Faith*, 95.

79. Richey, *Roman Imperial Ideology*, 187.

80. Wayne A. Meeks, "The Man from Heaven in Johannine Sectarianism," *JBL* 91 (1972): 44–72, esp. 69–71.

81. Raymond Brown, *The Community of the Beloved Disciple: The Life, Loves, and Hates of an Individual Church in New Testament Times* (New York: Paulist, 1979); Brown, *John*, esp. 1:lxx–lxxv; J. Louis Martyn, *History and Theology in the Fourth Gospel*, 3rd ed., NTL (Louisville: Westminster John Knox, 2003).

82. For a helpful foray into the *status questionis* of the Martyn-Brown reconstruction in Johannine studies, see the following essays and corresponding responses in John R. Donahue, ed., *Life in Abundance: Studies of John's Gospel in Tribute to Raymond E. Brown* (Collegeville, MN: Liturgical Press, 2005): Robert Kysar, "The Whence and Whither of the Johannine Community," 65–81; Hans-Josef Klauck, "Community,

to its Jewish origins and the Jewish symbolic world with which it richly interacts remains essential for understanding the Fourth Gospel, studies situating John within its Roman-imperial context represent one fruitful way of understanding the gospel's rhetoric under a paradigm different from that of an intra-Jewish conflict. Such studies have begun addressing the "massive yet unattended presence" of Rome as an indispensable interpretive matrix for the Fourth Gospel.[83] By depicting Pilate as strong and cruel throughout the scene yet genuinely afraid before the Son of God, John assures his readers that they placed their belief in someone more powerful than Rome and its agents, thereby advancing the gospel's aims of assuring followers of Jesus who experience powerlessness and alienation within their lived experience of empire.

John's Gospel affirms to its readers that even the strongest powers of the world are less powerful than Jesus. For John's narration to achieve its desired effect, Pilate must be depicted as strong and cruel yet also as afraid of Jesus, and the reason for Pilate's fear must be tied to Jesus's superiority over Pilate. For John's reader, Pilate represents Rome, the supreme power of the world. But since John's readers have aligned themselves with the God revealed by Jesus, that is, with the "truth" Pilate has rejected, John's Gospel seeks to assure its readers they chose rightly for Jesus and against Rome.[84] John's Gospel thus depicts Jesus as "greater than Caesar" in every

---

History, and Text(s): A Response to Robert Kysar," 82–90; Burton L. Visotzky, "Methodological Considerations in the Study of John's Interaction with First-Century Judaism," 91–107; Adele Reinhartz, "John and Judaism: A Response to Burton Visotzky," 108–16.

83. Commenting on the lack of attention to Rome in Johannine studies, Fernando F. Segovia states, "In terms of critical attention, the underlying geopolitical matrix involving the imperial-colonial framework of Rome and its impact on the production of the Fourth Gospel has not been addressed in any sort of sustained and systematic fashion. Rome may be said to hover in the background as a massive yet unattended presence" ("Johannine Studies and the Geopolitical: Reflections upon Absence and Irruption," in *What We Have Heard from the Beginning: The Past, Present, and Future of Johannine Studies*, ed. Tom Thatcher [Waco, TX: Baylor University Press, 2007], 283). Studies addressing this lacuna include Peter Claver Ajer, *The Death of Jesus and the Politics of Place in the Gospel of John* (Eugene, OR: Pickwick, 2016); Carter, *John and Empire*; Cassidy, *John's Gospel*; Moore, *Empire and Apocalypse*, 45–74; Rensberger, "Politics of John"; Rensberger, *Johannine Faith*, 87–106; Richey, *Roman Imperial Ideology*; Thatcher, *Greater Than Caesar*. For additional bibliography, see Carter, *John and Empire*, 18 n. 30.

84. Cassidy, *John's Gospel*, 84–88.

respect, as Thatcher argues, and offers a "rhetoric of distance" by which it encourages its readers to distance themselves from the pervasive influence of the Roman Empire, a point Carter develops.[85]

Rather than depicting an indecisive and weak Pilate, which would be a real contradiction according to what John's readers would expect from a Roman governor, John presents Pilate as ruthless and powerful. Yet John also makes clear that Pilate's power is tied to the world, not to the truth. While the members of John's audience themselves may not strike fear in any of Rome's representatives, by believing in Jesus, they staked their claim in a power ultimately more powerful than anything the world has to offer. As pointed out above, listening to the Jews' testimony about Jesus and not to Jesus's own self-revelation shows Pilate to be "of the world" and thus cut off from the source of Jesus's divine power (cf. 15:6). John's readers, however, abide in this power, since they abide in Jesus and Jesus abides in them (see 6:56–58; 15:1–10). Rome does not. The notice of Pilate's fear in 19:8, then, functions as reassurance to John's readers that God's victory through Jesus represents a real triumph against the powers of the world, even if the current reality of John's readers speaks to the contrary.

---

85. Thatcher, *Greater Than Caesar*, 3–17, esp. 4–11; Carter, *John and Empire*, 3–18, esp. 11–15.

The Resurrection Message and the Literary Shape of John 20–21

Yoshimi Azuma

Gail O'Day's *Revelation in the Fourth Gospel* remains a landmark work relating the literary shape of John to its theological message.[1] O'Day argues that theological meaning and narrative mode are inseparably intertwined and that the gospel narrative is the locus of revelation.[2] She writes, "Revelation lies in the Gospel narrative and the world created by the words of that narrative."[3] In her argument, the narrator's comments in 20:30–31 play an essential role. They "present the Gospel narrative itself as the locus of revelation for later generations."[4]

---

1. Gail R. O'Day, *Revelation in the Fourth Gospel: Narrative Mode and Theological Claim* (Philadelphia: Fortress, 1986).
2. Gail R. O'Day, "The Gospel of John: Introduction, Commentary, and Reflections," *NIB* 9:853. See also O'Day, *Revelation in the Fourth Gospel*, 93–94.
3. O'Day, *Revelation in the Fourth Gospel*, 94.
4. O'Day, *Revelation in the Fourth Gospel*, 93–94. See also O'Day, "Gospel of John," *NIB* 9:853. John Ashton agrees with O'Day in that the content of the Gospel of John is indistinguishable from its form and that the medium is the message. However, John Ashton (*Understanding the Fourth Gospel* [Oxford: Clarendon, 1991], 525 n. 55) criticizes O'Day for focusing on irony and not examining the medium of the whole gospel. Ashton regards the medium as the gospel that narrates the life of Jesus. See p. 525 n. 29. Christina Petterson (*From Tomb to Text: The Body of Jesus in the Book of John* [London: Bloomsbury T&T Clark, 2017], 134) agrees with O'Day and Ashton in that the medium is the message. Yet she questions Ashton's claim that the medium is the gospel that narrates Jesus's life. According to Petterson, this definition may suit Luke and Matthew but not John. Petterson argues that "resurrection discourses/dialogues" are situated in the post-Easter gap and present the teachings of the risen Jesus. The presence of the resurrected Jesus permeates the Gospel of John. Thus, for Petterson, the medium of John is resurrection discourses/dialogues that are gnostic in nature.

This essay explores John 20–21, a portion of the gospel in which the narrative mode has been underutilized as a source for John's theological message. Even O'Day's interpretation of these chapters does not adequately consider the relation of the narrative mode and the theological truth. O'Day regards the resurrection appearances as a sign that points to a theological truth. She says, "Like Jesus's other signs, the theological truth of the resurrection appearance lies not *in* the appearance itself, but *in that to which it points.* That is, the resurrection appearance stories are about something other than Jesus's miraculous return from death." Thus, the reader "is not summoned merely to believe in the resurrection, but to believe in the revelation of Jesus's identity and relationship with God, of which the resurrection is a sign."[5] In other words, the resurrection appearance as a sign points to the christological truth, namely, the identity of Jesus and his relation to God.

With this interpretation of John 20, O'Day seems to move away from her thesis that the narrative is the locus of revelation. The resurrection appearance narratives are only the pointer to the christological truth and themselves not the locus of revelation. The medium, the resurrection appearance narratives, is not inseparably intertwined with its message, namely, the christological truth.

By focusing attention again on the narrative features of John 20–21, I will argue that the theological message of the resurrection narrative is inseparably intertwined with its narrative mode. First, by using the narrative device of ellipsis, John does not narrate Jesus's resurrection and ascension and urges the reader to fill in the narrative gaps. Second, by using the narrative asides in John 20–21, John highlights the gospel narrative itself as a medium for understanding Jesus and his resurrection. Third, John makes strong connections between Jesus's last appearance in John 21 and Jesus's earlier sign narratives in John 6 and emphasizes the continuity between the incarnate Jesus and the risen/ascended Jesus. These narrative features are inseparably intertwined with the theological message that Jesus's resurrection and ascension demand human engagement and that the gospel narrative is the locus where one can encounter the risen and ascended Jesus.

Even though O'Day, Ashton, and Petterson agree that the medium is the message, they do not agree on what kind of medium John is.

5. O'Day, "Gospel of John," *NIB* 9:851 and 852, emphasis added.

The Structure of John 20–21

Reading John 20–21 from a literary perspective contrasts with much of twentieth-century scholarship, which argued that the gospel's original ending was at 20:30–31 and that John 21 was a later addition or an epilogue.[6] Even interpreters who use a narrative-critical approach see the discontinuity between John 20 and 21.[7] However, increasingly more scholars regard John 21 as a necessary part of the gospel narrative. These interpreters take different positions concerning the relation of John 21 to the whole gospel. While some scholars emphasize the narrative unity of John 20–21,[8] O'Day draws on the work of Edwyn Hoskyns in regarding

---

6. Most commentators regard John 21 as an addition by an ecclesiological redactor. Raymond E. Brown, *The Gospel according to John*, 2 vols., AB 29–29A (New York: Doubleday, 1966–1970), 2:1077–1082; Rudolf Bultmann, *The Gospel of John: A Commentary*, trans. G. R. Beasley-Murray, R. W. N. Hoare, and J. K. Riches (Philadelphia: Westminster, 1971), 700–706; Rudolf Schnackenburg, *The Gospel according to St. John*, trans. Kevin Smyth et al., 3 vols. (New York: Seabury/Crossroad, 1968–1982), 3:343–44.

7. Although R. Alan Culpepper admits that John 21 is "the necessary ending of the gospel," he regards John 21 as "an epilogue, apparently added shortly after the gospel was completed." *Anatomy of the Fourth Gospel: A Study in Literary Design* (Philadelphia: Fortress, 1983), 96. See also pp. 44–49, 66, 121–23, 197. Similarly, although Francis Moloney acknowledges that John 21 is an "integral part of the literary and theological unity of the Fourth Gospel" (242), he argues that John 21 is later added with a different point of view. He acknowledges the possibility that the same author with a different point of view later added chapter 21 (249). Francis J. Moloney, "John 21 and the Johannine Story," in *Anatomies of Narrative Criticism: The Past, Present, and Futures of the Fourth Gospel as Literature*, ed. Tom Thatcher and Stephen D. Moore, RBS 55 (Atlanta: Scholars Press, 2008), 237–51.

8. Charles Talbert regards John 20–21 as a narrative unit consisting of two parts with correspondences between 20 and 21. Charles Talbert, *Reading John: A Literary and Theological Commentary on the Fourth Gospel and the Johannine Epistles* (New York: Crossroad, 1994), 248–64. Beverly Roberts Gaventa takes a different position, arguing that John 20–21 provides dual endings for the gospel, "each of which has a distinct function and focus, and that at least some of the difficulties interpreters have identified in chapter 21 derive from the difficulties inherent in closure (or nonclosure, in this case). John 21 is best characterized, in the elegant phrase of David McCracken, as an 'archive of excess'" (242). Beverly Roberts Gaventa, "The Archive of Excess: John 21 and the Problem of Narrative Closure," in *Exploring the Gospel of John: In Honor of D. Moody Smith*, ed. R. Alan Culpepper and C. Clifton Black (Louisville: Westminster John Knox, 1996), 240–52.

John 20:30-31 as an end of John 20 and regarding John 21 as an end of the whole gospel.[9]

Although I also see the concluding function in John 21, I do not agree with O'Day in regarding 20:30-31 as an ending only to John 20. The narrator's comments in 20:30-31 refer to "this book" and provide concluding comments to the whole book. The narrator's comments in 20:30-31 lead the reader out of the narrative world, and in John 21:1 the reader reenters the narrative world. The final resurrection appearance narrative in John 21 is framed with the narrator's comments that bring the reader out of the narrative world.

My interpretation of John 20-21 adopts the narrative structure of Fernando Segovia, who considers 20:1-21:25 as the final narrative section of 18:1-21:25, which consists of three scenes: (1) the empty tomb and the appearance of Jesus to Mary Magdalene (20:1-18); (2) the appearances of Jesus to his disciples in Jerusalem (20:19-29); and (3) the appearance of Jesus to his disciples in Galilee (20:30-21:25).[10] Segovia regards the third scene as "a self-contained and coherent narrative scene consisting of three units" and identifies "a linear and progressive development" concerning the theme of the resurrection in relation to the role of the disciples in the world.[11] According to Segovia, the final appearance narrative in 21:1-23 is the "final farewell to the disciples prior to his final ascent to the Father and his full glorification or apotheosis with the Father (17:1-5)."[12]

While I agree with Segovia in seeing the development of the resurrection theme, my argument adds further depth to Segovia's conclusions by arguing that the reader sees the ascended Jesus after John 20:18. I argue below that the narrative form of the gospel may lead readers to understand

---

9. O'Day follows Hoskyns in regarding 20:30-31 as an end of John 20, and John 21 as an end of John 1-20. O'Day, "Gospel of John," *NIB* 9:854-55.

10. Fernando F. Segovia, "The Final Farewell of Jesus: A Reading of John 20:30-21:25," *Semeia* 53 (1991): 173-74.

11. Segovia, "Final Farewell," 173-74. Segovia also says, "the first scene establishes and proclaims the resurrection itself; the second scene begins to bring about the promised change of perception and understanding among the disciples, provides the occasion for the bestowal of Jesus's promised successor, and proceeds to outline the proper and correct role of the disciples in the world; the third scene provides a further development of the proper and correct role of the disciples in the world by focusing on the need for mission and on their relationship with regard to one another" ("Final Farewell," 174).

12. Segovia, "Final Farewell," 185.

that Jesus's ascension takes place in between his appearances to Mary Magdalene and to his disciples. Thus, Jesus's appearances in 20:19–23, 20:24–29, and 21:1–23 are presented as the appearances of the risen and ascended Jesus among the disciples, and not the final farewell before the ascension.

Ellipsis

John's language points to important elements of Jesus's story but does not narrate them explicitly. I refer to this literary device as ellipsis. Here, I discuss resurrection and ascension as events John leads readers to expect but does not explicitly narrate.

Resurrection

Jesus's rising from the dead is nowhere narrated. It is left as an ellipsis that is to take place sometime in between the end of the passion narrative in 19:42 and Mary's arrival at the tomb in 20:1 or the Beloved Disciple's arrival at the tomb in 20:4. In the end of the passion narrative, the narrator reports Jesus's burial in a new tomb in a garden on the day of preparation (19:41–42). The following scene continues to be at the tomb: "Early on the first day of the week, while it was still dark, Mary goes to the tomb and saw the stone removed from the tomb" (20:1).[13] The removed stone from the tomb suggests to the reader that Jesus may have risen from the dead and exited from the tomb by this point. However, whether Jesus has already risen from the dead and exited from the tomb before Mary's arrival at the tomb is not made clear in the narrative, because Mary, without seeing inside the tomb, leaves the tomb and runs to Peter and the Beloved Disciple to report the tomb robbery to them (20:2).

Thus, Jesus's resurrection could have taken place during Mary's leave from the tomb. The status of the inside the tomb is not made clear to the reader until the arrival of the Beloved Disciple at the tomb, who bends down to see the linen cloths lying in the tomb (20:5). The full view from inside the tomb, however, is not yet provided, since the Beloved Disciple does not enter the tomb (20:5). It is when Peter arrives and enters (20:6–7) that the full view from inside the tomb is provided to the reader: Jesus's body is not in the tomb, and only the linen wrappings and the face

---

13. All translations of John are mine.

cloths are left there (20:7). Certainly this can also be (mis)interpreted as the tomb robbery, as Mary's repeated words show (20:13, 15). It is also ambiguous whether the Beloved Disciple believed in Jesus's resurrection (20:8) at this point. However, the status of the inside of the tomb together with the removed stone suggest to the reader that Jesus has already risen from the dead and exited from the tomb.[14] The narrator's comments, "for they had not yet known the Scripture that it is necessary for him to rise from the dead [δεῖ αὐτὸν ἐκ νεκρῶν ἀναστῆναι]" (20:9), clarify to the reader that Jesus has already risen from the dead. Jesus's resurrection is to take place sometime in between the entombment and Mary's first arrival at the tomb or the Beloved Disciple's arrival at the tomb. The time when Jesus's resurrection takes place is left ambiguous in the narrative and left to the imagination of the readers.

While Jesus's rising from the dead or exit from the tomb is nowhere narrated, readers follow the characters' movement in and around the tomb before encountering Jesus. As O'Day points out, John draws attention to the empty tomb in a way no other gospel does.[15] The focus inside the tomb results from the narrative interaction between the Beloved Disciple and Peter. The tomb is a destination of their strange competition (20:3-4). The Beloved Disciple reached the tomb first but does not go in the tomb (20:4-5). Peter comes later and enters the tomb (20:6). Then, the Beloved Disciple also goes in (20:8). Although no reason for the hesitance of the Beloved Disciple to enter the tomb is given, his hesitance highlights the inside of the tomb as the destination.

In the latter half of the first section, in 20:11-18, the focus shifts from inside the tomb to outside the tomb, where the risen Jesus makes an appearance. This shift of focus is made through the perspective of Mary. Mary, while weeping, bent over to see inside the tomb, although she stays outside the tomb (20:11). She sees two angels in white clothes sitting in the tomb (20:12). Her movement in "turning" (20:14) highlights the shift away from inside the tomb to outside the tomb, where she sees Jesus stand-

---

14. The intertextuality with the Lazarus narrative supports this interpretation. In the Lazarus narrative, Jesus orders to remove the stone from the tomb (11:39) to bring Lazarus out of the tomb. Lazarus's resurrection is vividly narrated as an exit from the tomb, wearing the face cloth (σουδάριον) (11:44). The removed stone from the tomb and the leftover face cloth suggest to the reader that Jesus must have exited from the tomb.

15. O'Day, "Gospel of John," *NIB* 9:840.

ing (20:14). Her misunderstanding Jesus for a gardener (20:15) reminds the reader of the garden setting of the tomb (19:41). Through reading the narrative, the readers follow the characters' movements in and around the tomb and shift focus from inside the tomb to outside the tomb to encounter Jesus. The shift of focus from inside to outside the tomb enables the readers to complement the narrative gap.

To summarize, Jesus's resurrection is left as an ellipsis and nowhere narrated. It is to take place sometime in between the entombment and Mary's arrival at the tomb or the Beloved Disciple's arrival at the tomb. When exactly this takes place is left unclear. While Jesus's exit from the tomb is not narrated, the readers follow the movement of the characters into the tomb and can perceive the shift of focus from inside the tomb to outside the tomb to encounter the risen Jesus outside the tomb in the garden. This shift of focus enables the reader to vividly experience a transition from inside the tomb to outside the tomb to encounter the risen Jesus.

Ascension

Like Jesus's resurrection, Jesus's ascension is not narrated. Instead, clues in the text may lead readers to understand that Jesus's ascension has also occurred in the story, even though it is not explicitly narrated. In this section, I argue that there is a difference between Jesus's appearance to Mary in the first scene in 20:11–18 and Jesus's appearance to the disciples in the second scene in 20:19–29. The narrative leads readers to fill in the gap and assume that the ascension has taken place between the first and the second scenes (in between 20:18 and 20:19), and to see the ascended Jesus as the character animating the stories in 20:19–29 and in 21:1–25.

In 20:11–18, the second unit of the first scene, 20:1–18, Jesus prohibits Mary from touching him because of his transitory status before the ascension: "Do not touch me, for I have not yet ascended to the Father" (20:17). Jesus's transitory status, having not yet ascended, is the reason for Jesus's prohibition on touching him. Many interpreters support this interpretation that goes back to Origen.[16] Mary D'Angelo finds a similar notion,

---

16. Origen maintains that Jesus should not be touched because he is not yet fully risen. *Commentary on John* 6.287; 10.245; 13.179–80. Udo Schnelle also takes this position, saying Jesus "exists in an interim bodily state." Udo Schnelle, "Cross and Resurrection in the Gospel of John," in *The Resurrection of Jesus in the Gospel of John*, ed. Craig R. Koester and Reimund Bieringer, WUNT 222 (Tübingen: Mohr Siebeck

in Apocalypse of Moses, that touching the body of Adam after his death constitutes a problem.[17] D'Angelo argues that Jesus's prohibition in 20:17 should be interpreted in line with this idea.[18] This interpretation is confirmed by the content of Jesus's order to Mary: "Go to my brothers and say to them, 'I'm ascending [ἀναβαίνω] to my father and your father, my God and your God'" (20:17). The content of the proclamation is nothing other than Jesus's ascension in relation to the disciples.[19] Because Jesus has not yet ascended, Mary should not touch him but proclaim it to the disciples.

But in the second scene, 20:19–29, Jesus's appearances to the disciples contrast with his appearance to Mary in the preceding scene. Although Jesus's message to Mary was about the ascension in 20:11–18, after 20:19 Jesus no longer speaks about it. If the ascension has already taken place, it makes sense that Jesus no longer speaks about it.

In addition, Jesus's gift of the spirit to the disciples in 20:19–23 is best understood as something that takes place after the ascension. In the farewell discourse, Jesus foretells that the giving of the Spirit will happen after he returns to the Father (14:12, 16). The expectation may lead readers of 20:19–23 to conclude that the ascension has already happened.

2008), 144. Also, Harold W. Attridge says, "The verse does not indicate a problem with Mary, but with the situation of Jesus's transitional state. On his way back on high, he was simply not fit to be touched." Harold W. Attridge, "'Don't Be Touching Me': Recent Feminist Scholarship on Mary Magdalene," in *A Feminist Companion to John*, vol. 2, ed. Amy-Jill Levine with Marianne Blickenstaff (Cleveland: Pilgrim, 2003), 166.

17. Adam gives Eve instructions concerning the treatment of his body after his death and tells her that his body should not be touched before God takes his body (Apoc. Mos. 31:4). Mary Rose D'Angelo, "A Critical Note: John 20:17 and Apocalypse of Moses 31," *JTS* 41 (1990): 529–36, esp. 532.

18. "It is not necessarily the case that Mary would be ritually unclean if she were to touch him. Nor is it the case that *Apocalypse of Moses* evinces any concrete concern with the ritual pollution of Eve or Seth. But the touching of Jesus's or Adam's body in some way would constitute a violation, a danger not only to Mary or Eve but also to Jesus or Adam in his strange state, or perhaps to the holy and awesome process each undergoes." D'Angelo, "Critical Note," 534–35.

19. Jesus's ascension is proclaimed in relation to the disciples. Jesus calls the disciples "my brothers" for the first time in this gospel narrative. The repetitive expression, "my father and your father, my God and your God," highlights the sibling relationship between Jesus and the disciples and the filial relationship between God and Jesus, to which the disciples are now incorporated. Jesus's ascension concerns the disciples and their relationship with God; as he says in the farewell discourse, he will go there to prepare a place for the disciples (14:3).

Another change in the story is that Jesus no longer insists that his disciples should not touch him. In 20:19–23, Jesus appears amid his disciples in an enclosed space and shows his hands and side to them (20:20). Although the narrator does not report that the disciples actually touched Jesus, his display of his hands and side, the marks of crucifixion, indicates that there is no longer any problem with touching Jesus. Furthermore, Jesus's "breathing" on the disciples to give the Holy Spirit (20:22) shows Jesus's close physical interaction with the disciples. Apparently, there is no longer a problem with touching Jesus's body, which makes a strong contrast to Jesus's prohibition to Mary in the preceding scene.

Jesus's invitation to Thomas in 20:24–29 reinforces this contrast. Thomas's words to the other disciples, "Unless I see the mark of the nails in his hands and put my finger in the mark of the nails and my hand in his side, I will not believe" (20:25), emphasize Thomas's strong desire to physically confirm the marks of the crucifixion of the body of Jesus. Jesus's words to Thomas, "Put your finger here and see my hands. Reach out your hand and put it in my side. Do not be unbelieving but be believing," repeat Thomas's own words, revealing Jesus's knowledge of Thomas's words (20:27). Although the narrator does not state that Thomas actually touched Jesus, Jesus's invitation underscores that the prohibition on touching Jesus's body has ended. The appearances of a Jesus who has no problem with physical interactions with the disciples make a stark contrast with Jesus in the preceding scene with Mary.

This contrast may suggest to the reader that a change occurred in between the two scenes, between 20:18 and 20:19. In Molly Haws's words, "Clearly, the ban on touching has been lifted. Something has happened between the encounter at the tomb and his arrival in various locked rooms. Something has occurred to expand the possibilities of physical interaction with the risen Christ: Jesus's physicality has undergone a change in the interval between his 'Do not hold onto me' to Mary and his 'Put your finger here' to Thomas."[20] One possibility for this change is Jesus's expected ascension. The contrast in these scenes may suggest to the reader that Jesus's ascension takes place in between the first scene in 20:1–18 and the second scene in 20:19–29.[21]

---

20. Molly Haws, "'Put Your Finger Here': Resurrection and the Construction of the Body," *Theology & Sexuality* 13 (2007): 191.

21. Bultmann (*John*, 691) also sees the ascended one in 20:19–29. He says, "That Jesus in the meantime had ascended to the Father, as he had said to Mary that he

One additional difference may lead readers to assume that Jesus's ascension has occurred. Aspects of the third scene (21:1–23) heighten Jesus's divinity. In 20:19–23, Jesus gives the Spirit and sends the disciples to the world in the position of God. As many interpreters point out, Jesus's breathing the Spirit upon the disciples is portrayed as the second creation.[22] Similarly, Jesus's sending of his disciples parallels God's action: "Just as the Father sent me, I also send you" (20:21). Finally, Thomas's climactic confession, "My Lord, my God!" (20:28), is the only instance in any gospel for a human character to call Jesus God. The heightened divinity of Jesus after 20:19 leads the reader to see the ascended one in Jesus. These factors support the interpretation that Jesus's ascension has taken place prior to the scene. Jesus appears as the ascended one after 20:19 in the second and third scenes.

O'Day also sees the ascended one in Jesus after 20:19 and regards the resurrection appearance as a sign of Jesus's ascension. O'Day says, "It is not Jesus's resurrection appearances per se that reveal this truth, but his resurrection appearances as a sign of his return to God in glory."[23] In O'Day's interpretation, Jesus's resurrection appearances as a sign *point to* Jesus's ascension. It is true that the reader is urged to see the ascended one in the resurrection appearances in 20:19–21:23. However, I argue that O'Day's earlier impulse to explore the narrative mode of the gospel is also useful in John 20. By using ellipsis, Jesus's ascension is left as a narrative gap that requires the reader to complete. The reader is the only one, aside from Mary, who encounters Jesus in the transitory status before the ascension and listens to his prohibition on touching and the instruction to proclaim his ascension. The reader has already been conditioned

---

would (v. 17), and has now again returned to earth would be a false reflection—not only in the meaning of the source, but also in that of the Evangelist. Rather the sense is that he *has* ascended, and even *as such* he appears to the disciples; as such he is able to bestow the Spirit (v. 22), and as such he is afterwards addressed by Thomas as 'my Lord and my God' (v. 28)."

22. Sandra M. Schneiders points out that this story echoes both the creation story of Adam and the story of Ezekiel. She writes, "God had breathed the first human into life and new life into the dry bones in Ezekiel's vision, a clear indication that this New People … is indeed a *New Creation*." Sandra M. Schneiders, "The Resurrection (of the Body) in the Fourth Gospel: A Key to Johannine Spirituality," in *Life in Abundance: Studies of John's Gospel in Tribute to Raymond E. Brown*, ed. John R. Donahue (Collegeville, MN: Liturgical Press, 2005), 185.

23. O'Day, "Gospel of John," *NIB* 9:852.

to expect Jesus's ascension, just as they expected his resurrection. As the reader perceives the new details that allow the disciples to touch Jesus and that bring about the gift of the spirit, the reader may perceive that the ascension has occurred. In this way, the reader becomes involved in Jesus's ascension and becomes a participant in it. Together with Mary, the readers are given the mission to proclaim Jesus's ascension. The appearance narrative does not *point to* the ascension but *discloses* it to the reader within the narrative world.

To sum up, through the literary device of ellipsis, John does not narrate Jesus's ascension but leaves it as a narrative gap in between 20:18 and 20:19. Through the contrasting appearances to Mary and to the disciples, the reader can perceive that Jesus's ascension must take place in between the scenes. The reader is led to see the ascended one in Jesus in 20:19–20 and 21:1–23.

To summarize this section, neither Jesus's resurrection nor his ascension is narrated in the gospel. They are left as narrative gaps for readers to fill in. While Jesus's resurrection is not narrated, the reader follows the characters' movement in and around the tomb. Before encountering Jesus outside the tomb, the reader moves from inside the tomb to outside the tomb. While Jesus's exit from the tomb is nowhere narrated, the reader goes through this exit movement. Furthermore, Jesus's ascension is not narrated but is left as an ellipsis. The contrast in Jesus's appearances to Mary and the disciples may lead readers to conclude that Jesus's ascension is to take place in between the scenes. These narrative gaps require the active engagement of the reader to fill them.

Narrative Asides

Narrative asides throughout John 20–21 underscore the function the gospel narrative plays for readers as they seek to understand Jesus's resurrection. This portion of John includes three such asides: John 20:9; 20:30–31; and 21:24–25. In each insertion, the narrator emphasizes the identity or function of the gospel as Scripture.

John 20:9

Following the report of the belief of the Beloved Disciple in 20:8, the narrator comments on their knowledge of the Scripture in relation to the resurrection: "Then the other disciple, who reached the tomb first, also went in, and he saw and believed; for they had not yet known the Scripture [τὴν γραφὴν] that it is necessary for him to rise from the dead [ἐκ νεκρῶν ἀναστῆναι]" (20:8–9). Christina Petterson follows Francis Moloney's argument that the "Scripture" in 20:9 refers to the Gospel of John itself.[24] In John 2:22, the narrator has already associated Jesus's resurrection with the belief in the Scripture and the word of Jesus: "When he was raised from the dead, the disciples remembered that he has said these things and believed in the Scripture [τῇ γραφῇ] and the word that Jesus spoke." Grammatically, it is possible that early readers may have understood "the Scripture" and "the word that Jesus spoke" to refer to the same thing. Moloney argues that 20:9 refers back to 2:22, where the Scripture and the word of Jesus are collapsed, and that this plot reaches its climax in 20:29–31.[25]

The idea that the narrator identifies the gospel with Scripture is convincing for the following reasons. First, both in John 2:22 and 20:9, the narrator does not cite a specific scriptural passage. Second, it is quite possible to read 2:22 in a way that collapses the distinction between the Scripture and the word of Jesus. Third, understanding in this way explains why the Beloved Disciple and Peter, as characters within the narrative world, had not yet known the Scripture at this point. There is a gap between the knowledge of the characters and that of the readers of the Gospel of John. The narrator's asides draw attention to the significance of the medium, the Scripture, to understand the necessity of Jesus's resurrection.

John 20:30–31

At the end of chapter 20, the narrator explicitly comments on the purpose of this book: "Now Jesus did many other signs in the presence of his disciples, which are not written in this book [τῷ βιβλίῳ τούτῳ]. But these are written so that you may believe that Jesus is the Messiah, the Son of God, and that through believing you may have life in his name." Scholars have argued whether the signs that *are* written in "this book" include the

---

24. Petterson, *From Tomb to Text*, 35–36, 119–21. See also Francis J. Moloney, "'For As Yet They Did Not Know the Scripture' (John 20:9): A Study in Narrative Time," *ITQ* 79 (2014): 106.

25. Moloney, "'For As Yet They Did Not Know the Scripture,'" 105–6. See also Moloney, "The Gospel of John as Scripture," in *The Gospel of John: Text and Context*, BibInt 72 (Boston: Brill, 2005), 333–47.

resurrection (20:30).[26] I agree with O'Day in including Jesus's resurrection as the sign, since it is difficult to exclude what has just been narrated in John 20 from the signs written in this book.[27] However, I disagree with O'Day in regarding the signs as referring only to the resurrection appearances in John 20 and not broadly to Jesus's other signs recorded in this gospel.[28] The narrator refers to "this book" and has the whole book in its view, not just John 20.

I would also extend O'Day's logic regarding this passage to suggest that the narrative mode conveys the theological nature of the life Jesus gives to believers. O'Day argues that the resurrection is a sign of Jesus's identity and his relation to God. She limits the meaning of the resurrection to a narrowly christological sense: Jesus's identity in relation to God. However, Jesus's resurrection appearances are narrated primarily as the experience of the disciples and the new life given to them. Jesus's ascension reshapes the relationship between God, Jesus, and the disciples (20:17). By giving the Spirit to the disciples, Jesus recreates them anew (20:22). Jesus's resurrection appearances disclose not only Jesus's identity in relation to God but also his identity in relation to the disciples. Jesus's resurrection is a sign because it discloses the resurrection life Jesus gives to the disciples.

This soteriological dimension of the resurrection narrative, as well as the whole gospel narrative, is made clear by the narrator's asides. The narrator refers explicitly to both the christological and soteriological purposes of the gospel narrative. They were written "so that you may believe that Jesus is the Messiah, the Son of God, and that through believing you may have life in his name" (20:31). The purpose of the gospel narrative is not only to lead the reader to a christological confession but also to induce a soteriological experience of having life in his name.

---

26. Many interpreters do not regard the resurrection itself as the sign, since they find it theologically difficult. For example, Brown (*John*, 1059) argues that signs include the resurrection appearances in 20:1–28 but not the resurrection itself.

27. Petterson (*From Tomb to Text*, 125) notes that O'Day, like Brown, makes a careful distinction between the resurrection appearances and resurrection, not calling the resurrection itself a sign. However, while O'Day uses the expression "resurrection appearances" mostly, she also calls the resurrection itself a "sign." She says, the reader is "to believe in the revelation of Jesus's identity and relationship with God, of which *the resurrection is a sign*" ("Gospel of John," *NIB* 9:852, emphasis added).

28. O'Day, "Gospel of John," *NIB* 9:851.

John 21:24–25

At the end of John 21, the narrator again provides comments: "This is the disciple who is testifying to these things and has written them, and we know that his testimony is true. But there are also many other things that Jesus did; if every one of them was written down, I think that the world itself could not contain the books to be written [τὰ γραφόμενα βιβλία]" (21:24–25). The narrator ascribes the authorship to the Beloved Disciple and summarizes the content of the writing again as "things that Jesus did." Continuing from John 20:30–31, no distinction is made between the works of the incarnate and risen Jesus. If each one of the "things that Jesus did" was written, the world itself could not contain the books that would be written (21:25). While this is certainly a hyperbole, it also emphasizes the continuing nature of the works of Jesus. The narrator's comments in 21:24–25 do not state that this was the last appearance of the risen Jesus.[29] The comments that emphasize the amount of Jesus's deeds indicate an open character of Jesus's deeds. The risen and ascended Jesus continues to make an appearance among disciples and to work among them. Thus, recording all of what he did is virtually impossible, and what was written consists only a part of it.

In John 20:30–31 and 21:24–25, the narrator's words make the reader aware of the existence of the medium, the book. Patrick Counet argues that in 21:24–25 the text manifests itself as text.[30] Drawing on Counet, Petterson argues that the nature of the text as a medium is highlighted at the end of chapters 20 and 21. She argues that the narrator's comments are "two moments of externalization, where the text explicitly inserts itself as a mediator. The fact that this takes place at the end of the narrative means that writing takes on an unprecedented role, and its nature as a medium is highlighted."[31] She further says, "What takes place in these two chapters is the installment of Jesus's presence in the book proper. In both cases (20:30–31 and 21:24–25) the text here is inserted as *that* material order in which the resurrected one and the spirit can appear. The book has assumed

---

29. See Martin Hasitschka, "The Significance of the Resurrection Appearance in John 21," in *The Resurrection of Jesus in the Gospel of John*, ed. Craig Koester and Reimund Bieringer (Tübingen: Mohr Siebeck, 2008), 311–328, 313.

30. Patrick Chatelion Counet, *John, A Postmodern Gospel: Introduction to Deconstructive Exegesis Applied to the Fourth Gospel*, BibInt 44 (Leiden: Brill, 2000), 319.

31. Petterson, *From Tomb to the Text*, 129.

this presence throughout its narrative, but it is only here, via its externalization and becoming a book, that it is manifested in the earlier chapters."[32] By drawing attention to the gospel itself as the medium for experiencing the stories of Jesus, the narrative reasserts its own importance in drawing readers toward knowledge of the risen Jesus.

Echoes of Jesus's Life in John 21

The last scene, Jesus's resurrection appearance in 21:1–25, echoes the earlier gospel narrative of Jesus's ministry, especially the sign narratives in John 6. The reader is led to read the works of the risen and ascended Jesus in John 21 in light of the works of the incarnate Jesus and to see the continuity between the incarnate and the risen and ascended Jesus. At the same time, this continuity may lead the reader to go back to the beginning of the gospel narrative and read it again with the perspective of Jesus's resurrection and ascension.

First, the narrative of the fishing miracle and breakfast meal is presented as Jesus's revelation. It is framed with the narrator's words, with emphasis on revelation: "Jesus revealed himself to the disciples by the sea of Tiberias. He revealed himself in this way" (21:1); "This was the third time Jesus was revealed to the disciples after he was raised from the dead" (21:14). As O'Day points out, the verb "to reveal" (φανερόω) has already been used to address the revelatory dimension of Jesus's miracles (2:11; 9:3) and to summarize the purpose of Jesus's ministry (1:31; 17:6). Thus, the narrative of fishing and meal "should be interpreted in the light of the revelatory acts of Jesus's ministry."[33]

Second, the narrative of the fishing miracle and breakfast meal in John 21 has strong echoes of the sign narratives of feeding and walking on water in John 6. Both John 21 and 6 narrate a theophany story at the Tiberias sea, coupled with the meal story. As Martin Hasitschka points out, the place-name Tiberias is found only in John 6:1, 6:23, and 21:1.[34] In John 21, the words of the Beloved Disciple to Peter, "It is Lord [ὁ κύριός ἐστιν]" (21:7), reveal the identity of the risen Jesus to the disciples and bring them toward him (21:7–8). This echoes Jesus's self-revelation "I am" (ἐγώ εἰμι)

---

32. Petterson, *From Tomb to the Text*, 133.
33. O'Day, "Gospel of John," *NIB* 9:856.
34. Hasitschka, "Significance of the Resurrection Appearance in John 21," 312 n. 4.

at the Tiberias sea in 6:20,[35] which is presented also as a theophany.[36] Further, with the help of Peter, the risen Jesus provides the breakfast meal of abundant fish and bread to the disciples ("Jesus comes and takes bread and gives to them; so also the fish" [21:13]). In John, Jesus's last meal is related not to Jesus's death but to his resurrection.[37] This breakfast meal echoes the feeding miracle of bread and fish in John 6 ("Jesus took the loaves and, giving thanks, distributed them to those who were reclining; so also the fish, as much as they wanted" [6:11]), which is followed by the discourse on the resurrection.[38] It may be possible to see in both meals the allusion to the messianic banquet in which the resurrected dine with the messianic figure.[39] Furthermore, it is hard to miss the eucharistic overtones in this meal.[40] As Webster observes, while in John 6, the verbs are in the aorist tense, in John 21, the verbs are in the present tense, which is a dramatic narration that places the reader within the actions in the narrative.[41] In the end of the resurrection narrative, the reader is invited to take part in this breakfast meal with the risen and ascended Jesus and to taste the abundance of the resurrection life. The echo with the feeding miracle in John 6 accentuates the continuity of the risen and ascended Jesus and the incarnate Jesus. As O'Day says, "Jesus's gifts continue even after the events of his

---

35. C. K. Barrett (*The Gospel according to St. John*, 2nd ed. [Philadelphia: Westminster, 1978], 580) sees a correspondence to Jesus's self-identification "I am" (6:35; 8:24; etc.).

36. Susan Hylen, *Allusion and Meaning in John 6*, BZNW 137 (Berlin: de Gruyter, 2005), 134. Also see Gail O'Day, "John 6:15–21: Jesus Walking on Water as Narrative Embodiment of Johannine Christology," in *Critical Readings of John 6*, ed. R. Alan Culpepper, BibInt 22 (Leiden: Brill, 1997), 149–59, esp. 155.

37. As Liew says, "one finds in John's Gospel no narrative of the Last Supper before Jesus's crucifixion, but only a post-crucifixion and post-resurrection meal (21:1–14) to remember the dead and restore the living to life." Tat-siong Benny Liew, "The Word of Bare Life: Working of Death and Dream in the Fourth Gospel," *Anatomies of Narrative Criticism: The Past, Present, and Futures of the Fourth Gospel as Literature*, ed. Tom Thatcher and Stephen D. Moore, RBS 55 (Atlanta: Society of Biblical Literature, 2008), 179.

38. Only after revealing himself as God does Jesus speak of himself emphatically as the agent of the resurrection in the following discourse (6:40, 44, 54).

39. Jane S. Webster, *Ingesting Jesus: Eating and Drinking in the Gospel of John* (Atlanta: Society of Biblical Literature, 2003), 69–74.

40. O'Day, "Gospel of John," *NIB* 9:859.

41. Webster (*Ingesting Jesus*, 138) says, "The narrative lives on in the present."

'hour.'"[42] "The vast quantity of fish in the disciples' net and the gracious meal of bread and fish show that God's gift is available in the risen Jesus just as it was in the incarnate Jesus."[43]

Finally, the strong echoes of Jesus's sign narratives in John 6 not only emphasize the continuity between the incarnate Jesus and the risen and ascended Jesus but also encourage the reader to read the whole gospel narrative again with the perspective of Jesus's resurrection and ascension. The echoes of the ministry of Jesus may cause readers to reconsider the earlier passages in light of Jesus's death, resurrection, and ascension. John 21 sums up the whole gospel as a narrative of what Jesus did and encourages the reader to read this gospel narrative again.

Conclusion

In John 20–21 the theological truth of the resurrection narrative is inseparable from its narrative mode. First, by using ellipsis, John does not narrate Jesus's resurrection and ascension and leaves them as narrative gaps. By reading through the narrative, the readers follow the characters' movement in and around the tomb and move from inside to outside the tomb to encounter the risen Jesus outside the tomb. As for the ascension, through reading the narrative, readers may perceive a contrast between Jesus's encounter with Mary and his encounters with disciples and conclude that Jesus's ascension has taken place in between the scenes, 20:18 and 20:19. It is the reader who can perceive the contrasts between the scenes and fill in the narrative gaps. Second, by using the narrative asides, John highlights the role and purpose of the medium of the gospel narrative. Third, by echoing Jesus's sign narratives in John 6 in the final work of the risen Jesus in John 21, John emphasizes the continuity of the incarnate Jesus and the risen and ascended Jesus, urging the reader to reenter the narrative world with the resurrection perspective. Thus, the narrative mode is inseparable from its theological truths: Jesus's resurrection and ascension demand active human participation, and the risen and ascended one is the incarnate one who continues to reveal himself in the gospel narrative.

---

42. O'Day, "Gospel of John," *NIB* 9:864.
43. O'Day, "Gospel of John," *NIB* 9:864.

A Note on Ambiguity in the Book of Revelation

Patrick Gray

It is a truth universally acknowledged that nothing about the book of Revelation is universally acknowledged. Few texts generate so many or such divergent readings. A remark by Augustine near the end of his *City of God* indicates that this lack of consensus is not a recent development. "Now in this book called the Apocalypse," he writes, there are "many obscure statements, designed to exercise the mind of the reader; and there are few statements there whose clarity enables us to track down the meaning of the rest, at the price of some effort" (*Civ.* 20.17.13 [Bettenson]). It is not for lack of interpreters willing to put forth the effort over the centuries. To be sure, there are many who avoid the Apocalypse out of distaste for its bizarre literary qualities or to avoid becoming a footnote in its tragicomic history of reception, but there are just as many who devote prodigious intellectual energy to solving its many riddles.

This state of affairs is due in no small part to its pervasive and perplexing use of symbolic language. Who or what are the four horsemen, the twelve heavenly gates, the twenty-four elders, the seven lampstands, and 666, the so-called mark of the beast? And what about the animals—the lions, lambs, dragons, leopards, bears, eagles, locusts, scorpions, and birds—not to mention the hybrid creatures? Nor can everyone agree on how to handle the larger numbers: How long, exactly, is a thousand years, and can Mount Zion accommodate a multitude of 144,000?

The number of explanations put forward for each of these symbols is a function of their ambiguity. Although the symbols used by John are anything but transparent, ambiguity should not be understood as simply a synonym for vagueness or uncertainty. Furthermore, it is rarely the case that the interpreter is totally in the dark about what John is trying to signify. Quite often one faces the opposite problem of surplus meaning, when symbols point or pull the interpreter in two distinct directions. Alternative interpretations of many of the symbols he uses are distinct in the sense that they can be easily differentiated even when they are not distinct regarding the precise person, event, or location to which they refer. Desert imagery such as one finds in Rev 12:1–6, for example, can call to mind the segment of the created order where chaos reigns and unclean spirits dwell. But the desert motif may also suggest—as it does most memorably in Exodus—safety, liberation, and asylum.[1] Deserts have the capacity to evoke both of these mutually exclusive sets of associations, but the context makes it sufficiently clear that the desert is a place of safety for the woman in Rev 12:6. The ambiguity of John's language is thus frequently not an utter or absolute obscurity but a kind of relative obscurity from which the reader may reasonably hope for relief.

It is de rigueur in the secondary literature to highlight the literary or linguistic ambiguity that characterizes Revelation.[2] The ambiguity can be seen from the opening verse, where it is unclear whether "revelation of Jesus Christ" should be understood as an objective or subjective genitive (indicating Jesus as that which is being revealed or as the one who is making the revelation).[3] And the book ends on an uncertain note: Some manuscripts have John extending the grace of the Lord Jesus Christ to "all," while other scribes, perhaps "finding the word of universal grace too much to bear," limit it to "all the saints," an ambiguity that M. Eugene Boring sees as "symbolic of the provocative tension of Revelation as a whole."[4] David E. Aune calls attention to the ambiguity found at what might be called the macrocosmic and microcosmic levels. Guidance is often issued in riddles or in some other form demanding interpretation in the prophetic and oracular settings of Jewish and Greco-Roman antiquity similar to the likely *Sitz im Leben* of Revelation.[5] At the other end of the spectrum, Aune mentions the

---

1. G. B. Caird, *The Revelation of Saint John* (Peabody, MA: Hendrickson, 1966), 151–52.

2. See Lynn R. Huber, *Like a Bride Adorned: Reading Metaphor in John's Apocalypse*, ESEC (New York: T&T Clark, 2007); Susan Hylen, "Metaphor Matters: Violence and Ethics in Revelation," *CBQ* 73 (2011): 777–96.

3. The same ambiguity is present in Rev 1:2 with respect to the genitive phrases "the word of God" and "the testimony of Jesus Christ." See, e.g., K. T. Marriner, *Following the Lamb: The Theme of Discipleship in the Book of Revelation* (Eugene, OR: Wipf & Stock, 2016), 83. Unless otherwise indicated, all biblical translations are mine.

4. On Revelation's "wonderfully tensive ambiguity," see M. Eugene Boring, *Revelation*, IBC (Louisville: John Knox, 1989), 226.

5. David E. Aune, *Revelation 1–5*, WBC 52A (Dallas: Word, 1997), 15.

author's proclivity for using the *pronomen abundans*, that it, a personal or demonstrative pronoun that repeats the relative pronoun in a single relative clause, likely resulting from a Semitism that involves an indeclinable relative particle that is itself ambiguous and requires a personal or demonstrative pronoun for clarification.[6] These and other instances of ambiguity are often considered to be deliberate literary choices made by the author.[7] John, it has been argued, reflects an ambiguity about the fall of Jerusalem to the Romans, alternately viewing it as just deserts for the holy city for its rejection of Jesus or as the reason for its future destruction at the parousia.[8] Greg Carey argues that just as "John's ethos is at once egalitarian and authoritarian, so is the Apocalypse at once inviting and exclusive" and that consequently "conflicts among Revelation's contemporary readers in some measure derive from these ambiguities."[9] Elisabeth Schüssler Fiorenza may be correct when she observes that "literalist fundamentalists" and "scholarly scientific" interpreters mishandle the text and its ambiguities in unexpectedly parallel ways, but it is clear that this quality of Revelation has not gone unnoticed.[10]

On occasion, ambiguity itself occupies an ambiguous place in these and other studies. Ambiguity should be distinguished from ambivalence, with which it is sometimes confused. Language exhibits ambiguity; people experience ambivalence, which denotes simultaneous conflicting feelings toward a person or thing. John evinces very little conflict in his feelings about, for instance, Rome, Christ, or Satan. But, as has been documented, his language exhibits a great deal of ambiguity if one adopts William Empson's definition in his classic study, *Seven Types of Ambiguity*, as "any verbal nuance, however slight, which gives room for alternative reactions to the

---

6. Aune, *Revelation 1–5*, clxvi.

7. E.g., Richard Bauckham, *The Climax of Prophecy: Studies on the Book of Revelation* (Edinburgh: T&T Clark, 1993), 232; R. L. Thomas, *Magical Motifs in the Book of Revelation* (London: T&T Clark, 2010), 38. Harry O. Maier appreciates the "playful ambiguity" by means of which John "cleverly embed[s] himself in the Revelation he describes" (*Apocalypse Recalled: The Book of Revelation after Christendom* [Minneapolis: Fortress, 2002], 60–61).

8. C. M. Pate, *Interpreting Revelation and Other Apocalyptic Literature: An Exegetical Handbook* (Grand Rapids: Kregel Academic, 2016), 67–68.

9. Greg Carey, "The Apocalypse and Its Ambiguous Ethos," in *Studies in the Book of Revelation*, ed. S. Moyise (Edinburgh: T&T Clark, 2001), 163–64.

10. Elisabeth Schüssler Fiorenza, *The Book of Revelation: Justice and Judgment*, 2nd ed. (Minneapolis: Fortress, 1998), v.

same piece of language."[11] Empson clarifies the ways in which ambiguity can exercise a positive function, rather than simply resulting by default from poorly conceived and constructed sentences and paragraphs. Of special heuristic value for the present study are Empson's first and fourth types. The first type is the most general type that arises when a linguistic detail is effective in several ways at once. Contradictory meanings can be implied by the same piece of language. The fourth type is present when two or more meanings of a statement "combine to make clear a more complicated state of mind in the author."[12] John's state of mind is perhaps complicated though not conflicted. Furthermore, Empson's focus upon alternative reactions to the same piece of language is conducive to an analysis of Revelation's rhetorical qualities. John is almost certainly writing to provoke some kind of response, an assertion that does not in principle conflict with the claim that he has undergone some sort of visionary experience that he feels compelled to record.[13]

Thus understood, one may wonder whether John uses images, symbols, and language with multiple, often contradictory meanings and associations not in spite of the fact that they contain such a possibility for ambiguity, but for that very reason. If, on the other hand, it is not a conscious literary strategy on John's part, it is nonetheless possible to offer a thick description of the way in which ambiguity functions in the text. The description of the 144,000 standing with the Lamb in Rev 14:1–5 provides an interesting case study (see below). This scene appears to offer readers a foretaste of the glory they will experience in the future, but John's language also provides clues that the judgment of the wicked should be seen as the obverse of the salvation of the faithful. The full significance of his language cannot be set forth within the confines of one scene, however spectacular or however much the symbols he uses may suggest opposing meanings. Usually, the alternatives must be developed separately, which in part accounts for the frequent shifts in scene and character throughout the

---

11. William Empson, *Seven Types of Ambiguity*, 2nd ed. (New York: New Directions, 1947), 1.

12. Empson, *Seven Types of Ambiguity*, 133.

13. Whether the imagery came to him in the course of study, as part of his cultural heritage, or in a visionary experience is unclear. As Sophie Laws notes, "It is always important to distinguish between intention and function, and between the genesis of an image and its impact" (*In the Light of the Lamb: Image, Parody, and Theology in the Apocalypse of John*, Good News Studies 31 [Wilmington, DE: Glazier, 1988], 34).

book. John's language can never be all at once fully appreciated, because the multiple, very often contradictory ways of perceiving the same individual symbols or images are possible only by assuming certain perspectives. John depicts the opulence of Rome as harlotry so as to convince the reader of the proper way to regard it. From one perspective, the Lamb's deeds will appear in their full salvific glory. From another, the very same deeds will appear as its wrath. Both aspects cannot be experienced simultaneously. The reader is thus forced to choose one perspective, if only to make consistent sense of the chaotic story being told. Various characters may experience ambivalence, but the author wants his readers to overcome any conflicted feelings when they encounter ambiguity. Ways of seeing reflect where one stands, but they also have the power to shape one's actions. The only means John has at his disposal to affect his readers' ways of seeing is through the relating of his own vision. As seer-narrator, John provides the closest thing to an Archimedean point of reference, but because he has himself already committed to a way of seeing, he cannot empathize fully with the perspective embraced by those who follow the beast instead of the Lamb.

The Lamb and the 144,000

This dynamic comes into clearer focus upon a close reading of Rev 14:1–5, where the Lamb and the 144,000 are found on Mount Zion. The Lamb first appears in the description of the heavenly worship in Rev 4:1–5:14 and proceeds to break the scroll's seals in the subsequent chapters (6:1–8:5). The breaking of the seals unleashes a series of plagues on the earth while a faithful throng of 144,000 drawn from the twelve tribes of Israel celebrates a victory won by God and the Lamb. When the seventh seal is broken, seven angels appear with seven trumpets. The sounding of the seven trumpets ushers in more plagues, modeled upon the plagues visited by God on Egypt (8:6–11:19). A short description of a battle between the angels and a dragon is inserted within a longer account of the confrontation between the dragon and a pregnant woman in the heavens (12:1–17). Michael and his angels are victorious in heaven, while the dragon is cast to earth, bent on vengeance. Two beasts who act as the dragon's agents seduce, conquer, and control the whole world for forty-two months (12:18–13:18). The Lamb and the 144,000 reappear in Rev 14:1–5, followed by further warnings of judgment by angels who are poised to pour God's wrath upon the earth (14:6–16:21).

John introduces this new scene in Rev 14:1 with traditional visionary vocabulary. The combination of "I saw" with "behold!" strengthens the sense of astonishment. But in a book full of astonishing sights, it is perhaps more accurate to describe this formula as a cry of recognition. When the Lamb first appears in Rev 5:6, ἀρνίον occurs without the definite article. Here it is "the Lamb" (τὸ ἀρνίον); the reader is to understand that there is only one true Lamb, the one appearing in heaven "as if it had been slaughtered" (5:6; cf. 13:8). The beast whose heads John describes in Rev 13:3 is said to look "as if it had received a mortal wound" (ὡς ἐσφαγμένην εἰς θάνατον), but the NRSV obscures the fact that John uses the perfect passive participle of the same verb (σφάζω) for the Lamb (5:6; 13:8). In Rev 13:11, the second beast, who acts on behalf of the beast from the sea is described as having two horns "like a lamb" but speaking, eerily, "like a dragon." John's readers are not to be taken in by its lamb-like qualities. Agents of evil in Revelation often accomplish their purposes by becoming wolves in sheep's clothing, so to speak, by assuming certain attributes of God and his agents. This beast, faintly resembling a lamb, is able to deceive the whole world through the miracles it works and is thereby able to compel the inhabitants of the earth to construct an image of the first beast (13:14). The Lamb in Rev 14:1 stands in sharp contrast with the beasts John describes in the preceding passage. But it is a contrast that operates through both continuities and discontinuities suggested by the language the author employs. It is obvious to the reader, if not to every character in the narrative, that the beasts and the Lamb are not the same. John's language, recycling as it does certain words and images, invites the reader to compare opposing characters and to decide which is a parody or a perversion of the other.[14]

Describing it as "standing" (ἑστός) on Mount Zion is another means by which John connects this passage to earlier scenes in which the Lamb appears. When the Lamb is first introduced in Rev 5:6, it is by means of an ambiguous image: The Lamb is "standing as if it had been slain," with the phrase "as if it were slain" modifying the participle "standing." After the Lamb opens six of the seven seals in the following chapter and unleashes the wrath of heaven, those hiding in the hills raise the rhetorical question, "Who is able to stand?" (τίς δύναται σταθῆναι). Their cry "expresses

---

14. See J. E. Lunceford, *Parody and Counterimagery in the Apocalypse* (Eugene, OR: Wipf & Stock, 2009), 89–97.

the alarm of the conscious-stricken inhabitants of the earth" but not the thoughts of John.[15] The vocabulary of "standing" connects the presentation of the Lamb to the cry of those still on the earth when the sixth seal is broken. They do not yet recognize that the Lamb is indeed "able to stand." Almost immediately, John provides a partial answer to the question asked in Rev 6:17. The angels (7:1) and a great crowd (7:9) are said to be "standing" (ἑστῶτας/ἑστῶτες). A similar multitude stands with the Lamb in 14:1–5. Whether this great crowd is identical with the 144,000 in Rev 7:4 or with the 144,000 on Mount Zion in chapter 14 is the subject of long-standing debate.[16] In Rev 14:1, the Lamb and the 144,000 stand together and are no longer separated.

The first trait of the 144,000 John mentions is the name upon their foreheads. Since the name is the name of the Lamb "and of his father," it is unclear what that name is or whether there might not be two names. The perfect passive participle "written" (γεγραμμένον) is in the singular. This group stands over against the followers of the beast in chapter 13, who also bear a mark (χάραγμα) upon their brows. There are two beasts spoken of in chapter 13, but their followers receive only one mark. When the number of the beast is revealed (13:18), it is not entirely clear whether it belongs to the first or the second beast. The Lamb and his father are similarly conflated by virtue of the fact that they share a single name. God's ownership and protection of the 144,000 is signified by their sealing. Following so closely upon the branding described in Rev 13:16–17, the sealing with the divine name has further implications. Everyone—"the small and the great, the rich and the poor, the free and the slave"—receives the beast's mark.[17] Anyone without it is unable to participate in the economy. Those standing

---

15. R. H. Charles, *A Critical and Exegetical Commentary on the Revelation of St. John*, 2 vols., ICC (Edinburgh: T&T Clark, 1920), 1:183.

16. The history of interpretation is rife with conjecture. See Judith Kovacs and Christopher Rowland, *Revelation*, Blackwell Bible Commentaries (Oxford: Blackwell, 2004), 161–62. The options are briefly summarized by Craig R. Koester, *Revelation*, AYB 38A (New Haven: Yale University Press, 2014), 355.

17. The description of the 144,000 as being "without blemish" (ἄμωμος) in Rev 14:5 further accentuates the contrast with the followers of the beast. Throughout the LXX, ἄμωμος occurs in connection with sacrificial purity, but the adjective is an alpha privative of the noun μῶμος, which can refer not only to moral defect or physical blemish but also to a brand set upon something (LSJ, 1158). Therefore, an alternative translation of Rev 14:5b would be "they are without a brand."

with the Lamb appear to have opted out of the beast's economic system, since they do not bear its mark.

The description in Rev 14:1, then, anticipates and answers the obvious question that would arise regarding the fate of those who follow the course prescribed by John. They stand with the Lamb on Mount Zion, which appears here and nowhere else in Revelation. In a book where symbols are constantly reused, new symbols are striking. Mount Zion is mentioned in Ps 2, a psalm to which John also alludes in Rev 2:26–27. Zion originally referred to a portion of Jerusalem near the freshwater spring of Gihon and later designates the whole city of Jerusalem (Ps 76:1–2) or the western hill of the city, God's "holy mountain." A striking parallel is found in Heb 12:22–24. There the author tells his audience, "You have come to Mount Zion and to the city of the living God, the heavenly Jerusalem, and to innumerable angels in festal gathering, and to the assembly of the firstborn who are enrolled in heaven, and to God the judge of all, and to the spirits of the righteous made perfect, and to Jesus, the mediator of a new covenant, and to the sprinkled blood that speaks a better word than the blood of Abel." The "innumerable angels" and the "assembly of the firstborn" recall the 144,000. The motif of divine judgment appears in Rev 14:7. The references to Jesus and the sprinkling of blood relate to Jesus's self-sacrifice, which is described as "without blemish" ($ἄμωμος$) in Heb 9:14 and Rev 14:5. Jesus's portrayal as a lamb undoubtedly draws upon a sacrificial interpretation of Jesus's death, shared with the author of Hebrews. Both texts join judgment imagery associated with Mount Zion from Ps 2 with sacrificial imagery. That one place simultaneously evokes such disparate themes suggests that John wants his readers to interpret their experience in an unconventional way. What looks like sacrifice from one perspective looks like vindication from a slightly different angle of vision, though these are not antithetical perspectives since both are connected with hope in an early Christian context.

Mount Zion is perhaps an unexpected setting in which to find the Lamb and its followers. Other mountains in Revelation are precarious places. Among the catastrophes following the opening of the sixth seal, "every mountain ... was removed from its place" (6:14). In the aftermath, those hiding among the rocks would rather be buried by the mountains than face God and the Lamb's wrath (6:15–17). When the second angel sounds his trumpet, "something like a great mountain" plunges into the sea (8:8–9). The forces of the dragon in Rev 16:16 gather for battle at Armageddon, a Greek transliteration for the Hebrew "mountains of Megiddo." After the seventh bowl of wrath is poured out, "no mountains were to be found" (16:20). The scarlet beast upon which the whore of chapter 17 rides has seven heads representing seven mountains and seven kings (17:9), likely an allusion to the seven hills of Rome.[18] Mountains in Revelation therefore tend to function as sites, symbols, or even agents of evil and destruction. Zion's status as a place of refuge indicates that not all mountains are under the spell of evil forces.

The sound John hears in Rev 14:2 is not from the mountain, where the 144,000 are congregated, but from heaven. It is a singular voice or sound he hears from heaven, whether its source is a choir of angels or the 144,000 singing the new song (14:3). John writes that only the 144,000 can learn the song, not that they alone can sing the song. He may be suggesting that the Lamb is to teach them the "new song" he hears earlier (5:8–10; cf. 7:11–12). Or they may be singing "the song of Moses ... and the song of the Lamb" (15:3). Their identity as "those who had conquered the beast and its image and the number of its name" (15:2) is suggested by John's careful contrast of the 144,000 with those bearing the number of the name of the beast. They have learned the new song and stand "beside the sea of glass" before the heavenly throne (cf. 4:6). The song they are to learn in chapter 14 is thus given content in Rev 15:3–4. It will accompany the outpouring of God's wrath in chapters 15–16. Doxology and judgment are its dominant themes. Whereas these chords come together harmoniously for John, they likely clash in the ears of readers who align themselves either with the Lamb or the beast, not unlike the divergent reactions elicited from those who sympathize with the Israelites and the Egyptians by the Song of Moses in Exod 15.

Certain nuances in John's language in Rev 14:1–5 suggest an additional difference between the 144,000 and those bearing the number of the beast. First, the 144,000 are those "who have been redeemed from the earth" (οἱ ἠγορασμένοι ἀπὸ τῆς γῆς) and "redeemed from humankind" (ἠγοράσθησαν ἀπὸ τῶν ἀνθρώπων). John twice uses forms of the verb ἀγοράζω, "I buy." A more literal translation of these phrases would be "bought from the earth/humankind." This diction constitutes yet another connection between this scene and Rev 5:6–10, where the Lamb is praised for having "bought"

---

18. Given that the whore's name is Babylon the Great and that John elsewhere refers to Rome as Babylon, Bauckham's reading of the whore on the beast as the corrupting influence of Roman civilization riding upon the back of Roman military power is particularly apt (*Climax of Prophecy*, 343).

(ἠγόρασας) for God saints from every tribe, language, people, and nation. It reinforces the contrast drawn between the 144,000 and those bearing the mark of the beast since they do not have the beast's mark and therefore, according to Rev 13:17, are not able "to buy or sell" (ἀγοράσαι ἢ πωλῆσαι). An angel reminds John in Rev 14:9-11 that those able to buy and sell, by virtue of receiving the mark of the beast, are unable to be "bought" from the earth. The various meanings of the verb thus evoke the self-sacrificial mercy of the Lamb, the state of grace attained by the faithful, and the miserable fate awaiting the followers of the beast—as well as connecting the depiction of the 144,000 to the deliberations of the readers about their participation in the imperial economy.

Ambiguity and Revelation

As this cursory analysis of Rev 14:1–5 demonstrates, the ambiguity and allusiveness of John's language lend the book of Revelation an incredibly dense aspect. Nearly every phrase recalls a motif introduced earlier in his vision or foreshadows some later development. The images are shared in common with a wide range of biblical and noncanonical literature and come into clearer focus against the backdrop of Roman history and culture. This wide-ranging allusiveness amplifies the text's ambiguity, as the absence of interpretive alternatives would seem to permit only univocal readings. So much of Revelation's language can be interpreted in contradictory ways, and there is a palpable sense that there is a lot riding on the interpretive choices one makes, for John seems to imply that remaining neutral is not an option.[19]

Or perhaps it is that the interpretive choices one makes reflects some other, more important choice that has already been made and that in turn clarifies or even forces one's line of sight. John's rhetoric demands a commitment to a particular angle of vision.[20] By way of illustrating a similar

---

19. This theological imperative parallels the aesthetic principle laid out by C. S. Lewis: "The first demand any work of art makes upon us is surrender.... There is no good asking first whether the work before you deserves such a surrender, for until you have surrendered you cannot possibly find out" (*An Experiment in Criticism* [Cambridge: Cambridge University Press, 1961], 19).

20. It is not so much that the moral ethos or rhetoric of Revelation is "unstable" (Carey, "Apocalypse and Its Ambiguous Ethos," 164) but that the author's ambiguity forces choices on the part of its readers.

process, E. H. Gombrich compares literary criticism to the gestaltist's familiar drawing that from one angle resembles a duck and from another resembles a rabbit: "We can see the picture as either a rabbit or a duck. It is easy to discover both readings. It is less easy to describe what happens when we switch from one interpretation to another.... We are compelled to look for what's 'really there,' to see the shape apart from the interpretation, and this, as we soon discover, is not really possible."[21] The example of the duck-rabbit is well known from its use by Ludwig Wittgenstein, who refers to the phenomenon as "aspect dawning."[22] Like the text encountered by the readers of Revelation, the visual stimulus remains unchanged, yet the observer suddenly perceives as a duck what was once perceived as a rabbit or vice versa, as also occurs with optical allusions such as Schröder's stairs or a Necker cube.

Reading Revelation and processing its ambiguity is thus not a passive affair but is more closely linked with expectations, hopes, and fears than is often acknowledged. When the Lamb is first introduced as "the Lion of the tribe of Judah" and appears "standing as if it had been slaughtered" (5:5–6), the verbal and the visual cues pull in different directions. Likewise, it is easy enough to grasp the symbolism of washing one's robes and the efficacy of a lamb's blood in the context of Israelite worship, but readers may be confounded by the faithful having their robes "bleached" (ἐλεύκαναν) in blood (7:14). More broadly, Revelation has been read variously as a response to Roman persecution and as an anticipation or provocation of persecution, but it is difficult to adhere to both lines of interpretation simultaneously. To prefer one reading is necessarily to lose confidence in the other. The tenacity with which certain approaches to Revelation are maintained is a testimony to the power of perspective in this respect. To outsiders, the shortcomings and selective readings of, for example, the dispensationalist premillennial, postmillennial, and amillennial schools can be transparently obvious. Anyone who has attempted to point out the hermeneutical defects of one approach or the other can attest to the difficulty, if not futility, of the task.

Rightly or wrongly, these approaches focus on what Rudolf Bultmann labeled, with respect to the Fourth Gospel, the *Was* (the "what"

---

21. E. H. Gombrich, *Art and Illusion: A Study in the Psychology of Pictorial Representation* (New York: Pantheon, 1960), 5–6.

22. Ludwig Wittgenstein, *Philosophical Investigations*, trans. G. E. M. Anscombe (Oxford: Blackwell, 1958), 193–97.

or content) of revelation in the Apocalypse and not simply the *Dass* (the "that" or sheer fact) of its revelatory nature. Gail R. O'Day's analysis of the Johannine theology of revelation suggests that another category, the *Wie* (the "how"), which is well suited to the book of Revelation, regardless of the John to whom it is ascribed.[23] Rather than miring the reader in a "bog of indeterminacy," to use Robert Alter's phrase, the ambiguity of Revelation is integral to this *Wie*, or how John tells his story of "the things that must soon come to pass" (1:1).[24] If John is indeed using ambiguity to persuade his readers to commit to a way of seeing characterized by hopeful endurance, he is recognizing a principle articulated earlier by Paul. "Christ crucified," he writes in 1 Cor 1:23–24, is "a stumbling block to Jews and foolishness to gentiles, but to those who are called … Christ [is] the power of God and the wisdom of God." Paul realizes that Christ is an ambiguous symbol. There is only one Christ but a multiplicity of possible ways to regard and respond to him, though they are not equally desirable. Attempts to clarify with absolute precision the referential aspect of John's language miss the proverbial forest for the trees insofar as they become ends in themselves. An appreciation of the ambiguity of John's language alerts one to the relationship between the narrative mode or form in which John chooses to communicate his visions, the theological claims he makes, the practical aims he hopes to achieve, and the experience of the risen Jesus he seeks to convey.

---

23. Gail R. O'Day, "Narrative Mode and Theological Claim: A Study in the Fourth Gospel," *JBL* 105 (1986): 657–68.

24. Robert Alter, *The Pleasures of Reading in an Ideological Age* (New York: Simon & Schuster, 1989), 206–38.

Revealing Christ in Revelation

Lynn R. Huber

Readers of the Fourth Gospel and the book of Revelation have long wondered about the relationship between John the imagined author of the gospel and John the self-named author of the visionary narrative situated at the end of Christian canon.[1] While most current Johannine and Revelation scholars generally regard the connection as a remnant of early church tradition, the resonance between the two texts remains provocative. Among the similarities between these very different books is their focus upon revelation. Here I turn my attention to the ways that christological revelation occurs within the book of Revelation, specifically in the depictions of Christ as Lion *cum* Lamb and as the rider upon the white horse. In so doing, I employ Gail R. O'Day's insights into how the author of the Fourth Gospel uses irony to construct revelatory experiences. I maintain that John the author of Revelation, like the author of the gospel, uses irony to draw his audience into the process of interpretation, which subsequently reveals Christ and his significance.

Revelation in the Fourth Gospel

In her 1986 article "Narrative Mode and Theological Claim: A Study in the Fourth Gospel," O'Day extends the work of both Rudolf Bultmann and Ernst Käsemann, providing a helpful framework for discussing revelation within the Fourth Gospel.[2] In his monumental commentary, published in 1941, Bultmann famously emphasized the Fourth Gospel's revelation of

---

[1]. For the sake of clarity, when I refer to John I am referring to the author of Revelation and not the Fourth Gospel.

[2]. Gail R. O'Day, "Narrative Mode and Theological Claim: A Study in the Fourth Gospel," *JBL* 105 (1986): 657–68.

the *logos* in flesh. For the evangelist, "the very appearance of Jesus means that men are faced with the challenge to believe in him as the Revealer."[3] Operating with an "existential hermeneutic," Bultmann maintained that the Fourth Gospel's proclamation of this revelation prompts the gospel reader to respond to the revelation in faith.[4] This phenomenon, often characterized as *das Dass*, or "the bare fact," is for Bultmann the significance of revelation in the gospel. A student of Bultmann, Käsemann "turns the tables on [Bultmann]," according to O'Day, by arguing that the revelation of the gospel also includes content, *was*, or "what."[5] O'Day explains, "To Käsemann, the striking characteristic of the Johannine proclamation is that it contains one message that is rigidly and dogmatically repeated—the unity of the Father and the Son. This dogmatic reflection on Jesus' identity is the only object of faith for John, and one cannot therefore define faith solely on the basis of the situation of decision.... One cannot separate the fact of revelation from what is being revealed."[6] Through the process of revelation itself, the audience member encounters what is being revealed. The two elements, *Dass* and *was*, are intricately intertwined.

For O'Day, the connection between *Dass* and *was* is important for understanding the gospel, although she argues that these should not be detached from discussions of *wie*, or "how" revelation occurs in and through the narrative. The *Dass*, *was*, and *wie* of revelation are so intricately woven together that distinguishing between them misses the power of the Johannine narrative. Understanding revelation in the Fourth Gospel necessarily requires attending to how the narrative "presents Jesus as revealer and communicates [its] theology of revelation."[7] O'Day fleshes much of this out in her 1986 monograph, *Revelation in the Fourth Gospel*, emphasizing the author's deft use of irony as a mode of revelation.[8] Biblical scholars have tended to approach irony primarily as stable or dramatic irony, situations in which an audience's awareness stands in stark contrast to an obvious lack of awareness among those within a narrative or dramatic production. The Gospel of Mark, which highlights the inability of

---

3. Rudolf Bultmann, *The Gospel of John: A Commentary*, trans. G. R. Beasley-Murray, R. W. N. Hoare, and J. K. Riches (Philadelphia: Westminster, 1971), 207.
4. O'Day, "Narrative Mode and Theological Claim," 658–59.
5. O'Day, "Narrative Mode and Theological Claim," 660.
6. O'Day, "Narrative Mode and Theological Claim," 660.
7. O'Day, "Narrative Mode and Theological Claim," 661.
8. O'Day, "Narrative Mode and Theological Claim," 663.

those around Jesus to recognize his identity, is especially known for its use of dramatic irony.[9] However, irony actually describes a complex set of rhetorical tools involving obfuscation, according to O'Day. She explains that irony can occur whenever there is a disparity between text and context, text and cotext (or literary context), or text and other text.[10] Ironically, it is through a conflict in meaning that the ironic text creates meaning.

Employing irony within a narrative is risky, since it requires the audience to assume some interpretive responsibility for meaning to be effectively conveyed.[11] Given this, authors may, as the author of the Fourth Gospel does, signal that they are using irony through the use of double entendre, rhetorical questions, or other means.[12] Still, the audience member or reader is ultimately the one tasked with resolving the textual incongruities presented in the narrative. O'Day explains, "The incongruities and tension within irony draw the reader into the text and thereby into participation in this vision. Irony reveals by asking the reader to make judgments and decisions about the relative value of stated and intended meanings, drawing the reader into its vision of truth."[13] For example, when Pilate asks Jesus, "what is truth," before sending him to be crucified (18:38), the audience remembers Jesus's claim to be the truth and is prompted to answer the unknowing governor with either an affirmation or denial of Jesus's identity as the truth (14:6). Similarly, in John 4, a moment of ironic tension emerges when the Samaritan woman at the well asks "how" it could be that Jesus, a Jew, asks her, a Samaritan, for a drink (4:9). Even though the evangelist underscores the literal reality of the woman's claim, that conflict existed between Jews and Samaritans, Jesus's response to the woman ("If you knew") suggests that the "how" of her question could be understood another way, a way that points to Jesus's identity. If the woman *knew* his identity, she would recognize that he is the living water. In saying this, Jesus prompts the woman toward recognition of the revelation, and the gospel audience is prompted to respond with recognition. In this way, revelation within the Fourth Gospel typi-

---

9. David M. Rhoads, Joanna Dewey, and Donald Michie, *Mark as Story: An Introduction to the Narrative of a Gospel*, 2nd ed. (Minneapolis: Fortress, 1999), 60–61.
10. Gail R. O'Day, *Revelation in the Fourth Gospel: Narrative Mode and Theological Claim* (Philadelphia: Fortress, 1986), 26.
11. O'Day, *Revelation in the Fourth Gospel*, 30.
12. O'Day, *Revelation in the Fourth Gospel*, 28.
13. O'Day, "Narrative Mode and Theological Claim," 665.

cally includes communicating something ironic about Jesus's identity, such as his being both a Jew asking a Samaritan for a drink and the living water, as well as an invitation for the audience to participate in the revelation through recognizing this ironic identity.

Revelation's Revealing

Opening with the phrase *apokalypsis Iēsou Christou*, "a revelation of Jesus Christ," Revelation presents itself first and foremost as an unveiling (1:1). The word *apokalypsis*, transliterated into English as "apocalypse" and translated as "revelation," describes the act of removing a veil from (*apo*) something and thereby making it visible.[14] It is related to *anakalypsis*, the moment in the ancient Greek wedding when the bride's veil was lifted, revealing her to the groom for the first time.[15] By characterizing his narrative in this way, John foregrounds the revelatory aspect of the text—that which was once invisible/unknowable is being made visible/known.

The foregrounding of revelation in the text's opening lines belies the fact that Revelation has long been accused of being vague.[16] In fact, the book's opening line is unclear about whether Revelation is Jesus's act of revealing or whether Jesus is the object being revealed. Grammatically, there is a debate over whether the Greek genitive form *Iēsou Christou* should be translated as subjective or objective. Is Jesus the one who reveals, or is Jesus the one being revealed? Many commentators fall on the side of the subjective genitive, noting that Jesus is depicted as a link in a chain of Revelation's transmission from God to Jesus to an angel to John.[17] However, visions of Christ, depicted as Son of Man, Lion *cum* Lamb, and rider upon a white horse, consume a great deal of the text's attention. Through his narrative, John provides his audience with a sense of Jesus's identity and significance, essentially revealing him to those who hear. The christological claims of Revelation, furthermore, are central to understanding the

---

14. Lynn R. Huber, *Thinking and Seeing with Women in Revelation*, LNTS 475 (London: Bloomsbury, 2013), 10–11.

15. John Howard Oakley and Rebecca H. Sinos, *The Wedding in Ancient Athens* (Madison: University of Wisconsin Press, 1993), 30.

16. This accusation was leveled as early as the third century CE by Dionysius of Alexandria, according to Eusebius (*Hist. eccl.* 7.25.1–2).

17. E.g., Gregory K. Beale, *The Book of Revelation: A Commentary on the Greek Text*, NIGTC (Grand Rapids: Eerdmans, 1999), 183.

text's ethical imperatives.[18] Given that Revelation is a text that claims to be a revelation, which is often understood as unclear, and that the very first verse obscures the object/subject of revelation, O'Day's work on irony as revelatory mode seems an appropriate framework for exploring revelation within its pages.

Wie: How Revelation Reveals

As the opening verse of Revelation seemingly suggests, Jesus Christ acts as a revealer within the narrative. This happens a few different ways. One of the most obvious ways involves a vision of "one like a son of man," in which this figure of Christ reveals himself and speaks directly to John (1:12–20). Subsequently, the one like the son of man delivers to John seven messages for the angels of the seven communities that comprise Revelation's audience. In these messages (Rev 2–3), Christ reveals that he knows all that happens, good and ill, in their communities and that he plans on rewarding them accordingly. He promises eschatological rewards to all those who are victors or conquerors, like the crown of life (2:10) and new names (2:17; 3:12). It is hard to imagine a more direct form of revelation.

While there are these striking moments of Christ's relatively direct communication to the audience of Revelation through the seven messages, revelation in this text occurs primarily through John as a conduit. John describes himself undergoing a visionary and auditory experience while "in the spirit" on the Lord's Day (1:10–12).[19] John continually reminds his audience that this experience provides the content of the narrative by introducing many of his visions with the phrase "I saw" (*eidon*). John's role as revealer is facilitated by his being pulled up into the heavenly throne room (4:1), where the physical structure of the universe makes it possible for John to describe the way "the world looks when viewed through the eyes of God."[20] This viewpoint, moreover, leads to the ironic aspect of Revelation, as John is able to see things in a way that challenges the assumptions of those without the privilege of the God's-eye view.

---

18. Loren L. Johns, *The Lamb Christology of the Apocalypse of John: An Investigation into Its Origins and Rhetorical Force*, WUNT 2/167 (Tübingen: Mohr Siebeck, 2003), 176.

19. Unless otherwise indicated, all biblical translations are mine.

20. Gail R. O'Day, "Revelation," in *Theological Bible Commentary*, ed. Gail R. O'Day and David L. Petersen (Louisville: Westminster John Knox, 2009), 471.

Even though the first verse of the narrative outlines a simple chain of transmission (God → Jesus → angel → John → Jesus's slaves),[21] Revelation employs a number of different techniques to facilitate the revelatory process. In addition to John revealing through the process of narration, other voices abound throughout the text, including disembodied voices, choruses, and even objects. For example, the decorative horns on the altar before God voice a command to "release the four angels," who then proceed to kill a third of humanity (9:13–15). Revelation also uses techniques found in other apocalyptic and prophetic texts, such as otherworldly mediators, often called the *angelus interpres* (e.g., 17:1–2, 7–8; 19:9–10) to transmit knowledge. Even though it is difficult to ignore the revelations made by altar horns and angels, John is still the primary conduit for revelation in the text.

While John may be the primary mode of revelation in this book, the process of revelation demands audience participation. Throughout the narrative, John employs a variety of "grammars," to use the language of Giancarlo Biguzzi, or rhetorical tools that require the audience to participate in completing the meaning of the text. These grammars include textual lacunae that require audience members to fill in textual gaps or contradictions that invite the audience to accept or reject conflicting ideas.[22] The narrative also reveals through the use of simile and metaphor, including conceptual metaphorical mappings (e.g., IDOLATRY IS PROSTITUTION and A COMMUNITY IS A WOMAN).[23] Since John presents himself as making known things that have been unknown, he uses the known to help his audience see and understand. As a result, Revelation uses the word *hōs*, meaning "like" or "as," over seventy times and *homoios*, "like" or "similar to," at least twenty times.

---

21. Many modern translations (e.g., NRSV, NIV) use the English term *servant* to translate the Greek *doulos*, which refers to an enslaved person. For a discussion of the implications surrounding translating *doulos* as "servant" and not "slave" in the modern US context, see Clarice J. Martin, "Womanist Interpretations of the New Testament: The Quest for Holistic and Inclusive Translation and Interpretation," *JFSR* 6 (1990): 41–61.

22. Biguzzi outlines at least ten types of grammars employed in Revelation's text. Giancarlo Biguzzi, "A Figurative and Narrative Language Grammar of Revelation," *NovT* 45 (2003): 382–402.

23. For a discussion of Revelation's use of conceptual metaphor, see Lynn R. Huber, *Like a Bride Adorned: Reading Metaphor in John's Apocalypse*, ESEC (New York: T&T Clark, 2007).

John is often explicit in promoting the audience's participation in the revelatory event. There are times when he commands the audience, who hears the text read aloud (1:3), to see along with him. He does this through the repeated commands "Look!" or "Behold!," *idou* in Greek (4:1, 2; 5:5; 6:2, 5, 8; 7:9; 12:3; 14:1, 14; 19:11).[24] As Robyn Whitaker notes, Revelation is "one ancient author's attempt to give his hearers an epiphanic experience of God by igniting their imaginations and evoking their visual sense with his words."[25] In this way, Revelation's narrative mode bears some resemblance to the Fourth Gospel, as the audience is an active participant in the process of revelation.

O'Day's work on the Fourth Gospel, as discussed above, sheds light on the multiple ways that author employed irony. She explains that irony works, in part, because a text's author has a relationship with the audience that allows the former to use indirect communication. Because of the preexisting relationship, the author can count on the audience determining the correct meaning of the text.[26] At least this is the ideal. In the case of Revelation, John underscores his connection to the audience, describing it in terms of brotherhood and shared affliction (1:9). This connection sets up the possibility of irony as a revelatory technique. Despite this, the audience's ability to recognize what John intends through irony is far from certain.

Was: What Revelation Reveals

As mentioned above, the opening line of Revelation can be read as suggesting that the main object of revelation in the narrative is Jesus Christ.[27] In fact, throughout the narrative, Christ's identity is revealed in a number of different ways.[28] In addition to Christ appearing as one like a son of man,

---

24. Unfortunately, these commands are not evident in all English translations of Revelation, including the NRSV.

25. Robyn J. Whitaker, *Ekphrasis, Vision, and Persuasion in the Book of Revelation*, WUNT 2/410 (Tübingen: Mohr Siebeck, 2015), 1.

26. O'Day, *Revelation in the Fourth Gospel*, 29–30.

27. There are a number of book-length discussions of Christology in Revelation. See, for example, Johns, *Lamb Christology*, and Thomas Slater, *Christ and Community: A Socio-historical Study of the Christology of Revelation*, LNTS 178 (London: Bloomsbury, 1999).

28. Even though Revelation favors terms such as *Lamb* for describing Christ, it does use *Jesus Christ*, *Jesus*, and *Christ* some throughout the text. When *Christ* is used,

with hair like wool and eyes like flames of fire (1:14), Revelation's many hymns convey Christ's significance within the text (e.g., 5:9–14; 7:10–12; 11:17–18; 15:3–4; 19:1–8). Most notable, however, are the instances in which John describes seeing a figure that the audience must infer as being a metaphorical depiction of Christ.[29] In these instances, particularly the appearance of the Lion *cum* Lamb and the rider named faithful and true, John draws upon the audience's shared knowledge to present ironic portraits of the risen Christ.

"See, the Lion!"

Chapters 4–5 comprise the theological and christological heart of Revelation. In Rev 4, John offers a detailed description of the things he witnesses in the heavenly throne room, the center of which is the throne and the one who sits upon it, God. Among those in the throne room are four living creatures and twenty-four elders who offer hymns of praise that ascribe power, might, and glory to God. It is within the context of this throne room that John offers a revelation of Christ that is central to understanding the text as a whole.

After witnessing the worship of God upon his throne, a sight that John finds difficult to describe literally, John notices a sealed scroll in the divine right hand (5:1). Even though John can see writing on the outside of the scroll, the image of a rolled scroll with wax seals implies knowledge that is unknown and possibly inaccessible. The image offers a stark contrast to the idea of revelation and openness. The focus of the narrative tightens on the scroll when a mighty angel asks, "Who is worthy to open the scroll and break its seals?" (5:2). When no worthy candidate emerges, John weeps bitterly. He has been lifted into the heavenly throne room only to have its secrets withheld. In response to his grief, an elder from the throne room says, "Do not weep. See, the Lion of the tribe of Judah, the Root of David, has conquered, so that he can open the scroll and its seven seals" (5:5).

---

it seems to be employed more as a name than a title. Since Revelation seems relatively unconcerned with the life of the earthly Jesus, I will use *Christ* as a reference to Jesus Christ or the risen Christ.

29. A person could argue that the vision of the one like the son of man in chapter 1 functions in this way, since the text never explicitly identifies this figure as Christ. However, since this figure reveals himself to John directly, as opposed to appearing more as a character in the narrative, I am treating him differently here.

The command in 5:5, "See!" (*idou*), is directed at John; however, given that the text assumes oral performance (1:3), audience members hear the command directed to them as well. Everyone is invited to envision what John will see. The description of what will be revealed, "the Lion of the tribe of Judah, the Root of David," draws explicitly on traditions describing powerful and kingly leaders, including messianic figures (e.g., Gen 49:9–10).[30] In 4 Ezra, for example, the messiah appears as a lion who proclaims divine justice on behalf of the Most High (4 Ezra 11:37–46). Likewise, the reference to "the Root of David" alludes to traditions that associate a messiah with the line of David, such as in the gospels (e.g., Matt 1:1; Luke 2:4; 3:31). With all this in mind, John and his audience are prompted to envision a lion-like messiah coming to open the scroll. One can almost sense the relief. Moreover, as the Lion is described as having "conquered," a term used throughout chapters 2–3 as the ideal characteristic of Jesus followers (e.g., 2:7, 11, 17, 26; 3:5, 12, 21), the audience is prepared to meet their leader—the one who will show them how to conquer.

The expectations of John and his audience are immediately challenged when John tells us what he sees, "a Lamb standing as if it had been slaughtered" (5:6). The chasm between the audience's expectation and what is revealed could not be wider. Not only is a lamb conceptually antithetical to a lion, but also the image of the lamb *slaughtered* underscores this creature's powerlessness. As Stephen D. Moore observes, "At the center of the throne room that is the locus of absolute power in Revelation is a curious non-power, an abject inability, whose emblem is a butchered animal."[31] It is an image, moreover, that challenges ancient ideas about what it means to be powerful and strong. The implication is that the Lamb, along with those who follow the Lamb (14:4), conquer the beast by refusing to understand conquering or success on the beast's terms.[32]

---

30. Craig R. Koester, *Revelation: A New Translation with Introduction and Commentary*, Anchor Yale Bible 38A (New Haven: Yale University Press, 2014), 375.

31. Stephen D. Moore, "Ruminations on Revelation's Ruminant, Quadrupedal Christ; or, the Even-Toed Ungulate That Therefore I Am," in *The Bible and Posthumanism*, ed. Jennifer L. Koosed (Atlanta: SBL Press, 2014), 313.

32. Lamb imagery is something that the Fourth Gospel and Revelation share, although the texts employ different terms to reference this Lamb. In the Fourth Gospel, John the Baptist introduces Jesus by proclaiming, "Here is the lamb (*amnos*) of God who takes away the sin of the world" (John 1:29; cf. 1:36). The significance of this imagery culminates in Jesus's crucifixion on the day of preparation for the Passover,

Not only does this image engage Revelation's audience members by prompting them to envision the Lamb, who stands despite being slaughtered, described by John; it requires them to make an interpretive decision akin to those in the Fourth Gospel. In her discussion of the famous Samaritan woman scene in John's Gospel, O'Day offers words that could easily apply to Rev 5: "The text does not position the reader as observer, nor does it simply present propositions to which the reader is to give assent. Rather the narrative techniques of John 4:4–42 [or Rev 5:1–6] draw the reader into participation in the text. The invitation to discover Jesus' identity that Jesus extends to the woman (4:10) [or John] is extended to the reader also."[33] Like John, the audience members of Revelation are poised to make a decision about the paradoxical image before them. They are asked, Is this a case in which John sees the Lamb *instead of* the Lion, a biblical bait and switch? Or, is this figure both Lion and Lamb together? Using O'Day's understanding of irony, we can describe this an example in which a contradiction exists between both parts of the text itself (between what John *hears* and what he *sees*).[34] Resolving the apparent contradiction requires recognizing that the image of the Lion *cum* Lamb is ironic and not, in fact, a simple contradiction. It involves, moreover, associating this image with Revelation's understanding of Jesus Christ as the "firstborn of the dead" (1:5). The Lion *cum* Lamb embodies this paradox, as the one who died is the one who conquered.

"See, a White Horse and Its Rider!"

While the image of Christ as the conquering Lion who is simultaneously a slaughtered Lamb is arguably the most important christological image in Revelation, it is not the only revelation of Christ within the text. As Revelation approaches its climax, John has another vision of Christ, which features his final battle with the beast. The image is initially set up in Rev 17, when an interpreting angel explains to John that the kings of the earth "will make war on the Lamb, and the Lamb will conquer them, for he is Lord of lords and King of kings" (17:14). The audience is prepared to witness a final battle, a

---

when lambs were slaughtered for the Passover meal (John 19:31). In Revelation, John uses a diminutive, *arnion*, to describe the Lamb.

33. Gail R. O'Day, "The Gospel of John: Introduction, Commentary, and Reflections," *NIB* 9:572.

34. O'Day, *Revelation in the Fourth Gospel*, 26.

battle featuring not the Lion of Rev 5 but the Lamb. The text privileges here an image of weakness, only to have John subvert this through irony.

Immediately after a hymn that celebrates the destruction of Babylon and the coming wedding of the Lamb, John sees heaven opened and calls his audience to look with him (*idou*).[35] One expects to see the Lamb or his bride appear, since their wedding was just announced in the hymn (19:7). Instead, John and his audience witness a horse with a rider, who is called "faithful and true" (19:11). The image in Rev 19 is structured somewhat differently than that in chapter 5, as the movement from Lamb to rider is not structured quite as tightly as the movement from Lion to Lamb. However, John again invites his audience into the revelatory moment by using *idou*, and they are again called upon to resolve the tension between these images of Christ.[36]

In this passage, 19:11–21, John deploys a popular trope, the heroic king or victorious cavalryman, to depict the one who will come to destroy "the nations" (19:15). The rider wears multiple crowns or diadems, dons a robe dipped in blood, and leads the armies of heaven. This is an image of power and military strength. The image of a kingly figure or emperor upon a horse, ready for battle, was a typical way of representing masculine virtue or manliness, especially in Republican Rome.[37] In Asia Minor, the visual depiction of a god or hero on horseback, often called the "Thracian rider," was a common theme on gravestones and on votive reliefs.[38] The imagery

---

35. Unfortunately, English translations of Revelation are not consistent in how to translate the imperative *idou*, which can be literally rendered as "See!" The NRSV, in particular, vacillates and typically signals the presence of the imperative through the use of an exclamation point after "I looked," which translates the verb *eidon*.

36. One of the main interpretive questions surrounding this image is how it relates to the horse and rider that appear with the opening of the seven seals (6:2). In both cases, the horse being ridden is white, and the rider wears a crown, or crowns in the case of 19:12. Despite these similarities, contemporary scholars are divided on whether these figures should be read together. The description of the white horse and rider in Rev 6, along with three other horse and rider descriptions, which occur within the context of the opening of the seven seals, suggests that these four should be read together. This later horse and rider seem too far removed from the seals in the narrative to be connected. Koester, *Revelation*, 394.

37. Myles McDonnell, *Roman Manliness: "Virtus" and the Roman Republic* (Cambridge: Cambridge University Press, 2006), 149–54.

38. Nora Dimitrova, "Inscriptions and Iconography in the Monuments of the Thracian Rider," *Hesperia* 71 (2002): 209–29.

of a kingly rider similarly recalls the imagery of Ps 45: "Gird your sword on your thigh, O mighty one, in your glory and majesty. In your majesty ride on victoriously for the cause of truth and to defend the right; let your right hand teach you dread deeds" (45:3–4).

Aspects of this imagery suggest that this heroic rider represents Christ. He is called "faithful and true," which alludes to the character of the witness that Jesus is associated with throughout the narrative (e.g., 1:5; 3:14). Even though his name is unknown to those fighting against him (19:12), the audience is made aware that his thigh and robe are inscribed with the title "King of kings and Lord of lords" (19:16). This irony (the audience knows something unknown by those in the text) encapsulates Revelation's understanding of Christ as one who shares the heavenly throne of God (e.g., 7:17) and who is worthy of the obeisance associated with kingly figures (e.g., 5:11–14). Jesus Christ is also identified as "the ruler of the kings of the earth" at the same time he is described as "the faithful witness, the firstborn of the dead" (1:5). Further making it clear that this is an image of Christ, and specifically a messianic image, is John's description of the rider as warring against "the nations." The description of him subsequently ruling them "with a rod of iron" (see also 12:5) is a clear reference to Ps 2, in which God's "anointed," that is, the messiah, is told he will "break" the nations "with a rod of iron."

Ruling with a rod of iron is not the work of a benevolent ruler, and other facets of the rider's description reinforce this as an image of domination. For instance, the rider is described as treading the "winepress of the fury of the wrath of God the Almighty" (19:15), which draws a metaphorical connection between the color of wine and blood. The metaphor evokes an image from earlier in the narrative, when John describes the liquid from the "great winepress of the wrath of God" as flooding a city and becoming as high as a horse's bridle (14:19–20). This violent imagery continues as John describes the final standoff between the armies of heaven and those of the beast. An angel calls out to the birds of midheaven to gather for the "great supper of God," a possible realization of the Lamb's wedding banquet mentioned earlier in 19:9. However, this banqueting scene is horrific, as the birds gorge themselves on the flesh of those slain by the rider and his troops (19:21). Given this, the rider can easily be read as a description of Christ leading his followers into war against Satan.

Even though Revelation's depiction of the rider on the white horse seems like a clear reversal from the announcement that the Lamb will make war on the kings of the earth, on second look, the text is more ambiguous. It is possible, for example, that the blood that stains or colors Christ's garment is his own and not the evidence of violent actions. Perhaps these stains evoke Christ's role as the slaughtered or sacrificed Lamb (5:6), whose blood frees his followers from their sins (1:5). In this vein, Koester observes, "Christ's coming for battle does not signal a reversal in his character, as if the meek Lamb now becomes the vengeful warrior.... Instead, this victory completes the conquest of sin and evil that began with Christ's witness and crucifixion."[39] In other words, this image should be read as an image of love and justice.

Similarly, John's description of the sharp sword that emerges from Christ's mouth suggests a more ironic interpretation of the rider. While the sword implies violence, especially in a context of war, the fact that it comes from Christ's mouth suggests John is not describing a literal sword. Perhaps the sword represents Christ's "judging and purifying word."[40] The revelation of the rider's name as "the Word of God" supports this (19:13). Addressing this, Brian Blount notes, "After all, the primary weapon is a sword not of steel but of God's word.... This is the war of the Word, a war over which word, the word of whose lordship, is the true word. It is therefore on the level of testimony that the combat is waged."[41] The image of a messiah who does battle with weapons of the mouth is also found in other messianic texts. The author of 4 Ezra writes, for example, the messiah "neither lifted his hand nor held a sword or any weapon of war; but I saw only how he sent forth from his mouth as it were a stream of fire, and from his lips a flaming breath, and from his tongue he shot forth a storm of fiery coals" (13:9–10). John, it seems, is employing a traditional metaphorical association in which weapons or potential weapons (e.g., swords, fire, coals) serve as a way of characterizing words of judgment.

This vision of the rider seemingly stands in stark contrast to that of the Lamb, and scholars disagree about the image's significance, whether it should be read as a description of violence or as reference to metaphorical judgment.[42] Within the narrative, however, the audience seeing the Lamb who appears as the rider is seemingly asked to hold these images together.

---

39. Koester, *Revelation*, 765.
40. M. Eugene Boring, *Revelation*, IBC (Louisville: John Knox, 1989), 147.
41. Brian K. Blount, *Revelation: A Commentary*, NTL (Louisville: Westminster John Knox, 2009), 354.
42. Susan E. Hylen, "Metaphor Matters: Violence and Ethics in Revelation," *CBQ* 73 (2001): 778–79.

These are the same Christ, the blood on his robe is his blood and the blood of those he defeats with the sword of his mouth. Recalling O'Day's emphasis on the need to consider not just what the text reveals but also how it reveals, it is necessary to acknowledge that the image of Christ as warrior employs the language of violence as a revelatory tool. In this vein, Susan E. Hylen reminds us that even if the image of the rider upon the horse is read metaphorically, "the violent content of Revelation's metaphors is not magically transmuted into something nonviolent."[43] Even if John imagines the final battle between Christ and the powers of evil as a "war of words," the audience is still forced to think of this conflict in terms of war. The audience's imagination, as Hylen notes, is constrained by the imagery and forced to think of "God's accounting of justice as a zero-sum game" that demands the subjugation or annihilation of the defeated other.[44] For John at least, this image of Christ rests alongside the image of the slaughtered Lamb who will marry his bride.

As mentioned earlier, some of Revelation's earliest interpreters wondered whether the text should even be called a "revelation," given its tendency to obscure more than clarify (Eusebius, *Hist. eccl.* 7.25.1–2). This conundrum points to the complex way that revelation occurs within Revelation. Revelation occurs within ironic moments in which the audience is invited into the interpretive process. In this text, one is encountered by the image of a slaughtered Lamb who slaughters, a Lion who is a Lamb, a future groom who is a king in a bloody robe. For John, these are all equally images of Christ that the believer is asked to hold in tension. This does not mean that John suggests Christ is literally coming to shed the blood of his enemies on earth any more than he is saying that Christ was or is an actual lamb. All of these images are metaphorical; however, the dissonance created in these images requires the audience member or interpreter to engage the text creatively. As O'Day says of the Fourth Gospel, this narrative "does not just mediate the revelation ... but *is* the revelation."[45] All that is left is for the audience to see and understand how these ironic depictions of the divine illuminate the worlds in which they live.

---

43. Hylen, "Metaphor Matters," 780.
44. Hylen, "Metaphor Matters," 780.
45. O'Day, "Narrative Mode and Theological Claim," 668.

Part 2

Nicodemus, Misunderstanding, and the Pedagogy of the Incarnation in Chrysostom's *Homilies on John*

William M. Wright IV

An important contribution of Gail O'Day to Johannine studies has been her analysis of the essential role played by the Fourth Gospel's literary and rhetorical strategies in its theological presentation. Through its various literary and rhetorical techniques, the gospel draws its readers to participate actively in its narrative world as they interpret the meaning of the gospel's language. In doing so, O'Day argues, the gospel literarily reproduces for its readers the dynamic encounter with the revelation of God in Jesus that the narrative itself describes.[1] Put differently, the gospel has been composed so as to place its readers in a position similar to those individuals in the narrative who encounter Jesus. She writes, "Through the dynamics of the Johannine revelatory narrative, the fourth evangelist is able to recreate the revelation experience for the reader, engaging the reader in the text in the same way that Jesus engaged those whom he encountered."[2]

This alignment between readers of the gospel and individuals who encounter Jesus in the gospel points to a certain fittingness between the Fourth Gospel's literary and rhetorical technique and the reality of the incarnation. As the individuals in the gospel narrative are challenged to understand Jesus and receive him in faith and discipleship, so does the gospel put before its own readers a challenge: "Through this participation [in the gospel's narrative dynamics], the reader can then decide about what the text means, about its portrait of Jesus as revealer, and can decide

---

1. See Gail R. O'Day, *Revelation in the Fourth Gospel: Narrative Mode and Theological Claim* (Philadelphia: Fortress, 1986), 93–114.
2. Gail R. O'Day, "Narrative Mode and Theological Claim: A Study in the Fourth Gospel," *JBL* 105 (1986): 668.

whether to accept or reject his revelation."[3] There is, in other words, a theological congruence between form and content in John's Gospel. As O'Day puts it, "In order to understand *what* John says about Jesus and God, then, one must attend carefully to *how* he tells his story.[4]

O'Day's observations about the theological function of the gospel's literary and rhetorical dynamics have some interesting similarities with the Johannine exegesis of one of early Christianity's most rhetorically attuned readers: Saint John Chrysostom. In this essay, I will examine John Chrysostom's interpretation of Nicodemus and the Johannine motif of misunderstanding. Similar to O'Day, Chrysostom sees Nicodemus's misunderstanding as having an important theological function that is deeply connected to the incarnation. For Chrysostom, the motif of Nicodemus's misunderstanding—and Jesus's response to it—exemplifies the basic pattern of God's pedagogical "accommodation" (*synkatabasis*) to humanity that both the biblical text and the incarnation express.[5] Chrysostom's exegesis helps us appreciate what O'Day has pointed out in her own way: the theological relevance of John's literary strategies and their deep congruence with his teaching about the incarnation.

Before turning to Chrysostom's interpretation of Nicodemus, a sketch of divine accommodation (*synkatabasis*), a theological notion very important in Chrysostom's exegesis generally and his interpretation of Nicodemus specifically, is in order.[6]

---

3. O'Day, *Revelation in the Fourth Gospel*, 96.

4. Gail R. O'Day, "The Word Become Flesh: Story and Theology in the Gospel of John," in *Literary and Social Readings of the Fourth Gospel*, vol. 2 of *What Is John?*, ed. Fernando F. Segovia, SymS 7 (Atlanta: Scholars Press, 1998), 69.

5. The term *synkatabasis* carries a variety of nuances in Chrysostom's usage that cannot all be captured by a single English term (e.g., accommodation, condescension, adaptation). For discussion, see David Rylaarsdam, *John Chrysostom on Divine Pedagogy: The Coherence of His Theology and Preaching* (New York: Oxford University Press, 2014), 29–30.

6. For discussion (to which I am indebted here), see Hans Boersma, *Scripture as Real Presence: Sacramental Exegesis in the Early Church* (Grand Rapids: Baker Academic, 2017), 69–80; Bertrand de Margerie, S.J., *The Greek Fathers*, vol. 1 of *An Introduction to the History of Exegesis*, trans. Leonard Maluf (Petersham, MA: Saint Bede's, 1993), 189–212; Robert Hill, "St. John Chrysostom's Teaching on Inspiration in 'Six Homilies on Isaiah,'" *VC* 22 (1968): 19–37; Hill, "Chrysostom's Terminology for the Inspired Word," *EstBib* 41 (1973): 367–73; Hill, "The Incarnation of the Word in Scripture," *Compass Theology Review* 14 (1980): 34–38; Hill, "On Looking Again at Sunkatabasis," *Prudentia* 13 (1981): 3–11; Hill, "Introduction," in John Chrysostom,

Divine Accommodation (*Synkatabasis*) in Chrysostom

For Chrysostom, divine accommodation is a form of pedagogy whereby the transcendent God adapts his speech and action to the limited capacities of human beings. This basic notion does not originate with Chrysostom, but, as David Rylaarsdam has documented, it has roots in both the Greco-Roman rhetorical tradition and in early Christian exegesis.[7] For instance, Quintilian speaks of the need for rhetoricians to adapt their speech to a particular setting and audience: "Oratorical ornament is in fact varied and manifold, requiring different forms for different contexts; consequently, unless it is adapted both to circumstances and to persons, it will not only fail to lend distinction to the oratory, but will ruin it"(*Inst.* 11.1.1 [LCL]).[8] Similarly, Rylaarsdam calls attention to passages in Origen, Athanasius, and the Cappadocians, which speak of God's accommodation or adaptation of his teaching to human capacities. Thus, in *Hom. Jer.* 18, Origen speaks of God accommodating himself to the level of human beings in the way comparable to how an adult condescends to a child's level. He writes,

> whenever the divine plan involves human matters, it carries the human intellect and manners and way of speaking. And just as we, if we are talking with a two-year-old child—for it is impossible, if we observe what is fitting for the age of a full-grown man, and when talking to children, to understand the children without condescending [*synkatabainontas*] to their mode of speech—something of this sort also seems to be the case with God whenever he manages the race of men and especially those still *infants* [cf. 1 Cor 3:1]. (*Hom. Jer.* 18.5 [PG 13:476, Smith 198–99])[9]

In order for humans to understand anything of God's dealings with them, God must lower himself and adapt his communication and action to the limited comprehension of human beings.

Scholars of Chrysostom's exegesis have pointed out that his account of divine accommodation presupposes his doctrine of divine incompre-

---

Homilies on Genesis 1–17, FC 74 (Washington, DC: Catholic University of America Press, 1986), 13–19; Rylaarsdam, *John Chrysostom on Divine Pedagogy*, 13–99.

7. See Rylaarsdam, *John Chrysostom on Divine Pedagogy*, 18–30.
8. Reference owed to Rylaarsdam, *John Chrysostom on Divine Pedagogy*, 20.
9. Reference owed to Rylaarsdam, *John Chrysostom on Divine Pedagogy*, 26.

hensibility.[10] In September of 386, as a newly ordained priest in Antioch and about five years before his homilies on the Gospel of John, Chrysostom gave a series of sermons known as *On the Incomprehensible Nature of God*.[11] These sermons were directed against the enduring beliefs of Anomians (also known as Heteroousians), who held that the Son was of an essence entirely different from that of the Father (hence, hetero-ousia) and (on account of Eunomius's theory of verbal signification) that human beings can know God in the same way that God knows himself.[12] Against the latter claim, Chrysostom, like the Cappadocians before him, placed great emphasis on the incomprehensibility of the divine essence. Consider, for instance, Chrysostom's remarks in *Anom*. 3:

> Let us call upon him, then, as the ineffable God who is beyond our intelligence, invisible, incomprehensible, who transcends the power of mortal words. Let us call on him as the God who is inscrutable to the angels, unseen by the Seraphim, inconceivable to the Cherubim, invisible to the principalities, to the powers, and to the virtues, in fact, to all creatures without qualification, because he is known only by the Son and the Spirit.... It is not pretense or vain boasting to say that the creator is beyond the grasp of all creatures. (Chrysostom, *Anom*. 3.5–6 [PG 48:720, Harkins 97])[13]

Chrysostom thus affirms both the incomprehensibility of God and the correlate inability of all creatures, including the highest ranks of angels, to comprehend God the creator.

This account of divine incomprehensibility is of a piece with the radical transcendence of God the creator from all creation, a belief that the doctrine of a free creation *ex nihilo* entails. God the creator brings and sustains all things in existence by a totally free act of his will and without any kind

---

10. De Margerie, *History of Exegesis*, 1:189–99; Rylaarsdam, *John Chrysostom on Divine Pedagogy*, 14–18.

11. Following *The SBL Handbook of* Style, I will use the abbreviation *Anom*. for this work (otherwise known as *Contra Anomoeos*). On the dating of these groups of sermons, see J. N. D. Kelly, *Golden Mouth: The Story of John Chrysostom—Ascetic, Preacher, Bishop* (Ithaca, NY: Cornell University Press, 1995), 60–62, 90.

12. So Kelly, *Golden Mouth*, 60–61. On these Heteroousians, see Lewis Ayres, *Nicaea and Its Legacy: An Approach to Fourth-Century Trinitarian Theology* (Oxford: Oxford University Press, 2004), 144–49.

13. Reference owed to Rylaarsdam, *John Chrysostom on Divine Pedagogy*, 16.

of dependence upon creation.[14] God the creator is radically distinct from the world, and since God is not "a 'kind' of thing at all," he does not rival or compete with created realities in any respect.[15] This understanding of God as radically transcending creation has been shown to be a key premise informing pro-Nicene theology of the fourth century and beyond.[16]

To explicate the incomprehensibility of God to creatures, Chrysostom appeals to biblical evidence from both testaments. He cites Paul's identification of God as the one who "dwells in unapproachable light, whom no one has ever seen or can see" (1 Tim 6:16; John Chrysostom, *Anom.* 3.8–13 [PG 48:720–21, Harkins 98–101]).[17] Chrysostom takes the "unapproachable light" and the inability of people to see God as indicating that God is radically incomprehensible to human beings. He then explains that God is similarly ineffable to the angels—and thus picking up the above quoted reference to the seraphim and other ranks of the angelic hierarchy. To do so, Chrysostom asks why in Isaiah's prophetic call vision the seraphim around God's throne cover their faces with a pair of wings (cf. Isa 6:2). The reason for this covering, Chrysostom argues, is that the created, angelic nature cannot perceive the divine essence. Such perception is beyond their natural capacities as creatures. Instead, Chrysostom states, "What [the seraphim] saw was a condescension [*synkatabasis*] accommodated to their nature" (*Anom.* 3.15 [PG 48:722; Harkins 101]). Chrysostom goes on to provide a summary statement of *synkatabasis*: "What is this condescension [*synkatabasis*]? God condescends whenever he is not seen as he is,

---

14. Robert Sokolowski has masterfully explored this theological tenet in terms of what he calls "the Christian distinction between God and the world." See Robert Sokolowski, *The God of Faith and Reason: Foundations of Christian Theology* (Notre Dame: University of Notre Dame Press, 1982), 1–30; Robert Sokolowski, *Eucharistic Presence: A Study in the Theology of Disclosure* (Washington, DC: Catholic University of America Press, 1993), 34–54; Robert Sokolowski, *Christian Faith and Human Understanding: Studies on the Eucharist, Trinity, and the Human Person* (Washington, DC: Catholic University of America Press, 2006), 38–50.

15. Sokolowski, *God of Faith and Reason*, 42. On the noncompetitive, noncoercive nature of God's relationship to the world, entailed by the distinction, see Robert Barron, *The Priority of Christ: Toward a Postliberal Catholicism* (Grand Rapids: Brazos, 2007), 17, 204–7, 226–29; Robert Barron, *Exploring Catholic Theology: Essays on God, Liturgy, and Evangelization* (Grand Rapids: Baker Academic, 2015), 65–67.

16. See Khaled Anatolios, *Retrieving Nicaea: The Development and Meaning of Trinitarian Doctrine* (Grand Rapids: Baker Academic, 2011).

17. Unless otherwise noted, all biblical citations are taken from the NRSV.

but in the way one incapable of beholding him is able to look upon him. In this way God reveals himself by accommodating what he reveals to the weakness [*astheneia*] of vision of those who behold him" (*Anom.* 3.15 [PG 48:722; Harkins 101–2]). Several interrelated things stand out here. First, Chrysostom identifies accommodation as the form of divine revelation or pedagogy. The radically transcendent God is incomprehensible to creatures. If God is to be known by creatures in some manner, then God must accommodate himself to the capacities of the creatures and communicate in ways intelligible to them. Hence, the notion of divine incomprehensibility segues theologically into the notion of divine accommodation. Furthermore, Robert Hill points out that Chrysostom frequently speaks of divine accommodation as "a manifestation of the goodness (*philanthrōpia*) and providential care (*kēdemonia, pronoia*) of God."[18]

Second, Chrysostom underscores the fittingness of divine accommodation on account of the limited capacities, or "weakness" (*astheneia*), of creatures. As regards human beings, this weakness has different forms. To explore this weakness, Chrysostom cites the example of Daniel, who was overwhelmed at an appearance of an angel (Dan 10:5–9; Chrysostom, *Anom.* 3.18 [PG 48:722; Harkins 103]).[19] Following the biblical text, Chrysostom acknowledges that Daniel was a holy, righteous man. Thus, Chrysostom writes, "let no one think that [Daniel] experienced this [fear and weakness] because of his sins or a bad conscience.... Clearly, then, the blame for his condition belonged to the weakness [*astheneia*] of his nature" (*Anom.* 3.18 [PG 48:722, Harkins 103]). As Rylaarsdam points out, Chrysostom here indicates that such human weakness can be ascribed not only to the natural limitations of created nature but also to the damaging effects of sin on humanity.[20]

Chrysostom sees God's accommodation to human beings throughout the whole of the divine economy and especially in the ways that God speaks with humans. De Margerie observes that, for Chrysostom, God communicated by way of the spoken word with Adam, Noah, and the patriarchs.[21] However, de Margerie continues, "As humanity began to degenerate, the Creator did not totally turn away from it, but to those who were now living somewhat estranged from him he sent a letter, through

---

18. Hill, "On Looking Again at *Sunkatabasis*," 5; italics removed in parts.
19. The reference is from Rylaarsdam, *John Chrysostom on Divine Pedagogy*, 17 n. 32.
20. Rylaarsdam, *John Chrysostom on Divine Pedagogy*, 17–18.
21. De Margerie, *History of Exegesis*, 1:192.

the agency of Moses, to recall them to his friendship."[22] This letter is sacred Scripture.

Sacred Scripture, therefore, is a form of divine accommodation, whereby God makes his word known to human beings through intelligible, human discourse. For instance, in his *Hom. Gen.* 3, Chrysostom states the following about the description of God's creating on the first day: "Do you see the degree of considerateness [*synkatabasei*] employed by the blessed author, or rather the loving God [*philanthrōpos theos*] through the tongue of the author, instructing the race of men to know the plan of created things … and who was the creator of all, and how each came into being" (*Hom. Gen.* 3.6 [PG 53:34; Hill 42]). The verbal discourse of Scripture, for Chrysostom, is a form of God's accommodation to human weakness by which he educates human beings. Chrysostom continues, "since mankind was yet untutored and could not understand more elaborate matters, the Holy Spirit accordingly explained everything to us by moving the author's tongue in such a way to take account of the limitations [*astheneian*] of the listeners" (3.7 [PG 53:34; Hill 42]).

Chrysostom sees the various figures of speech, images, anthropomorphisms, obscure and challenging passages, and modes of discourse in the Scripture as serving this pedagogical purpose. For instance, commenting on the creation story in Gen 1, Chrysostom sees the text presenting God the creator in a manner similar to the way that a human craftsman plans, makes, and takes pride in a work.[23] "For Chrysostom," de Margerie writes, "all such biblical expressions pointed to the condescension of a spiritual being who merely wished to provide us with the means of attaining him, through metaphors suited to our materiality."[24]

This program of divine pedagogy, given through various forms of divine accommodation, culminates in the incarnation. A passage in Chrysostom's *Hom. Matt. 26:39*, which treats Christ's prayer to the Father in Gethsemane, illustrates this point and connects the incarnation to many other aspects of divine accommodation (PG 51:31–40; *NPNF* 1/9:199–207).[25] He states the following: "The doctrine of the incarnation was very

---

22. De Margerie, *History of Exegesis*, 1:192–93.
23. Chrysostom (*Hom. Gen.* 3.10 [Hill 43]) states, "This blessed author spoke this way out of considerateness for the way human beings speak."
24. De Margerie, *History of Exegesis*, 1:195.
25. Reference taken from Rylaarsdam, *John Chrysostom on Divine Pedagogy*, 93–94.

hard to receive. For the exceeding measure of his lovingkindness and the magnitude of his condescension [*hyperbolē tēs philanthrōpias autou, kai to megethos tēs synkatabaseōs*] were full of awe, and needed much preparation to be accepted" (PG 51:36; *NPNF* 1/9:204–5).

Chrysostom identifies the incarnation as the supreme form of divine accommodation and the greatest expression of God's *philanthrōpia*. God's love and accommodation in the incarnation was so great that God sought to prepare people for it ahead of time. Hence, Chrysostom cites a number of Old Testament texts in which he sees God slowly preparing a people and forming expectation for the incarnation of the Word.[26] Chrysostom also underscores the magnitude of the divine accommodation in the incarnation by connecting it to God's incomprehensibility that surpasses the capacities of all creatures. He states: "For consider what a great thing it was to hear and to learn that God the ineffable, the incorruptible, the unintelligible, the invisible, the incomprehensible ... the weight of whose condescension [*synkatabaseōs*] not even the Cherubim were able to bear but veiled their faces by the shelter of their wings, that this God who surpasses all understanding ... deigned to become man, and to take flesh formed of earth and clay, and enter the womb of a virgin ... and suffer all things to which man is liable" (PG 51:37; *NPNF* 1/9:205).

Among the purposes that Chrysostom discerns in God's accommodation is to elevate human beings to participate in heavenly life. Redolent of Athanasius's famous statement in *On the Incarnation*, Chrysostom sees the descent of the Word as resulting in the elevation of human beings.[27] Commenting on John 1:14, Chrysostom states:

> He became the Son of Man, though he was the true Son of God, in order that he might make the sons of men children of God. In truth, to mingle the high with the low works no harm to the honor of the high but raises the lowly up from its very humble estate. Accordingly, this is also true in the case of Christ. He in no wise lowered his own nature by this descent, but elevated us, who had always been in a state of ignominy and darkness, to ineffable glory. (*Hom. Jo.* 11 [Goggin 106])[28]

---

26. Chrysostom cites Gen 49:9; Isa 7:14; 53:2; 9:6; 11:1; Bar 3:35–37; and Ps 72:6.

27. Athanasius, *Inc.* 54 (PG 25b:192): "For [the Word] became human so that we may become divine [*Autos gar enēntheōpēsen, hina hēmeis theōpoiēthōmen*]."

28. Reference taken from Johannes Quasten, *Patrology*, vol. 3: *The Golden Age of Greek Patristic Literature from the Council of Nicaea to the Council of Chalcedon* (Westminster: Newman, 1960), 439.

As we shall see in Chrysostom's interpretation of Nicodemus, the divine accommodation in the incarnation also serves to direct humans to a proper understanding of God and heavenly realities.

In summary, accommodation (*synkatabasis*) is, according to Chrysostom, a form of divine pedagogy. The incomprehensible, transcendent God adapts to the various forms of weakness (*astheneia*) that beset humans and communicates in ways intelligible to them. Chrysostom sees this mode of divine pedagogy displayed across the divine economy in God's discourse with human beings, in the language of Scripture, and preeminently in the incarnation. Through this pedagogical accommodation, the transcendent God manifests his *philanthrōpia* and aims to elevate human beings to a proper contemplation of himself and to participate in heavenly glory. With this sketch of Chrysostom's notion of *synkatabasis* in place, I now turn to his interpretation of Nicodemus in his *Homilies on the Gospel of John*.

Chrysostom's Interpretation of Nicodemus

Nicodemus appears in three scenes in John's Gospel. He first appears in John 3, where he is introduced as "one of the Pharisees" and "a leader of the Jews" (3:1). He comes to Jesus at night and engages him in a dialogue. This exchange features Jesus's teaching about acquiring a new life from heaven and Nicodemus's misunderstanding of Jesus's words. The second appearance of Nicodemus is in John 7, within a meeting of the Jewish leadership in Jerusalem (7:45–52). Here, Nicodemus subtly defends Jesus against other Jewish leaders who rush to condemn Jesus without the investigative process mandated by torah. Nicodemus appears for a third and final time at the cross after Jesus's death. Along with Joseph of Arimathea, Nicodemus prepares Jesus's corpse for burial with an extravagant amount of spices and entombs him (19:38–42). Nicodemus is also to be counted among those secret believers among the Jewish leadership in Jerusalem who do not publicly profess their belief on account of their fear of losing socioreligious relationships and their desire for honor from others (12:42–43).

Nicodemus is an ambiguous character in the Fourth Gospel.[29] On the one hand, Nicodemus approaches Jesus favorably, engages with him in

---

29. See Susan Hylen, *Imperfect Believers: Ambiguous Characters in the Gospel of John* (Louisville: Westminster John Knox, 2009), 23–40; R. Alan Culpepper, "Nicodemus: The Travail of New Birth," in *Character Studies in the Fourth Gospel: Narrative*

theological discussion, subtly defends him before his opponents, and performs the culturally significant task of burying him. And yet, Nicodemus repeatedly fails to understand Jesus and does not openly profess belief in Jesus because of his fear and desire for honor.

As we shall see, in his exegesis, Chrysostom preserves the ambiguity of Nicodemus and capitalizes upon his weaknesses in order to highlight the loving accommodation of God manifest in the incarnation.[30]

Scene 1 (John 3:1–15)

Chrysostom's interpretation of John 3:1–15 appears in his *Hom. Jo.* 24–27.[31] When Chrysostom comes to the introduction of Nicodemus in John 3, he provides a brief rehearsal of the three scenes in John wherein Nicodemus appears. In many ways, Chrysostom's remarks on Nicodemus in *Hom. Jo.* 24 sets much of the tone for his subsequent handling of Nicodemus. From the outset, Chrysostom identifies Nicodemus as a sympathetic, though imperfect, figure in the gospel.

He begins by stating that Nicodemus "was well disposed toward Christ, not, indeed, as much as he ought to have been" (*Hom. Jo.* 24 [PG 59:144, Goggin 234]). While Nicodemus seeks out Jesus, he does so at night, and Chrysostom takes this timing as reflecting Nicodemus's fear. By so interpreting Nicodemus's coming to Jesus at night at a secretive meeting, Chrysostom identifies Nicodemus as one of the secret believers among the Jewish leadership mentioned in John 12:42–43.[32] This group, the gospel narrator states, did not openly profess their faith in Jesus because of their

---

Approaches to Seventy Figures in John, ed. Steven A. Hunt, D. Francois Tolmie, and Ruben Zimmermann (Grand Rapids: Eerdmans, 2016), 249–59.

30. While Chrysostom maintains the ambiguity of Nicodemus, I do think that Chrysostom (like John the Evangelist) is ultimately more favorable to Nicodemus than he is unfavorable.

31. For secondary discussion of Chrysostom's exegesis, see Chrysostomus Baur, O.S.B., *John Chrysostom and His Time*, 2 vols., trans. Sr. M. Gonzaga, R.S.M. (Westminster, Newman, 1959), 1:206–26, 315–29; de Margerie, *History of Exegesis*, 1:189–212; Kelly, *Golden Mouth*, 83–103; Wendy Mayer and Pauline Allen, *John Chrysostom*, ECF (London: Routledge, 2000), 3–52; Quasten, *Patrology*, 3:424–82, esp. 439–40; Rylaarsdam, *John Chrysostom on Divine Pedagogy*; Robert Louis Wilken, *John Chrysostom and the Jews: Rhetoric and Reality in the Late Fourth Century* (Berkeley: University of California Press, 1983).

32. See John Chrysostom, *Hom. Jo.* 52, 68.

fear of becoming *aposynagōgoi* and out of their love for honor—or public praise (12:43).

Chrysostom also sets up Nicodemus's slowness to understand Jesus's words by declaring, he was "not in the proper frame of mind but still held back by Jewish weakness [*astheneias*]" (*Hom. Jo.* 24 [PG 59:144, Goggin 234]). Chrysostom's habitual anti-Jewish sentiments are visible in this statement.[33] However, he does not consider weakness to be a specifically Jewish trait. As we have seen, Chrysostom often uses "weakness" (*astheneia*) in his account of divine accommodation to denote the limitations and incapacities of sinful human beings to grasp divine realities. Such weakness is due to an admixture of human finitude, sin, and sin's consequences. Rylaarsdam points out that Chrysostom counts "fear" (*phobos*) among those emotions that have become disordered by sin.[34] In addition to Nicodemus's fear, Chrysostom also speaks of his inner moral disposition when contrasting him with those leaders who opposed Jesus and worked for his death. Chrysostom says, Nicodemus "was much more worthy of pardon than those whose actions were dictated by malice [*ponērian*]"(*Hom. Jo.* 24 [PG 59:144, Goggin 234]). Nicodemus may be afraid and incomprehending, but he is not motivated by "malice" (*ponēria*).

As one beset by weakness and suffering the consequences of sin, Nicodemus reflects the basic condition of fallen humans to whom God accommodates himself in order to elevate them to heavenly realities. Given this positioning of Nicodemus, it is not surprising that Chrysostom speaks of Jesus's *philanthrōpia* and accommodation in order to teach Nicodemus: "But the mercy of God [*philanthrōpos theos*] ... did not reject [Nicodemus] or censure him, or deprive him of His teaching, but even discoursed with him very kindly and revealed to him the most sublime teachings, obscurely, to be sure, but nevertheless revealed" (*Hom. Jo.* 24 [PG 59:144, Goggin 234]).

For Chrysostom, the exchange with Nicodemus exemplifies the larger salvific process of divine accommodation that God undertakes with respect to the whole of humanity. Chrysostom sees Jesus accommodating his

---

33. John Chrysostom is notorious for the anti-Jewish invective in his preaching, typified in his sermons directed against Christians attracted to Judaism (his sermons known as *Adversus Iudaeos*). For historical perspective, see Kelly, *Golden Mouth*, 62–66; Wilken, *John Chrysostom and the Jews*.

34. Rylaarsdam, *John Chrysostom on Divine Pedagogy*, 17. Cf. John Chrysostom, *Hom. Gen.* 9.8–10.

teaching on divine realities to Nicodemus's present state, which is marked by spiritual weakness and a limited ability to understand. He thus summarizes Jesus's pedagogy of accommodation in the opening of his *Hom. Jo.* 27: "when Jesus is at the point of arriving at teachings that are sublime he frequently restrains himself in consideration of the weakness [*astheneian*] of his hearers, and does not dwell for long on subjects befitting his greatness, but rather on those which condescend [*synkatabasin*] to their lowliness" (*Hom. Jo.* 27 [PG 59:158, Goggin 259]).

This process of accommodated pedagogy holds true especially as regards Nicodemus's misunderstanding of Jesus and Jesus's corresponding response to Nicodemus. To begin with, Chrysostom regards Nicodemus's address of Jesus as "Rabbi" and "a teacher from God" along with his appeal to Jesus's miraculous "signs" (John 3:2) as well-intentioned though ultimately wanting. They display Nicodemus's lack of understanding. As Chrysostom sees it, Nicodemus thinks of Jesus in primarily earthly categories, focuses on his miraculous signs, and thinks that Jesus wields powers that are delegated from God (like a prophet does) (see John Chrysostom, *Hom. Jo.* 24 [Goggin, 234–35]).

Jesus, for his part, responds to this well-intentioned though inaccurate greeting of Nicodemus with gentleness. He goes on to accommodate his language to Nicodemus's limited understanding in order to elevate his thinking. Jesus does this by speaking in enigmatic discourse and riddle speech.[35] Hence, Jesus speaks of the need to be "born again from above" in order to "see the kingdom of God" (John 3:3). According to Chrysostom, Jesus's enigmatic discourse is a mode of divine accommodation because it engages his audience and prompts them to inquire further: Jesus "wished to make His hearers more inclined to ask questions and to cause them to be more attentive" (*Hom. Jo.* 24 [Goggin 237]).

Nicodemus responds in the proper manner. He continues to engage Jesus's enigmatic teachings, displaying a "thirst for knowledge" and "respect for Christ" (*Hom. Jo.* 24 [Goggin 237, 239]). But he continues to show his misunderstanding by asking how being "born again" would be possible for an adult. This question about physical birth shows that Nicodemus still thinks of Jesus and his teaching within categories of this world. Accordingly, Chrysostom reads his words in John 3:4 regarding the

---

35. Chrysostom writes (*Hom. Jo.* 24 [Goggin 236]), Jesus "by speaking in riddles raised him [i.e., Nicodemus] up from his earthly thoughts."

"How?" of this second birth as expressing incredulity and doubt (*Hom. Jo.* 24 [Goggin 238]).

In the moral exhortation with which he closes this homily, Chrysostom holds up Nicodemus as a moral example from whom Christians should learn. The exhortation in *Hom. Jo.* 24 focuses on the need for people not to subject divine truths and realities to human standards and conventions.[36] This tendency, according to Chrysostom, bedevils all human beings who have been wounded by sin. Nicodemus does not understand Jesus and his teachings at first because he does exactly this—he subjects Jesus's words to worldly understanding and conventions. When Nicodemus first heard Jesus's words about being born, Chrysostom states, "he did not think anything great of it, but something human and earthly. He was, therefore, blinded and plunged in doubt" (*Hom. Jo.* 24 [Goggin 240]). A corrective for this mistake is for people to be open and receptive for "illumination to come from above." This requires a person to have "both a well-disposed soul and an upright life" (*Hom. Jo.* 24 [Goggin 240]).[37] Though Chrysostom does not make the connection explicit in his exhortation, the interpretation of Nicodemus in *Hom. Jo.* 24 seems to identify him as one who displays both the lack of understanding and something of the proper disposition befitting those open to heavenly teaching and illumination. One might say, therefore, that insofar as Chrysostom instructs his audience to follow his exhortation, he invites them to learn from the example of Nicodemus: some things to avoid and other things to imitate.

Chrysostom's other homilies on John 3 continue this dual motif of Nicodemus's misunderstanding and Jesus's gentle accommodation. As we have seen, Nicodemus thinks of Jesus's words about a second birth in terms of worldly, physical birth (cf. John 3:4). Jesus, for his part, recognizes Nicodemus's misunderstanding and speaks so as to elevate his thinking to heavenly realities (*Hom. Jo.* 25 [Goggin 243]).[38] Accordingly, Jesus

---

36. Chrysostom thus opens the exhortation: "let us not examine into the things of God by reasoning and let us not submit divine things to the order prevailing among us, nor subject them to the necessity of nature, but let us think of them all reverently, believing as the Scriptures have said" (*Hom. Jo.* 24 [Goggin 239]).

37. His Greek phrasing here reads *psychēn eugnōmona kai orthon ... bion* (PG 59:147).

38. Thus, Chrysostom states, Jesus spoke in such a way so as "To lead away from this idea which was dragging him [i.e., Nicodemus] earthward, and to show that he was not speaking of this kind of birth."

employs two worldly examples—water and wind—to lead Nicodemus to grasp the heavenly nature of this birth about which he speaks. Thus, commenting on Jesus's words in John 3:6-8, Chrysostom states the following: "By saying 'Do not wonder', [Jesus] took note of the other's trouble of soul, and recalled to his mind a material object that is somewhat insubstantial [i.e., the wind]. For, by saying 'That which is born of the Spirit is spirit' He had begun to lead him away from things of the flesh" (*Hom. Jo.* 26 [Goggin 253]). Jesus uses the example of the wind—a worldly reality that is "insubstantial"—to help move Nicodemus's thinking from worldly realities to heavenly realities.

Yet as Chrysostom reads it, Nicodemus's question, "How can these things be?" (John 3:9), indicates that he still does not quite understand Jesus. Chrysostom sees Christ shifting his pedagogical strategy with Nicodemus by issuing a rebuke to him in 3:10: "Are you a teacher of Israel, and yet you do not understand these things?" Even though Jesus changes his tone and pedagogical strategy, Chrysostom still regards this move as a form of divine accommodation.[39] Jesus accommodates his remarks to the state of his audience in order to bring him to a different, higher mode of understanding. Indeed, given the roots of *synkatabasis* in the Greco-Roman rhetorical tradition, it is fitting that in the exhortation to *Hom. Jo.* 26, Chrysostom holds up Jesus as providing an example for the patient teacher or the preacher who may fail to persuade.[40] Even though Chrysostom highlights Nicodemus's misunderstanding, he insists that Nicodemus's responses to Jesus do not proceed from vice. He writes, "See how [Jesus] nowhere accused [Nicodemus] of malice, but merely of slowness and stupidity" (*Hom. Jo.* 26 [Goggin 255]).

The last substantive remarks about Nicodemus in Chrysostom's homilies on John 3 appear in a rhetorical comparison between Nicodemus and Nathanael. This comparison, which praises and criticizes both individuals, centers on how each interacted with Jesus. For instance, Chrysostom contrasts the situations wherein both individuals first encountered Jesus. On the one hand, Nathaniel was brought to Jesus by another disciple, but

---

39. Rylaarsdam (*John Chrysostom on Divine Pedagogy*, 79–80) explains that for Chrysostom divine accommodation can be given in a variety of tones (gentle or stern) and for a variety of purposes.

40. Chrysostom (*Hom. Jo.* 26 [Goggin 257]) writes, "By this mode of action He was giving us also the example of unceasing gentleness, and teaching us not to show displeasure, not to be indignant, when we preach to men and do not persuade them."

Nicodemus sought Jesus out of his own accord. Nathaniel also came to Jesus somewhat begrudgingly, but Nicodemus came to Jesus with much "eagerness" (*Hom. Jo.* 28 [Goggin 275]). Chrysostom also contrasts the responses of Jesus to each individual. Jesus spoke very briefly to Nathaniel, but he spoke at length to Nicodemus. The difference in the length and manner of Jesus's words to each, according to Chrysostom, is accounted for by the fear that did or did not beset each of these two. Nathanael was not beset by fear, but Nicodemus, who came to Jesus at night, was filled with fear. Thus, Chrysostom writes, "since [Nicodemus] was still held back by fear, [Jesus] prudently did not reveal everything to him, but stirred his mind so as to cast out fear by fear by saying that he who does not believe is judged and that persistence in unbelief proceeds from the consciousness of a wicked life" (*Hom. Jo.* 28 [Goggin 275–76]).

Chrysostom's interpretation of the other two episodes in John featuring Nicodemus do not display the same concern for divine accommodation. Nevertheless, Chrysostom does comment on Nicodemus's moral disposition and development, which extend the interpretation given thus far.

Scene 2 (John 7:45–52)

The second scene in John's Gospel where Nicodemus appears is a meeting of the Jerusalem leadership in 7:45–52. Here the temple guards, whom the authorities dispatched to arrest Jesus, return empty-handed and amazed at his teaching. A group of leaders rebuke both the guards for having been "led astray" by Jesus and also the festival crowd for their ignorance of torah (7:48–49). In their remarks about the temple guards and the crowd, these authorities distinguish themselves from both groups: "Has any one of the authorities or of the Pharisees believed in him?" (7:48)—with the expected answer being "no." In response, Nicodemus speaks up and says, "Our law does not judge people without first giving them a hearing to find out what they are doing, does it?" (7:51).

With this question, Chrysostom sees Nicodemus as going on the offensive against other Jewish authorities. He writes, "Nicodemus in consequence attacked them ... [and] was proving, to be sure, that they neither knew the law, nor carried out the law" (*Hom. Jo.* 52 [Goggin 46]). That is, Nicodemus's question shows that these leaders, who strongly oppose Jesus, are themselves displaying the very ignorance of torah for which they condemn the crowds. Chrysostom continues, "if [the law] prescribed that no one put a man to death without first giving him a hearing, and if these men had striven to do this before giving a hearing, they were transgressors of the law" (*Hom. Jo.* 52 [Goggin 46]).

Moreover, the very presence of Nicodemus at this meeting further illustrates the ignorance of these authorities. As stated above, the Jewish leaders who oppose Jesus ask rhetorically, "Has any one of the authorities or of the Pharisees believed in him?" (John 7:48), and the syntax of their phrasing expects a negative answer. Yet standing among them and debating the matter is Nicodemus, a Jewish leader who is also a secret believer. Their protest in 7:48 has the effect of displaying their lack of knowledge.

At the same time, however, Nicodemus's words to the leaders that oppose Jesus are measured and cautious. While Nicodemus does offer a defense of Jesus, it is not a full-throated, robust defense. Chrysostom again attributes this to Nicodemus's fear and again identifies him as one of the secret believers among the leadership. Despite his fear, Chrysostom regards Nicodemus (like the other secret believers) as a genuine disciple, and he even sees Nicodemus as displaying a measure of courage here.[41]

Chrysostom's text of John does not include the pericope of the woman caught in adultery (John 7:53–8:11), and so he takes Jesus's teaching about being "the light of the world" and believers "not walking in the darkness" (8:12) as a kind of response to Nicodemus's words. Chrysostom writes that with these words, Jesus "was spurring on and encouraging Nicodemus, because he had spoken up bravely" (*Hom. Jo.* 52 [Goggin 47). While Chrysostom does not identify Jesus's words here as a form of accommodation, they nevertheless show a level of appropriateness to Nicodemus's circumstances.

Similar to what we have seen in his homilies on John 3, Chrysostom regards Nicodemus here as favorable but also flawed. Nicodemus acts bravely and offers a defense of Jesus before those authorities who oppose him and slander other groups who disagree with them. Nevertheless, it is a cautious and measured defense, for out of fear, Nicodemus still wishes to keep secret his being a follower of Jesus.

Scene 3 (John 19:38–42)

The final scene in which Nicodemus appears is Jesus's burial. Once again, Chrysostom sees Nicodemus's actions here as a blend of heroism and

---

41. Chrysostom (*Hom. Jo.* 52 [Goggin 46]) writes of the secret believers, "Not yet, to be sure, did they admit it as openly as they ought; nevertheless, they were followers of Christ."

misunderstanding. Chrysostom calls attention to the fact that Nicodemus participates in Jesus's burial whereas none of the twelve apostles do. Significantly, Chrysostom sees Nicodemus's actions as a public display of bravery and something of a development in his character. In the previous two episodes in which Nicodemus has appeared, Chrysostom had made mention of Nicodemus's fear. But in this scene, Chrysostom states that Nicodemus "came despite his fear" to participate in Jesus's burial (*Hom. Jo.* 85 [Goggin 437]). Fear no longer inhibits Nicodemus, and thus he participates in the public action of burying Jesus.

Although Nicodemus overcomes his fear and acts bravely and with "tender affection" toward Jesus, his actions here still display a measure of misunderstanding (*Hom. Jo.* 85 [Goggin 437]). Chrysostom sees this evidenced in the extravagant amount of spices that Nicodemus brings to the burial. He writes, "they brought those spices which are most likely to preserve the body for a long while and not permit it quickly to become the prey of corruption, a procedure which indicated that they thought nothing out of the ordinary of him" (*Hom. Jo.* 85 [Goggin 437]). Thus Nicodemus and Joseph of Arimathea perform a public gesture of kindness toward Jesus. But the extravagance of the burial suggests that they do not regard him as anything more than a man and are not expecting anything to happen after Jesus's death.

Conclusion

Gail O'Day invites us to view the Fourth Gospel's literary and rhetorical dynamics as being deeply connected to the reality of the incarnation. Comparably, John Chrysostom sees the motif of misunderstanding in the Nicodemus episodes as closely connected with the incarnation. For Chrysostom, Nicodemus's misunderstanding is caught up in the larger process of divine accommodation whereby the transcendent God teaches limited and weak human beings. O'Day has argued that through literary techniques such as irony, the gospel draws its audience into its narrative world and invites them to engage more deeply with its presentation of Jesus. Similarly, Chrysostom sees Jesus inviting Nicodemus to engage him more deeply through his enigmatic discourse, riddle speech, and symbolic examples. Both the language of Scripture and the incarnation proper are means by which God accommodates to the level of human beings in order to draw them into right relationship with himself.

Both O'Day and Chrysostom in their respective ways point to the theological congruence between the literary mode of the Fourth Gospel and the reality of the incarnation. The incarnation is at the core of the gospel's content, and it also informs the gospel's literary and rhetorical strategies. These strategies in turn facilitate for readers an encounter with the Word of God, analogous to those had by individuals in the gospel narrative itself.[42] For it is through the words of the gospel, with its literary and rhetorical dynamics, that readers of later generations can come into genuine contact with the Word of God who "became flesh and lived among us" (John 1:14).

---

42. See also William M. Wright IV, "Inspired Scripture as a Sacramental Vehicle of Divine Presence in the Gospel of John and Dei Verbum," *Nova et Vetera* [English edition] 13 (2015): 155–80.

A Gospel Homiletic

Karoline M. Lewis

In *Revelation in the Fourth Gospel: Narrative Mode and Theological Claim*, Gail R. O'Day argued that the literary devices used by the Fourth Evangelist help the readers understand John's theology.[1] Specifically, O'Day addressed the function of irony as a means by which John communicates a theology of revelation. That is, the *how* of John's theology of revelation is most appropriately expressed through the literary device of irony. Or, in other words, irony is necessary to comprehend the fullness of theological revelation in the Fourth Gospel.

As the subtitle of the book suggests, O'Day's thesis was that the literary device of irony is a technique or narrative mode that makes a theological claim. On the heels of Alan Culpepper's groundbreaking work on literary criticism and John, *Anatomy of the Fourth Gospel*,[2] O'Day's research contributed to what would be a long and significant trajectory in Johannine scholarship on the various literary features in the Fourth Gospel and how these devices add to the communication of the possible meanings of and in the text.

Of course, this attention to literary issues in John's Gospel mirrors the trend in biblical scholarship in general addressing the relationship between literary/narrative sensibilities and biblical interpretation. These literary and narrative studies have, therefore, demonstrated how the rhetorical form and style of a biblical text also communicate the message, arguing that the full meaning of a biblical text cannot be located only in its content but is also known in how the content is organized and expressed.

---

1. Gail R. O'Day, *Revelation in the Fourth Gospel: Narrative Mode and Theological Claim* (Philadelphia: Fortress, 1986).
2. R. Alan Culpepper, *Anatomy of the Fourth Gospel: A Study in Literary Design* (Philadelphia: Fortress, 1983).

As a result, John's Gospel is not unique in employing various literary and narrative modes and methods by which to tell the story of Jesus. The biblical writings are replete with literary techniques that reinforce arguments, augment themes, and contribute to the overall reception of the message. At the same time, how John employs these devices is unique to the Fourth Evangelist's own theological constructs and commitments. Tending to John's use of certain literary features to communicate particular theological claims is, in part, the legacy of Gail R. O'Day.

At the same time, beyond the academic study of the Fourth Gospel within the realm of biblical research and scholarship, as one book of the sixty-six in the Bible, John is also considered Scripture by the church. As such, John's Gospel is not only the object of study in scholarly guilds and biblical research but is also a resource for the church's proclamation. In the history of the preaching of the church, there has been due diligence given toward approaching the biblical texts with a kind of generosity that respects the particularity of each book in the canon. For example, the uniqueness of material evident in Matthew and Luke, assuming Mark as a source, is then critical for the faithful preaching of these writings. Tending to the unique elements of each gospel writer is essential for both the hermeneutical and homiletical task.

This essay will ask whether there is an embedded homiletic in biblical texts, and if so, how do we access that imputed homiletic? The test case for the thesis will be the Gospel of John so as to determine criteria for how biblical texts communicate their proclamative purposes. If, as O'Day has argued, the narrative mode of biblical texts makes a theological claim, then that narrative mode might also make a claim about how God's revelation can and should be preached.

Challenges to Preaching John

The Fourth Gospel is well known among preachers for its homiletical challenges. Early on in its history, John's unique presentation of Jesus, consistently compared to the synoptic portraits, resulted in almost insurmountable difficulties in the interpretation of John. Rather than being seen for how these differences communicate the Fourth Gospel's distinct message, navigating the noted Johannine differences has relegated John's homiletical potential. As a result, a good amount of energy has been spent on observing and explaining the differences between the four gospels, without ever reaching a sense what kind of meaning a passage might actually have for the gathered community. When these differences are consistently presented as difficulties for the preacher, no wonder apprehension is a consistent response to the possibility of having to tackle a sermon on the Fourth Gospel. Indubitably, the differences in and of themselves are not enough to provide the substance of a sermon, and yet emphasizing these differences has perhaps overstated the issue and unduly complicated the preaching of the Fourth Gospel.

The primary nature of these differences, of course, is theological. It is clear that the Fourth Evangelist is working out his portrait of Christ in terms and categories that do not align with the Christologies presented in Matthew, Mark, and Luke. The variances, of course, are not limited to John's portrait of Jesus but include stark dissimilarities in soteriology, eschatology, and pneumatology. Negotiating the particularities of theology in Scripture is a challenge many preachers are either unwilling or ill-equipped to execute, and the default strategy is more often than not to rely on what is familiar or what is known, neither of which is often John. As a result, John's specific theological presentations are viewed through the lens of the synoptic perspective, thereby skewing John's specialized sense of the revelation of God in Christ.

It does not help matters that embedded in the theology of the Fourth Gospel are two problematic categories that complicate its interpretation and, in particular, its proclamation. The first is the perceived anti-Semitism in the Fourth Gospel, and this connection between the Fourth Gospel and the justification of anti-Semitism makes preaching the Fourth Gospel all the more complicated.[3] While the preacher might want to preach a corrective sermon to explain John's anti-Jewish rhetoric, this acting homiletic does not seem enough, or appears to be taxing, for the weekly sermon. Does the preacher apologize? Does the preacher offer an explanation? It is easier, therefore, to avoid preaching John altogether than to have to figure out how to talk about its sordid history related to the justification of anti-Semitism.

The second element in John's theology that obfuscates its preaching is the assumed theological exclusion in the Fourth Gospel, an exclusion manifested in a verse like John 14:16, "Jesus said to him, 'I am the way, and

---

3. For a comprehensive collection of essays on the anti-Jewish language in John and John's relationship with first-century Judaism, see R. Alan Culpepper and Paul N. Anderson, *John and Judaism: A Contested Relationship in Context* (Atlanta: SBL Press, 2017).

the truth, and the life. No one comes to the Father except through me."[4] Or John 3:3, "Very truly, I tell you, no one can see the kingdom of God without being born from above," seemingly insisting that salvation is beyond anyone's grasp unless being born again. Even the infamous John 3:16 finds its way into parlance that justifies a radical rejection of any person who does not believe in Jesus. Once again, preachers find themselves trying to solve years of misuse, even hurtful use, and misinterpretation within the confines of a Sunday sermon, and therefore, they choose to preach elsewhere. The sense of exclusion perceptible in John's Gospel is also exacerbated by the argument that John presents a high Christology. The Jesus in John seems unapproachable, a Jesus so divine so as not to be accessible, and a Jesus that indeed is in a place so as to judge and condemn. A Jesus like this is not often one you want to bring into the pulpit.

Possible answers to these homiletical challenges remain at issue when it comes to approaches to preaching John. Consistently, homiletical methods for John's Gospel have resulted from responding to the topics outlined above in the history of the interpretation of the Fourth Gospel. As a result, suggestions for how to preach the Fourth Gospel arise from reaction to John's hermeneutical and theological challenges. Preaching John has become less about constructing a particular homiletic, or gleaning best practices for preaching John, and more about arguing for a homiletical strategy to solve its hermeneutical challenges.

As such, to address the challenges noted above, one answer to preaching John has been to map out the differences in John's theological world. Knowing these differences becomes the primary tactic for preaching John. To "move into the world envisioned in John's Gospel" will then adequately appreciate John's unique presentation of Christ's ministry, and therefore, the preacher will be able to make the move to proclamation.[5] Once the preacher recognizes and appreciates this different theological universe, then the means by which to preach the Fourth Gospel will be clearer. The answer to peaching John, therefore, is to enter sufficiently into John's symbolic world. In doing so, the preacher will have a better handle on the content of John's theology, and thus, more understanding of subsequent theological categories. The assumption is that increased knowledge and

---

4. Unless otherwise indicated, all biblical translations are from the NRSV.
5. David Fleer and David Bland, eds., "Moving into the World Envisioned in John's Gospel," in *Preaching John's Gospel: The World It Imagines* (Saint Louis: Chalice, 2008), 2.

awareness of John's theology will directly lead toward more security and ease when preaching on the Fourth Gospel.

Another related homiletical strategy proposed to address the difficulties of John's narrative is that knowing the whole of the gospel will assist in interpreting individual pericopes of the gospel. Thus, Robert Kysar, in his book *Preaching John*, writes, "the better we know the whole of the Gospel of John, the better we will understand its individual parts."[6] Certainly, this is true. The structure of John's Gospel has often been described as a spiral, less linear and more circular—thus establishing mutual interpretive possibilities between passages and sections within the narrative itself. That is, it is almost impossible to interpret a segment of John without instantaneously connecting the immediate passage with other allusive portions in the gospel.

Once again, the interpretive necessity of making connections between passages in the gospel is certainly apparent, but is this also a homiletical clue to preaching John, a homiletical necessity for the proclamation of John? In other words, proposed strategies for preaching John have primarily focused on how to interpret the content of John's Gospel, the *what* of the message and the meanings thus prescribed. Unquestionably, noting the specific nature of John's theology is a helpful strategy, both for interpretation and proclamation. However, this strategy focuses primarily on the content of the gospel. Knowing the what of John's theology ends up being sufficient for how to preach the gospel.

The *how* of John's Gospel, that is, its narrative mode, not only communicates its theology but also communicates its homiletic. While it might be overextending in the space of this essay to argue for an overall homiletic present in John's Gospel, there are enough rhetorical devices used by the Fourth Evangelist to suggest various purposes for and ways of preaching John.[7] The literary devices employed in the Fourth Gospel should also come into play when assessing how John should be preached. As such, to access the means by which to preach John demands a different starting point than differentiating John's theology from the Synoptics or establishing reliable accesses to interpret said theological content. This starting point, therefore, can be the narrative mode of the Fourth Gospel, its literary and rhetorical elements that might indeed reframe and reposition how

---

6. Robert D. Kysar, *Preaching John* (Minneapolis: Fortress, 2002), 9.
7. For an introductory sense of the various purposes of preaching, see Jana Childers, ed., *Purposes of Preaching* (Saint Louis: Chalice, 2004).

to preach John. Rather than begin with the *what* of John's Gospel as central to John's homiletic, this essay will suggest that beginning with *how* can reimagine a homiletic for John's Gospel.

Literary Devices as Homiletic Strategy

The literary device of irony does not exhaust John's method for communicating a theology of revelation, and a list of literary devices will not deplete how these features relate to the preaching of John. At the same time, noting the ways in which some of these literary devices might communicate a Johannine homiletic suggests that addressing the how of the text can also assist in the how of preaching. That is, the literary mode of the Fourth Gospel cannot or should not be separated from its homiletic.[8] Or, in other words, John's homiletic must take into account the how of the gospel—the rhetorical features that communicate the what of John's theology. Three rhetorical features will have to suffice for the purpose and goal of this article. Again, while the study of literary devices in John's Gospel has been directly connected to John's theological themes, this essay suggests that an intentional study of literary devices in John's Gospel can also suggest connections to preaching John.

Repetition

The first literary device on which this essay will focus is the use of repetition in the Fourth Gospel. Repetition as a literary feature has several functions, occurring in a variety of schemas or patterns as classified by ancient rhetoric in the works of Cicero, Quintilian, and Aristotle.[9] These kinds of repetition include repetition of letters, syllables, and sounds; repetition of words; and repetition of clauses, phrases, and ideas. Repetition as means by which to communicate a particular homiletic at work in a text can occur at both a microlevel and a macrolevel. On a microlevel, the prominent use of repetition within an isolated passage in the Gospel of John might communicate certain homiletical directions. This can be the repetition of the same word or the repetition of similar words.

---

8. O'Day, *Revelation*, 32.

9. For an overview of basic rhetorical devices and concise definitions, see Richard A. Lanham, *A Handlist of Rhetorical Terms: A Guide for Students of English Literature* (Berkeley: University of California Press, 1968).

For example, John 12 repeats words related to the smell of the perfume Mary uses to anoint Jesus: the cost of the perfume, the amount, that it was "pure nard," and that "the house was filled with the fragrance of the perfume." The repetition of abundance intimates that a sermon on the passage should create an experience of abundance, particularly, the ability to smell what Jesus smelled.

On a macrolevel, repetition can also set up allusions between textual units that create mutual interpretive possibilities, aid in memory, and therefore reiterate a primary point. At the same time, repetition creates the experience of the repeated word itself. That is, the repeated word sets up an effect and establishes the very experience the word communicates. In the Gospel of John, one of the most often repeated words, used over forty times in the narrative, is *menō*. English translations make it hard to detect this repetition, with multiple synonyms used, such as "remain," "stay," "abide," and "continue." What does this communicate about preaching John? It means that a sermon that is distinctively Johannine will create the sense of what it feels like to abide in the Father, to abide in Jesus.

The function of repetition also needs to account for a word's placement in any narrative. For example, in the Gospel of Mark, the location of the verb *schizō* (1:10 and 15:38) creates an *inclusio* that links Jesus's baptism and Jesus's crucifixion. With this rhetorical device, Mark intimates both how to interpret these events and also what a sermon should do. For John, the specific placement of "grace," only four times in the narrative and all in the prologue, then asks not just the meaning of the term itself but also, what does this concentrated use in the prologue mean for preaching John? The "grace upon grace" in 1:16 foreshadows 10:10, "I came that they may have life and have it abundantly," but, on a larger scale, the theme of abundance going forward in the narrative, captured in each of the signs of Jesus in the gospel (2:1–11; 4:46–54; 5:1–46; 6:1–14, 15–21, 22–71; 9:1–10:21; 11:1–44). The miracles performed by Jesus, always referred to in the Fourth Gospel as signs, are over-the-top, abundant, grace-upon-grace signs, most explicitly described in the abundance of details. These details, therefore, that communicate abundance create the feeling of abundance. Thus, the first sign Jesus performs is turning water into wine, but it is the abundance of repetitive details that secures the grace-upon-grace certainty—six jars, each having a capacity of twenty to thirty gallons, filled to the brim of the best wine when you least expect it (2:1–11). The man Jesus heals in John 5 has been ill for thirty-eight years, the average life span of a Jewish male in first-century

Palestine (5:1–46). The blind man in John 9 has been unable to see since birth and "not in the history of the world has a man born blind been able to see" (John 9:32). The final sign in John, the raising of Lazarus, is certain to note that Lazarus has been dead four days, when Jewish belief held that the soul left the body after three days (11:1–44). The raising of Lazarus is once again a sign of abundance.

Outside of the designated signs performed by Jesus, abundance becomes an event by which to identify Jesus. In John 21, the disciples are unable to recognize who Jesus is until the abundant catch of fish. Once again, the repetition of details communicates abundance: a net full of fish; the net had to be hauled to shore; large fish; at the count of 153. What this abundance reveals about Jesus's identity, therefore, becomes a critical homiletical question.

The rhetorical schematic of the isolated use of "grace" in the prologue, with then Jesus's first sign being an experience of John 1:16, suggests, as a result, a particular homiletic for John's Gospel. That is, a sermon, based on and from the literary mode of the Fourth Gospel, could therefore create the same experience of grace upon grace. The rhetoric not only communicates the meaning of the signs and the purpose of Jesus's ministry but also indicates that preaching John should take on the function of putting the listener in the place of being the recipient of grace upon grace.[10] Grace is not the topic of the sermon but a sensorial experience.

Another schema of repetition is the repetition of ideas or images. These repeated ideas establish connection points between passages where the reciprocity of these ideas sets up the need to interpret one passage in relationship to the other. For example, there is a direct correlation of a similar idea or image of an enclosed and safe space, in chapter 10 as the sheep pen and in chapter 18 as the garden. Just as Jesus as the door/good shepherd prevents the thieves and the bandits from getting into the sheep pen, Jesus leaves his disciples safe in the garden, handing himself over to the Roman soldiers and the police representing the chief priests who threaten the disciples. These ideas and images, however, are not random but indicate the need to make the connection between one passage and the other. To interpret one passage necessitates the connec-

---

10. Critical to preaching is not only the focus or core affirmation of the sermon (the primary message) but also what the preacher intends the sermon to do or the function of the sermon. For this distinction, see Thomas G. Long, *The Witness of Preaching*, 3rd ed. (Louisville: Westminster John Knox, 2016).

tions with the other. To preach one passage insists that the other be taken into account.

On another level, however, the nature of the repeated ideas or imagery in John is relational. The ideas consistently communicate the notion of relationship, particularly, a relationship with Jesus, and with God through Jesus. The images indicate elements of the relationship that suggest closeness and intimacy, as well as nurture and sustenance. For example, the predicate nominative "I am" statements in John revolve around maintaining and sustaining the relationship between Jesus and his disciples. These statements propose that Jesus is the source of that which we need for our lives to be supported. Thus, Jesus is the origination of the basic needs for human survival—light (I am the light of the world [John 8:12]), bread (I am the living bread/bread from heaven [John 6:35]), safety (I am the door/gate [John 10:7]).

Two central images are clearly relational, "I am the good shepherd" (John 10:11, 14) and "I am the vine" (John 15:1). The image of the good shepherd in chapter 10 occurs in Jesus's discourse concerning the healing of the man born blind and interprets the sign. Jesus has been the good shepherd for the blind man, thus making the blind man a sheep in Jesus's fold. Jesus as the good shepherd, therefore, cannot be interpreted and preached only through the lens of first-century Palestinian pastoral practices but is fundamental to how John imagines the relationship between Jesus and believers. A sermon should match this closeness and intimacy in tone.

The image of the vine portrays an intimacy between Jesus and his believers that represents mutual need. Furthermore, Jesus's presentation of this image takes place in the Farewell Discourse, when Jesus tells his disciples of his impending departure and comforts them with the claim, "I am the vine, you are the branches" (15:5). The statement communicates something about Jesus and something about us, but their similarity and repetition also suggest that if these repetitive images revolve around relationship and intimacy, then a Johannine homiletic will be one that will seek to undergird that relationship.

In conclusion, the use of repetition as a literary device in the Gospel of John not only communicates the gospel's key themes and main content but also points to the means by which this content might play out in a sermon. The repetitions establish connections between passages creating mutual interpretive possibilities. The Fourth Evangelist suggests that neither passage can be interpreted or preached without the other.

Dialogue, Conversation, and Discourse

Another literary device critical to John's story of Jesus is the use of dialogue, conversation, and discourse. Rhetorically, these many dialogues have the effect of engaging the reader or listener in the conversation and in the narrative setting. The most prominent placement of these dialogues is in the larger structural pattern present around the signs in John. Jesus performs a sign, which is then followed by a dialogue and then a discourse from Jesus that interprets the sign. Chapters 7–8 present a critical dialogue between Jesus and the Jewish leaders about Jesus's identity and the purpose of Jesus's ministry. The conversation between the Samaritan woman at the well and Jesus dominates their encounter in John 4.

In addition to advancing the plot, unpacking themes, and developing characters, what might be a homiletical function or purpose for these conversations? The dialogues indeed engage the readers of the narrative, drawing them into the story, putting them in the story, so as to imagine how they might respond to an encounter with Jesus. At the same time, these conversations suggest a way of preaching that should employ a form for the sermon or a sermon design akin to a conversation. That is, the sermon should unfold in such a way that represents the progress of the conversation and the growth that can be tracked. For example, in both John 4 and in John 9, the woman at the well and the man born blind advance in their recognition and understanding of who Jesus is in the conversation, from a simple identification, to prophet, to Messiah. A sermon on these passages, therefore, should do the same, designed so as to create the same progress narrated in the text.

One of the more vexing homiletical challenges of John's Gospel is the length of the discourses spoken by Jesus. They can seem repetitive and almost unnecessary. Jesus does not seem to be saying anything new. Furthermore, they do not appear to move the plot forward or to state anything novel theologically. Critical to note, however, is that the discourses are part of a larger structural pattern in the Fourth Gospel, as noted above, where Jesus performs a sign (not a miracle) that is followed by a dialogue about the nature and meaning of the sign, to which then Jesus responds with an interpretive discourse, sometimes intermixed with additional conversation. Case in point, the bread of life discourse, which occurs in Year B of the Revised Common Lectionary, means four Sundays in a row preaching from John 6, or five Sundays if John 6:1–21, the feeding of the five thousand and Jesus walking on water, is included. The homiletical exasperation is, in part, because of the penchant of the preacher, as discussed above, to focus on the content of the discourse. However, as this essay argues, tending to the content alone of the Johannine narrative cannot suffice for its proclamation. One way to address the preaching of the discourses is to take seriously the discourse, or Jesus's interpretations, as a literary device that then determines how it should be preached.

In doing so, homiletical results surface. First, the discourses have a pattern in which there is a gradual unfolding of what the sign means. Might, then, the sermon do the same? That is, the sermon form then maps out the moves in the discourse toward layers of meaning. Second, the discourses, as interpretive in nature, surprise as to the meaning of the sign. A sermon on the discourses, therefore, will calculate the juxtaposition of the initial impact of the sign with the levels of meaning Jesus reveals.

Misunderstanding

One final literary device that suggests a homiletic for John's Gospel is the Fourth Evangelist's use of misunderstanding, a prominent literary feature in the Fourth Gospel.[11] The misunderstandings are a common reaction to Jesus's discourses in which he attempts to reveal his true identity. As Culpepper notes, "The most significant function of the misunderstandings, however, is to teach the readers how to read the Gospel."[12] And yet, as the biblical texts are fundamentally oral in nature, and from the viewpoint of preaching, analysis of the misunderstandings in John advise a way of preaching that would duplicate the experience narrated in the text. In this regard, misunderstanding evokes for preaching a kind of engagement with the text at hand where listeners are caught in their own misunderstanding. What does this misunderstanding feel like? Is there a resolution? In other words, a sermon that seeks to explain or make clear Jesus's words, that has as its goal understanding or clarification, works against the text homiletically.

Conclusion

The literary and narrative features of biblical texts on which biblical scholarship has focused in the past forty years have contributed significantly to

---

11. For a list of the misunderstandings in John, see Culpepper, *Anatomy*, 161–62.
12. See Culpepper, *Anatomy*, 165.

the interpretation of texts and to how meaning is determined. The above summary points to how the literary features of texts contribute to the meaning of the content, the material at hand, the *what* of the text. At the same time, this trend in biblical scholarship has worked with the biblical texts as texts that are read silently alone and not voiced aloud.[13] Attention to the rhetorical schemas of the biblical texts from a starting point of the inherent orality of Scripture suggests that these devices will also determine oral interpretation and homiletical possibility.

The biblical texts as authoritative within a community of proclamation have been relegated to written interpretation rather than meaning incarnated in the preached word. As a result, the preacher should be tasked with not only tending to how the narrative mode makes a theological claim but also how that narrative mode determines the ways in which the theological claim gets preached. Gail R. O'Day insisted that how texts work should make a difference for their homiletical import, thereby illuminating an intersection essential to meaningful proclamation.

---

13. Donald H. Juel, "The Strange Silence of the Bible," *Int* 51 (1997): 5–19.

EDITORS' INTRODUCTION: Thomas Long points out how the language of John suggests overlapping time zones. Some of the stories John tells—in this case, the story of Jesus turning water into wine—occur in their own moment in time. But John narrates the story in a way that suggests that the time is simultaneously the time of God's creation. This literary pattern of multiple times occurring at once gives rise to theological meaning, as the events of the wedding at Cana are read in relationship to divine events. The message of the sermon stems from the observation that the interruption of one time period with mention of another adds meaning to the story. Long relates this observation about time in John to moments in life when God's eschatological time is almost visible in human experience.

Learning How to Tell Time

Thomas G. Long

Isa 62:1–5; Ps 36:5–10; John 2:1–11

People who have a lot of experience with weddings, I'm thinking about ministers, florists, caterers, wedding planners, mothers and fathers of couples, people who know something about the intricacies and complexities of a wedding ceremony, these people share a piece of secret knowledge. Namely, whenever there is a wedding, something is going to go wrong. You can count on it. It might be large, it might be small, it might be hidden from view, it might be out there for everybody to see, but there are simply too many details between the ordering of the invitations and the throwing of the rice for there not to be at least one little glitch in the service.

We could probably have fun this morning, going around the room, telling wedding stories. Stories of fainting brides and splitting tuxedo pants, intoxicated ushers and soloists singing "O Promise Me" while the candles quietly catch the greenery on fire. Years ago, I went to a very traditional wedding in North Carolina, where the father of the bride was a rough-hewn, burly construction worker, ill-accustomed to fancy ceremonies and understandably anxious about this one—so much so that he spent several days before the wedding, staring into the shaving mirror and practicing his one and only line: "Her mother and I do. Her mother and I do." When the wedding actually came around and the minister intoned, "Who giveth this woman to be married to this man?," the father startled all of us by announcing, "*My* mother and I do."

People who know about weddings share a piece of secret information: whenever there is a wedding, something is going to go wrong. So it should not come as a surprise to us that at this wedding, a wedding where Jesus and his disciples and his mother were on the guest list, something went wrong. What went wrong at this particular wedding was they ran out of wine. Presumably, there were enough melon balls and finger sandwiches, but the claret was exhausted before the receiving line was.

In ancient Jewish society, wine was not just a beverage. It was a sign of joy, a sign of gladness, a sign of the very presence of God, so what they ran out of at Cana was blessing. There was a wedding at Cana, and there was a problem. So, what else is new? People who know weddings know the secret.

But careful readers of the Gospel of John also share a piece of secret knowledge. Whenever Jesus is present at an event, nothing is ever as ordinary as it may seem. In fact, Jesus brings the extraordinary to human affairs. The first clue we have that something extraordinary is at work is not in the fact that they ran out of wine.

That's ordinary. But in the strange conversation that Jesus has with his mother, she says, "Look! They've run out of wine!" To which Jesus does not say, "Well, mother, what do you expect, it's a wedding, and something is—" In fact, he doesn't call her "mother" at all. He doesn't call her "Mary." He becomes strangely formal and distant. He calls her, "*Woman.*"

"O, Woman, what is this to you and me," or as one translation puts it, "What is this *between* you and me? My hour has not yet come. My time is not yet here." Now there is a phrase designed to make ears of the careful listener to the Gospel of John perk up, because they know how very important the whole theme of time is to John's Gospel, in fact, much different from the other gospels. In the Gospel of John, we actually have two time frames operating simultaneously. There's ordinary clock time.

It's a few minutes after eleven o'clock on a Sunday morning in October. Ordinary time. But above, it is God's time. Eternal time. And like a sewing machine, eternal time keeps penetrating down into ordinary time, creating signs and wonders of the fullness itself. Another way to put it is, if you're going to be able to tell time in the Gospel of John, you have to wear two wristwatches: one to tell ordinary time and one to tell God's time.

What time is it? What time is it? What time is it at the wedding at Cana? Well, you look at one watch, and it's an ordinary wedding on an ordinary day in a dusty little Galilean village. You look at the other watch, and "on the third day, there was a wedding at Cana." *On the third day*, there was a wedding. On the third day, he was raised again. Is this a wedding story or an Easter story?

What time is it? You look at one watch, and we have a routine wedding with an ordinary problem going about the punch bowl. You look at the other watch, and this is the wedding feast we have all been waiting for: the marriage feast of the Lamb, where fullness and abundance abound, and the bridegroom himself is present.

What time is it? What time is it? "O, Woman, what is this between you and me? What time is it to you?" In that moment, she becomes more than Mary, more than his mother. She becomes Woman. She becomes Eve at the dawning of the new creation. In that moment, he becomes more than Jesus, more than her son. He becomes her Lord and ours, the Lord of all time and space, if she knows how to tell time. She then turns to the servants, and what she says indicates very well that she knows exactly how to tell time. Pointing at her son and her Lord, she says, "Obey him." And you know what happened: He transformed the water in the jars of purification into more wine than a hundred Canas could drink, to the delight of the guests and the astonishment of the caterer, who said, "This is the best wedding I've ever been to; the best wine was saved for last." But the disciples discerned that the eternal had entered the ordinary, and his glory was disclosed.

What time is it? The capacity to tell time is essential to the accomplishment of our mission. We simply cannot get up every day and put one foot in front of the other, unless we know that the ordinary trudgings of life, the fragments and breakages of our human community, are infused with the possibility of the glory of God.

The old preacher, George Buttrick, used to love to tell about the church in New York City that had, right over the communion table, a stained glass window that they had gotten out of a supply house catalog. It was a stained glass window depicting the biblical image of the new Jerusalem coming down from heaven like a bride adorned for her husband, and there it was in all of its gaudiness. Streaks of gold, aquamarine rivers of life, emeralds and pearls, angels floating around, and the congregation *hated* it. That wasn't the city they lived in. They didn't have streets of gold. They had streets of crime. They didn't have aquamarine rivers. They had the East River and the Hudson. They didn't have emeralds and pearls. They had tenements and squalor. It was too pious, too otherworldly. But then, said Buttrick, over time, the colors in that window began to fade so that ever so slightly, you could see through it, the outline of the skyscrapers and tenements of the city of New York beyond. It was then, said Buttrick, that the window began to take on power, as God's city and their city, God's time and their time merged. One city was the place of mission, the other the image of hope.

What time is it? What time is it? You may remember that wonderful experience in the life of Thomas Merton, a Roman Catholic contemplative monk, when he was walking in downtown Louisville, Kentucky, on an ordinary day, and coming to a busy intersection, and suddenly, God's time and ordinary time merged for him. He said this about it:

> In Louisville, at the corner of Fourth and Walnut, in the center of the shopping district, I was suddenly overwhelmed with the realization that I loved all these people, that they were mine and I was theirs, that we could not be alien to another even though we were total strangers. It was like waking from a dream of separateness.... We're in the same world as everybody else; the world of the bomb, of race, hatred, the world of technology, mass media, big business, revolution, and all the rest. Yet, so does everybody belong to God. And if only they could realize this, there's no way of telling people that they're walking around, shining like the sun.[1]

What time is it? What time is it? At the church where I worship in Atlanta, we have had for years an overnight shelter during the cold winter months for homeless folks. Several years ago, they didn't have enough helpers, so they asked for volunteers from the congregation, and I volunteered for a night in February. I knew I couldn't do it by myself, so I asked an old friend of mine if he would help me out that night. He's not a

---

1. Thomas Merton, *Conjectures of a Guilty Bystander* (Garden City, NY: Doubleday, 1966).

member of our congregation; he goes to another church, but he and I have been friends for years. And he's a little bit embarrassed about having a minister as a friend. In fact, he will sometimes begin conversations, "Hey, I'm no theologian, but it seems to me that...." Well, anyway, we arrived for our night in February. It was a bitterly cold night. We put peanut butter and jelly sandwiches and cups of tea on a table, and when all was ready, we opened the door to the cold winter night, and in came several hundred folks, eager to find the warmth of the place and some food and a place to sleep. When everybody had gotten their food, they made nests. We had no cots in those days, just cardboard pallets. They made nests to sleep on. And then I said to my friend when everybody was down, "One of us has to stay up all night. What shift do you want? Do you want the first shift or the second?" And he said, "While these folks are still awake, I'd like to get to know them. I'd like to hear their stories. Let me take the first shift." I said, "Fine. I'm going to the staff room and get some sleep. You wake me up at about two o'clock in the morning." Two o'clock in the morning, he shook me awake. Even though the room was dark, I could feel excitement on his body. "What is it?" I said. "I'm no theologian," he said, "but I think Jesus Christ is out there."

I think my friend had learned how to tell time.

Does anybody here have the correct time?

EDITORS' INTRODUCTION: Teresa Fry Brown shapes the form of her sermon to the narrative order of the healing story in John 5. She leads the listener verse by verse through the Johannine story. As she does, she also describes each detail as part of a modern story, bringing the listener's story into contact with John's story. The connections between the passage and the present expand, rather than narrow, the possibilities for meaning, as Fry Brown identifies various points of connection, and multiple meanings in the passage.

Stop Waiting, It's Time for an Attitude Adjustment

Teresa Fry Brown

John 5:1–14 (5–9)

Attitude—manner, disposition, feeling, position, posture, thought
Adjustment—alter, move, transform, change

There is a story, in the gospel as attributed to John, regarding our active faith.
God already has provided a means for us to do justice now
It is up to us to get up and do it.

Wedged between the encounter of the woman at the well and the healing of the government official's son and the feeding of the five thousand is John, the son of Zebedee and Salome, aka Son of Thunder's account of the paralyzing effect of waiting for someone to do what God has already equipped us to do and a lesson about the reality that not everyone wants us to get well.

"After this there was a Jewish festival, and Jesus went up to Jerusalem" (John 5:5).
After the healings in Galilee, Jesus arrives in Jerusalem on the Sabbath
It was not the time for a feast of the Lord—Passover, Pentecost, or Feast of the Tabernacles
The church folk wanted to kill him and were always looking for dirt to get rid of him

It is said, when we are about God's work, it is as if we have a large target on our back
The more work we do for what is right, the more people will try to attack us

If everyone likes you, better check your papers to see why?

In Jerusalem near the Sheep Gate in the north city wall is a pool with the Aramaic name Bethsaida. It had five covered porches,
In the northern wall of Jerusalem, there was a double pool, called Bethsaida, used to transfer water from the Springs of Siloam
Stairs led down into the pool
Intermittently the water moved as the underground spring filled one of the pools
The urban myth was that an angel was "troubling the water"
The first one in the pool when the water moved would be healed.

"And a crowd of people who were sick, blind, lame, and paralyzed sat there" (5:3).
Sheltered from the sun by five porticos, alcoves, porches
But the text says, there was a Jewish festival in progress

Probably not the liturgical holidays but a local feast day—like Friends and Family, Usher's Anniversary, Choir Day, Pastor's Appreciation

The leaders of the temple had heard about Jesus
Became threatened because he was meeting the needs of people

The widows
Those whose husbands, fathers, and brothers had died
Those who were unable to work due to societal standards regarding the "weaker sex"

The poor
Those who cleaned the inns but could not afford to stay there
The ones who harvested the food but could not shop at Whole Foods or Sprouts

The orphans
Those whose parents had died, deserted, exploited, or abused
Those whose parents kicked them out because they did not understand their relationships

The strangers, immigrants
Those who did not speak clear Aramaic
Those who were not regular temple worshipers
Those who were merely looking for a new opportunity to live free
But heard someone wanted to build a wall to keep them out

Jesus was an equal opportunity minister
Jesus was a perpetual justice preacher
Jesus was barely thirty years old
Jesus did not have a long track record with the temple
Jesus was a carpenter's son with a passion to change lives
Jesus was a conduit for the teaching of God

Some translations say hundreds *waited*
Unable to move
Unable to stand
Unable to gain equal access to benefits
Sick, not well, out of sorts, incapacitated, hopeless, helpless,
Waiting to be the first in the pool
Waiting for someone to assist them
Waiting for someone or for something to help them.
We are not told how long they had waited but
They *waited*
They understood their condition
Wanted to be healed
But they *waited*

Looking longingly at a pool of unattainable possibilities
Of inaccessible privilege

Of untenable power
Contagious postponing aggregation–*waited*
Infectious waiting congregation–*waited*
Self-quarantined pausing people–*waited*
Communicable stagnant parishioners–*waited*

Hundreds *waited* among the porticos with a variety of issues, burdens, problems, barriers, and obstacles
Some overwhelmed with what next to do about
Militaristic budgetary priorities while millions of children go to bed hungry
Recidivism of gender attitudes seeking the return of Victorian values and the rebuilding of a man's castle
Superficial talking heads posturing about whether or not domestic violence is a crime or a fallacy while three women and one man are killed daily at the hands of an intimate partner
Lifesaving care available for some, while others must decide between food and drugs.
Generational discrimination evidenced in media presentations of youth culture and the expendability of elders

WAITING for permission to go into the water
WAITING for the next great leader to lead them to an imagined status change
WAITING for enforcement of the law of the land
WAITING for the next cycle of liberative movements

Still others facing
Death from diseases only "those people" contract
Destruction of entire cultures for broadening imaginary earthen boundaries
Depression from the unyielding societal weight of otherness
Disappointment in human promises written on counterfeit campaign pledges
Denial of faith resultant from fire sales on blessing and abuse of ministerial power
Declarations that the real, pure DNA, verified family tree, patriots must take back their land
WAITING for actualized dreams and visions

Stop Waiting, It's Time for an Attitude Adjustment

WAITING, hearsay evidence of a possibility of change

The text describes them as sick, paralyzed, immobile,
Going through
Privilege reserved
Restoration delayed
Love vacated
Benefits denied
Healing evaded
Justice deferred
Wholeness postponed
Languishing on the fringes of society
Overlooked even by their own friends and families
Seemingly they could not do anything … but *wait … wait … wait*

In the text
"A certain man was there who had been sick for thirty-eight years" (5:5).
Reportedly the life expectancy during the time of Jesus was fifty.
There is a man at the pool who had been sick for thirty-eight years, longer than Jesus had been alive
There is no indication of how he became ill
Nothing about his family or friends
How he arrived at the pool,
What he did while he was there
He was one among hundreds
Whatever the case, he had been sick for thirty-eight years, incurable, permanent, hopeless, poor, outcast
Waiting at the pool
Oversleeping, worn out, fatigued, fatigued, fatigued, nightmares at the possibility of having to attend one more discussion, sermon, group, meeting, lecture, petition, protest, lecture, conference, seminar
change the more they remain the same.

When Jesus *SAW* him lying there,
knowing that he had already been there a long time,
he asked him, "Do you want to get well?" (5:6).
Jesus picked him out of the crowd
No indication of his temple affiliation, just a man lying by the pool
Jesus did not wait, he saw him and initiated conversation and conversion

Did not wait for TMZ to play a grainy tape of how the man arrived at the pool
Did not wait for a photo opportunity to deal with the issue
Did not wait for a budget meeting to cover the cost of the potential healing
Did not become a part of a panel of so-called experts with preconceived notions of how those people get in those circumstances in the first place
Did not wait to see what law would cover his encounter with the man.
Did not wait for an armor-bearer to clear the way to get to the man.
Did not check to see if he had viable health care coverage.

Jesus knows even about our daily little deaths, disappointments, and disturbances
Jesus sees and knows without our having to ask
Jesus meets us where we are with our particular, peculiar, individual, and collective needs
Jesus has instructions for
Those who feel tired of injustice
Those who love but are not loved in return
Those who do what is right but are punished because of the actions of others.
Those who are unable to read and write,
those who live in substandard or unsafe housing,
those who lack protection for leveraged and abused bodies,
those who languish in prison cells,
those who fear attending schools due to bullying or bullets,
those who face horrendous choices between nourishment or medical care
those who work for less than a living wage yet are ignored by those who benefit most from their labor
those who clean hotels but cannot afford to stay one night
those who are objectified based on the levels of melanin in their beings
those with willfully ignored claims of sexual harassment

We have a Savior who considers our individual needs and makes a way for our resurrections
Who levels the ground at the foot of the cross.
Jesus SEES and KNOWS
In the text, Jesus
knew this man's story,
his daily routine,
his questions about life's unfairness,

his acceptance of his situation, his story,
but does not tell it, expose the man's business,
kept his confidence
There is no indication the man had ever heard of Jesus
What is more important is that Jesus knew him!!!!

Jesus asked him "Do … you … want … to … get well?" … "Do … you … want … to … get well?"
Can't you see his face like when people ask us a question that seems on the surface to be unnecessary
I imagine he thought, "Man, don't you see me laying here with all these other sick, paralyzed people
Do you think I like being here?"
But the man launches into an explanation of his condition,
He does not answer Jesus's question

He went on autopilot, excuse mode
Saying what he thought people wanted to hear rather than seeking a solution for his issue
"I don't have anybody to put me in the pool.
When the water is disturbed
I can't get to the pool fast enough
No one will help me
By the time I get there, somebody else is already in" (5:7).

Too often our beds
Our personal history
Our mistakes
Our words
Our mistakes
Our inadequacies
Our family history
Our relationships
Our secret behaviors
Our past
Our fears
Our attention to what they say
Our attendance at the sidewalk or hallway meeting
Our successes

Our failures
Our selves
Become beds of impossibility, immobility, improbability, impotence
Listening to the voices of others
Believing the hype
Reciting Tweets without research
Believing Facebook posts without evidence of truth
Forwarding Messenger change letters threatening those who chose to delete
Moving from church to church to church never knowing God for ourselves
Following the crowd without even noticing how much of ourselves are dying
Living below our inheritance
Incapacitated spiritually, mentally, socially, and physically
Hiding from unsubstantiated fears
Crippled by the actions of others
Eating off someone else's table
Living out someone else's dreams

In the text, Jesus does not touch the man
Anoint the man
Have the man spin around in circle three times
Write a check
Give his neighbor a high five
Or engage in thirty seconds of so-called Crazy praise
Jesus did not tell the man to recite some formulaic incantation
Jesus never tells him to get in the water
Did not say, Touch the water
Write a check for water
Wait for an insurance co-pay to be approved
Wait for legislation approving certain people to use the pool
Jesus does not go through a long committee meeting
Did not ask for money or budget approval
Did not consult the latest media doctor
Did not ask the man why he was resisting a healing
Did not Instagram, Snapchat, Tweet, or FB the healing
Did not put him down for a referral
Did not tell him what to do afterward

Jesus uses six words to cancel all that
Six words to change the man's attitude about his position

Stop Waiting, It's Time for an Attitude Adjustment

Six words to refocus our attention on the promise
Six words to help us reclaim our identity
Six words to move us toward transformation
Jesus asked, "Do … you … want … be … made … whole?"
Do you want to get better?
Do you want to change position?
Do you want justice or injustice?
Do you want to live differently?
Do you want to think new thoughts?
Do you want to be well?
How many times has Jesus asked us that very question?

In the text,
Jesus is about to give the man something he did not ask for but needed
Jesus was about to demonstrate HE was the power of water
The healing water
The saving water, the quenching water
The cleansing water
The only water needed was Jesus words
It was the Sabbath, but Jesus did not wait
He could have waited until dark and healed the man early Monday, but why wait
It was within the law to heal someone on the Sabbath if it was a life and death situation, but why wait?
Jesus knew the political pundits and power brokers would say he thinks he is above the law, would again try to kill him, but why wait?
Jesus knew at times church folk care more about the law, order of service, what the bulletin or the screen says than saving lives in the church—Why wait?
Three commands for healing,
Three commands for becoming whole
The man had been sick for thirty-eight years
Jesus said, "Get up!"
The man had been by the pool for thirty-eight years waiting for someone else to help him, do what he thought he could not do for himself
Jesus said, "Pick up your mat!"
The man had been using excuses, complaining about his lack of healing, his immobility, his inactivity, his bodily
Jesus said, "Start walking!"

Don't wait for an angels-acknowledged miraculous event, special day, particular hour
Don't wait for the water to bubble up—right environment, right time
Don't wait for someone else to help you—this time it is all about you

Three commands adjust our attitude
Get up!
Pick up your mat!
Start walking!

This time there were no excuses
He did not wait
This time he did not hesitate
He did not transfer his inactivity on someone else

Too many times people want healing, prayers answered
Blame others for their condition
answer to their prayer
new life
but after
Vivid 3D cinematography
surround sound
digitally remastered scenes so when we post, it goes viral
custom design miracles
no repentance
no sweat equity
no tears
no pain
no rehabilitation

Something happened in that moment
In that encounter that changed his mind
Shifted his point of view
Adjusted his attitude
Transformed his thoughts

He got up (had been sick thirty-eight years, perhaps never walked before)
But he stood up
Picked up his pallet

And started walking
and he was healed immediately

My Brothers and my Sisters
What if we chose to stop our waiting, whining, and wailing?
What if we stopped waiting
For a convenient time
An appropriate space
The beneficial access
The suitable condition
The proper venue
A new prophet
A new sacrificial lamb
A tragedy on our own steps
The right place
The right circumstance
The right law

What if we stopped waiting and followed this template healing, to wholeness, to God-given rights, to justice.
Get up, stand up
Pick up our stuff
Walk
Remember some people do not want to see us get better
Others deciding when "with all deliberate speed" is necessary
Those in power always seem to have an answer for deferring justice:
It's not time
Maybe next time
We already have one
The last one we had did not work out
The people do not want
You are overqualified
Those things that control us when we are lying by the pool
Inequality
Injustice
Hatred
Hopelessness
Inadequacy
Prejudice

Oppression
Discrimination
Greed
Disappointment
Poverty

Like in the text,
When the Jewish leaders understood that the man had been healed they immediately focused on church law. It's Sunday
More interested in doctrine than deliverance
Rules than redemption
Chronos/Kairos
You are not supposed to carry anything today
Who would dare go against the law to heal you, today?
No concern about the man's health but who supplanted their authority.

Maybe that's what's wrong with many of our churches, today—no one is being healed
Not everyone will be happy when your attitude is adjusted
Who will they talk about after they say
Why does he deserve healing?
I asked God, and nothing happened?
I remember them from before
Why is she so happy?
They didn't do as much at church as I did, now look at them, it's not fair.
What are we going to do with that ministry, now that everyone is better?

Look the text:
The man did not know who Jesus was but knew who healed him
Jesus shows up in the temple later and
said, "See! You have been made well.
Don't sin anymore in case something worse happens to you."
You have been freed from what bound you
Don't go back, it will be worse next time
Don't go back to the pool experienced
Don't pick up the stuff that weighed you down before
Poet and philosopher George Santayana once said, "Those who do not remember the past are doomed to repeat it."
The debt, the pipe, the bottle, the ego, the habit, the arrogance

The belief you were only three-fifths of a person
The debilitating stereotype
The suffocating thought that you can't learn
The gut-wrenching thought, belief, lie will never get better
The old tape that says no one cares
Don't depend on others to do what you can do for yourself
When the leaders harassed Jesus for breaking their laws
 Jesus replied, "My Father is still working, and I am working too"

Just like the man at the pool, God sees us and knows our struggle yet continually calls us in our current situations to do the miraculous
God calls on us to get up, pick up whatever has been a hindrance to your wholeness

Like Jesus's encounter with the man at the pool
God
Does not ask for our credentials, connections, clique, committee, or club
Does not ask who our people are, where we live or how much money we make

God changes our position and gives us authority (prerogative to take a given action)
Don't worry about what others say
God is still working on our behalf
Ready for a divine realignment of our thoughts, words, actions
Prepared for spiritual cataract surgery so we can see God and not our problems.
Moving to override the noise of the world that keeps us from hearing God's directions.
God is calling for each of us to be transformed by the renewing of our minds
To end our whining about life and live
Time to get our lives together

The text indicates that if we want equal access before the law, powers, and principalities
If we want to transform the world

Time to stop waiting around by the poolside of impossibility
Our souls drying out under the heat of oppression and injustice

Lying around
Waiting
waiting for someone to free us
waiting for something to happen
waiting for the next election
waiting for someone else to make us happy
waiting for a knight in shining armor,
waiting for a celebrity look-alike spouse
waiting for a talk-show savior
waiting for a new media-defined leader
waiting for the next megaconference, annual revival, or speaking tour
waiting for someone to die

Jesus is saying to us today
Don't wait for someone to trouble the water
Get up
Pick up your stuff
Do the work
Transforming what was not of God into what is of God
God is no respecter of persons

Jesus demonstrated this by picking a man out of the crowd of hundreds to change his life, to begin his movement, change, transformation,
We serve a just God who is still working miracles even in an unjust world
Get up
Pick up
Walk
Mahatma Gandhi once said, "You must be the change you want to see in the world."

We need to rejoice in the fact that God does not always give us what we deserve
God supplies just what we need, when we need it
God wants more than a hashtag or T-shirt campaign after a crisis has begun
Get up
Pick up whatever is holding you down
Start walking

Stop Waiting, It's Time for an Attitude Adjustment

Walk

God is calling for preemptive, prophetic, powerful actions that avert issues
God is calling for each of us to get up, step up, and speak up so someone can live
Someone's life can be revived
Someone's life can be transformed
Someone's life can be blessed
Get up
Pick up
Move up
Let us covenant tonight to adjust our attitudes
Let us work individually and collectively to
Never go back to the way it used to be
Never return to our pools of complacency
Never go back to strange fruit and cargo holds
Never go back to separate but never equal
Never go back to boy and gal
Never go back to the back of the bus
Never go back to enter only by the back door
Never go back....

I'm glad that when death seemed to be on the earthly throne
Sin seemed to have the last word
Pool existence was all we knew
God still was working
God did not wait for our invitation
God in the flesh recognized our dilemma
God came to us as we lay in the stench of our wrongdoing
God senses the bitterness of our tears
God loves us enough to
Move on our behalf when we could not or would not move ourselves
Even now our Prince of Justice
The same Jesus at the pool
This same Jesus says
Time to adjust our attitude
Get up
Pick up our mats
And walk

Not tomorrow
But right now! Stop waiting, time for an attitude adjustment.

I am reminded of two lines of the 1975 social-activist anthem written by MacFadden and Whitehead and sung by Teddy Pendergrass of Harold Melvin and the Blue Notes
Wake up everybody no more sleepin' in bed
No more backward thinkin' time for thinkin' ahead....
The world won't get no better if we just let it be
The world won't get no better we gotta change it yeah, just you and me.

Time for an attitude adjustment!!

EDITORS' INTRODUCTION: Veronice Miles's sermon takes up the literary context of the footwashing story as a way of illuminating its meaning. She brings to mind all that the disciples have heard and experienced before Jesus begins to wash their feet, as a way to understand their responses. Miles also draws on historical context—the role of slaves in footwashing—to describe how Jesus's act would have appeared to the disciples in their context. Together, the literary and historical aspects help her to connect the experience of the disciples to the listeners' experience.

Disciple, Will You Let Me Wash Your Feet?

Veronice Miles

John 13:1–17, 34–35; Exod 13:3–10

Today is Maundy Thursday, and over the past thirty-eight days we have taken stock of our lives and considered where we stand as people who endeavor to live as followers of Jesus. We have denied ourselves some guilty pleasure, some habitual practice, some cultural ritual to which we had become attached, drawing near to the one whose identity we claim as our own. We have seen the footprints of Jesus in spaces and places and among peoples and communities we had scarcely noticed before, awakening us even more to God's expansive love for all who dwell upon the earth.

The season of Lent has also brought moments of great joy *and* deep sorrow, hope *and* disappointment. And though we have endeavored to remain faithful, we have also faltered. Yet we come on the evening of this thirty-eighth day, committing ourselves anew to walk with Jesus wherever he may lead us.

Tonight we come to the table with Jesus and his disciples as they eat their last meal together. We have come to know this meal as the Last Supper, an adaptation of the Passover Seder, and indeed the three Synoptic Gospel writers characterize it as such. Matthew, Mark, and Luke tell us that Jesus and his disciples gathered to observe the Passover, to eat the meal during which the ancient Hebrews recalled their time of enslavement in Egypt and God's deliverance on their behalf.

Today, families still gather at the table on the first night of the Passover to eat a meal prepared with unleavened bread, bitter herbs, the shank-bone of a lamb, and other such symbols in memory of their ancestors' preparation for the exodus journey. The meal begins with a question from a child: "*What makes this night different from every other night?*" In response, they eat the bitter herbs and unleavened bread as they recount, with mournful yet determined hearts, their ancestral story. With the lingering taste of bitterness in their mouths, each new generation vows "*we shall never forget.*" Remembering always the struggles of their people as slaves in the land of Egypt.

As African Americans and people with a similar legacy, we take note of this ritual gathering. For we too might do well to taste the bitterness from time to time ... to let it linger on our tongues as we vow to "*never forget*" the death-dealing realities and struggles of the enslaved peoples upon whose shoulders we stand today, our ancestral mothers and fathers.

The meal begins with bitterness, but it does not end there. The Passover Seder is a two-part meal, and in the second half of the meal, the people replace the bitter herbs with wine. As the sweet taste of the wine flows over the tongues, the joy of liberation and hopeful anticipation overwhelms their sorrow, and the evening becomes a time of rejoicing, for they are slaves no more.

That's the story as recorded by Matthew, Mark, and Luke—the occasion for the communion ritual we will celebrate tonight as we remember the bitterness of crucifixion, the hope of resurrection, and stand in anticipation of the day when all peoples will experience God's liberating presence.

But John tells a different story. John will not permit us this joyful celebration. He will not invite us to taste the bitter herbs of sorrow or sip the wine of hope-filled liberation—not yet. He will not allow us to rush quickly past the moment in chapter 13 as though it does not matter, to ignore the pan of water *or* Jesus stooping there in front of us as though we cannot see him. Instead, John invites us to sit at table for an everyday meal between

Jesus and his disciples on the days prior to the Passover. And if perchance we should see Jesus stooping there, John urges us to let him wash our feet.

The *Last Supper* that John recalls is not a reinterpretation of the Passover Seder. It is a gathering at which Jesus teaches his disciples one final and definitive lesson about the dispositions of heart and mind and concrete practices necessary for a life of discipleship. A lesson that we, these twenty-first-century followers of Christ, might consider as we also seek to live as Jesus's disciples.

We meet the disciples at the table, eating, drinking, and a bit perplexed over Jesus's growing preoccupation, or so it seems, with his own mortality. He had been speaking about his death *a lot*, claiming, "the ruler of this world will be driven out. And I, when I am lifted up from the earth, will draw all people to myself" (John 12:31b–32). But his disciples did not understand.

Jesus's death was imminent. He knew that the culmination of his earthly ministry was at hand and that the cross of crucifixion awaited him. He understood that he would have to leave those whom he loved more than life itself, and that created for him a sense of urgency. Though sure of his own identity and destination—that he had "come from God and was going to God"—he was not at all certain his disciples understood the significance of his life and ministry or of their own identity as his disciples (John 13:3).

They knew him, sure enough, but they didn't *know* him. They had traveled with Jesus from one remote village to the next, had looked on in amazement as he multiplied fish and bread and fed more than five thousand people. They had traveled through Samaria with him, certain that his conversation with a woman at the well in Sychar would spell his ruin or all their deaths. Even in Jerusalem, when Jesus interrupted a crowd prepared to stone a woman to death as the stench of their own sins lingered in the air, his disciples were *right there*, silently watching their teacher at work. Later, when they were curious about the relationship between physical limitations and sin, Jesus revealed the absurdity of the question by reminding them that he is "the light of the world," God's agent of love, grace and reconciliation for all people, and especially for those who are broken and torn (John 9). But his disciples did not understand.

Not many days later, despite Jesus's assumption that his friend Lazarus was probably already dead, the disciples made the short but treacherous journey to Bethany with Jesus and witnessed an unanticipated resurrection. A few days later, Bethany became the staging ground for Jesus's triumphal entry into Jerusalem, and yes, the disciples walked beside him, cheering with the crowd: "Hosanna! Blessed is the one who comes in the name of the Lord—the King of Israel!" (John 12:13).

They had been with Jesus, had watched him work and listened to his teachings, but they had not yet put their hands to the plow. They had been good observers and faithful companions but had not truly become his disciples. Discipleship required something more of them, requires something more of us—more than association and observation, more than simply naming the name of Jesus or claiming a salvific heritage, more than standing back while Jesus does the work. Discipleship requires us *to immerse* ourselves into the continuing work of Jesus in our world today, *to permit* God's ongoing ministry in Christ—God's justice and reconciliation—to give shape and meaning to our lives. But like many of us today, Jesus's disciples did not understand.

Jesus makes it plain. With the meal preparation still in progress, Jesus gets up from the dinner table, ties a towel around his waist, pours water into a basin and prepares to wash the disciples' feet. At first glance, Jesus's actions appear to us as a simple act of hospitality, a common practice of the time. In ancient communities where people wore sandals as they walked throughout the countrysides and along the dusty roads of their communities, it was customary to wash the feet of guests as they entered the house. The host, the mistress or master of the household, would offer guests a basin of water to wash their feet or, in affluent homes, instruct household servants to wash the feet. It was also common practice for servants to wash their masters' feet or, as a gesture of honor, for students or disciples to wash their teachers' feet. But there was no precedence for masters washing the feet of their slaves or teachers washing the feet of their students.

So, Peter *was* right! It was neither customary nor proper for a teacher or a renowned rabbi, much less God's chosen one, to wash the feet of his followers. Nonetheless, Jesus, as though a student and not a teacher, a slave and not a king, a commoner and not God's chosen, stands there with towel in hand to wash each of his disciples' feet.

But Peter was also wrong! He did not get it, did not understand why the one whom he esteemed so highly would assume the posture of a servant and wash the feet of those who should have been paying him a debt of gratitude. Peter missed the point. Jesus was not engaging in the compulsory activity of a slave. This was not a self-abnegating gesture by someone who felt insecure about his identity. And his actions were not some subtle denunciation of messianic expectation. Jesus's actions were a call to discipleship, an outpouring of grace and demonstration of love that exerted a claim upon the lives of those whose feet Jesus washed.

For, "*unless I wash your feet,*" Jesus told them, "*you have no share with me.*"

What might it mean for us to surrender our feet to Jesus today, for us present-day disciples to permit Jesus to stoop down right in front of us and wash our feet? Not to dip us in baptismal waters or fill us with the Holy Spirit and fire, but for Jesus to call us by name and wash our feet, just our feet. Not to purify our hands or anoint our head, but to perform this simple act of service by washing our feet.

What would it mean if the one who loves us so deeply and cares for us so completely, the one who under threat of death would not turn back from proclaiming the gospel of salvation and hope, what if this one washed our feet?

What if Jesus himself stooped down in the center of our great cathedrals, small houses of prayer, or the gathering space we occupy today; what if he stooped down in the midst of our altars and in the face of ornate regalia, if he stooped down in front of us, knowing our faith and doubts, fears and faults, hurts and hopes, and said, "let me wash your feet"?

What if the one whom John says was with God in the beginning interrupted our pretentiousness about our status as Christians and *grabbed hold of our feet* just at that moment when we are about to forget that we are created to live as an expression of divine presence? What if Jesus knelt down right in front of us and washed our feet?

What if you and I found ourselves in a Judas-like position, in some quagmire of infidelity and deceit or wandering far from God like prodigal daughters and sons who have lost our way, and Jesus, with the love and care that a mother gives to her children, began to wash our feet as though we had never left the fold?

What if the one who, *on Friday*, will hang on Calvary's cross, the one whom we call Messiah and Savior, stooped down, poured water in a basin, and, with hands dripping wet with love and mercy, began to wash our feet, washing our feet and immersing us into his life as though we were already what he desires us to be?

"*Unless I wash your feet,*" Jesus said, "*you have no share with me.*"

That's what Jesus's disciples discovered—that despite their failures and faults, doubts and fears, despite Judas's betrayal and lack of fidelity, despite Peter's impending denial, Jesus wanted to wash their feet, wants to wash our feet, all of us, as though we are already the image of discipleship to which he calls us. And that's what he did, right there at this everyday meal; Jesus washed their feet.

"Do you know what I have done to you?" Jesus asks (John 13:12), shrouding his ministerial invitation in a question and awaiting our response, *beckoning* us to follow his example of humility and service by doing the work of the ministry and acknowledging that we are not greater than the one in whose name we have come, *preparing* us to live the life of faith in humble service to our sisters and brothers, *binding* us to each other with fetters of love that cannot be broken, and *reminding* us that we are disciples of that preaching/teaching/healing prophet who gave his life on Calvary. And we shall never forget.

And so we say yes, because we have been claimed by this outpouring of grace and demonstration of love. Yes, we hear your beckoning call. Yes, we want to be your disciples. Yes, we understand and are ready to serve, ready to get our hands wet in the water of love, ready to embody humility and grace, ready to live as an expression of our identity in you.

Yes, Jesus, we will let you wash our feet!

EDITORS' INTRODUCTION: Ted Smith's theological message is built on close attention to the Greek verb tenses in Revelation. He teases out aspects of John's vision of the new Jerusalem as a way of revealing God's action in the past, present, and future. Smith connects Revelation to the listener's present by proclaiming that God's past, present, and future action shape contemporary events in similar ways.

The Time of Revelation

Ted A. Smith

Emory University, All Saints' Day 2018

Grammar geeks, Greek freaks, partisans of the perfect passive participle, this text is for you! But not only for you.

Saints! Sinners! (I'm assuming significant overlap between these categories.) This text is for you. But it is not only for you.

All you with tears running down your faces, all you who cry out for justice, all you who live with death, all you who thirst for God, this text is for you.

***

> Then I saw a new heaven and a new earth; for the first heaven and the first earth had passed away, and the sea was no more. And I saw the holy city, the new Jerusalem, coming down out of heaven from God, prepared as a bride adorned for her husband. And I heard a loud voice from the throne saying,
>
> > "See, the home of God is among mortals.
> > He will dwell with them;

> they will be his peoples,
> and God himself will be with them;
> he will wipe every tear from their eyes.
> Death will be no more;
> mourning and crying and pain will be no more,
> for the first things have passed away."
>
> And the one who was seated on the throne said, "See, I am making all things new." Also he said, "Write this, for these words are trustworthy and true." Then he said to me, "It is done! I am the Alpha and the Omega, the beginning and the end. To the thirsty I will give water as a gift from the spring of the water of life." (Rev 21:1–6 NRSV)

***

This word comes to us in fearful times, times defined by fear. A gunman in Pittsburgh feared that Jews were conspiring to replace him, and so he murdered people at prayer. Now Jewish people fear—not without reason—that once again a society is curdling into violent anti-Semitism. Fear inspires violence that generates fear. A white majority fears becoming a minority and so sends ICE to the factory and troops to the border. They—and here I must say *we*, as this is done in my name, even if I would resist it—send police into the streets to stop and frisk and give rough rides and incarcerate and fire shots that kill Black and Brown neighbors. In a Kroger in Louisville, in a man's own home in Dallas, in a church in Charleston, in every kind of space, fearful white hands take up violence outside the law, too often with the sanction of law. Even against children. Even against grandparents. And so Black and Brown people—even children, even grandparents—fear, and not without reason. In our age, fear begets violence begets fear.

The seer of Revelation—whom we might as well call John the Revelator—lived in times that were not unlike ours. Fearful times, violent times. Scholars dispute the details. But the outline is clear. Whether the violence came from mobs, individuals, or official imperial forces, the pattern was familiar: fear begat violence begat fear. That old spiral of death.

Into this fearful, violent world, John the Revelator saw a "holy city, the new Jerusalem, coming down out of heaven from God, prepared as a bride adorned for her husband" (21:2). This city has a wall. But the wall is not made to keep people out. For the wall has twelve gates—twelve gates to the city, hallelu!—twelve gates that are always open during the day, and in that city it is never night. The walls aren't designed to keep people out. In John's vision, people from all over the world stream into the city to offer praise.

These walls aren't made to keep people out because they are not built out of fear. Where God reigns, there is no fear. The walls are built for praise. They are made of jasper, adorned with jewels; they are made not to be effective barriers but beautiful offerings. Glorious! They are made to invite praise and offer praise themselves. They are the walls of a city without fear.

Verse 2 makes it plain: We don't build up this new Jerusalem. It comes down from God. It is good to vote—we have *got* to vote, and to work to undo all the powers that would keep people from voting—but the new Jerusalem is not voted in by a blue wave, or a red wave, or a blue tsunami with a red undertow, giving us the divided government Americans historically prefer. No. The new Jerusalem comes from God.

And so the question posed by the new Jerusalem is not, How do we build it? but, When is it coming?

Revelation does not give a simple answer to that question. In fact, if there is one surefire way to be a fool, it is to name a date. ("It's coming Tuesday!" "Oh ... did I say Tuesday? I meant *next* Tuesday." "Actually, I meant 'Tuesday' in an *allegorical* sense.") And it's not just that no one knows the day or the hour. It is that it's hard even to say whether Revelation thinks the new Jerusalem has already come, will come someday, or is coming right now. Revelation doesn't answer this question simply. Instead, it gives us a tangle of tenses—present, future, and at least two kinds of past. Because that's what it takes to tell the whole gospel truth.

Some things are clearly in the past. John the Revelator narrates the story of his vision in the aorist: "*I saw* a new heaven and a new earth.... *I saw* the holy city.... *I heard* a loud voice from the throne." I saw. I heard. The vision happened in the past. This is not a small point. It means that the *vision has been given*. The endless chatter of fear and violence has already been interrupted by a gospel word. Just that interruption is already a kind of deliverance. Because the way the spiral of fear and violence works is to make us think that it is the whole of reality, that this pattern of fear begetting violence begetting fear is all that there is, so we might as well knuckle under and join the fray. But the vision John passed on to us—the vision we have already received—breaks that spell. It says this spiral will not go on forever. Death will not have the last word. From past revelation, we already know this about the future. And that makes all the difference for the present.

But that's not all that Revelation puts in the past. It's not all that has already been accomplished. The text also uses the past to talk about the defeat of the powers of this age. The first things, verse 1 says and verse 4 repeats, have already passed away. "It is done!" verse 6 says, in the perfect tense. The perfect tense, which, you grammarians know, conveys past action with continuing effect. *A past action with continuing effect.* The strife is over, the vict'ry won. It's past. It's done. And its effects continue. Hate, violence, fear, and death might still stagger around. But they are zombies, walking dead, already defeated, not long for this world. Their time is already past.

If Revelation puts some moments in the past, it puts others in the future. There is a string of future tense in verses 3 and 4. Verse 3 promises the fullness of the presence of God. In the future tense, God *will* dwell with them. They *shall* be God's people. God *will* be with them. And verse 4 makes plain the effects: God *will* wipe away every tear. Death *will be* no more. There *will be* no more mourning or crying or pain. The fullness of redemption will bring communion with God and an end to every kind of suffering. All this is in the future tense. It is not yet, present now only as promise. We have the promise—thanks be to God!—but we still have the tears. (*Don't we know it.*)

Sin, death, fear, and violence—all the powers of this age—have already been defeated. Past tense. And communion with God, a communion so close that there is no more crying then—that is in the future, soon and very soon. But what is in the present?

The present tense is the rarest of tenses in these verses. But it is also at the heart of them. For it is in the present tense that the one on the throne speaks. That one on the throne: his name is Jesus. And he says, "Behold, I am making all things new." Right now. In the present tense. That's *poiō*, for those of you following along in your Nestle-Aland critical editions. *Poiō*, "I am making." Revelation promises that Jesus is at work, even now, in the present, making all things new. And Jesus goes on in that same present tense, saying: "I am the Alpha and the Omega, the beginning and the end." I am, Jesus says, from the throne, in perfect harmony with the "I am" that Moses heard from the burning bush. "I am," Jesus says. Right now. In the present. Jesus is, right now, the Alpha and the Omega. And not just for this moment, this now, but for every now that ever will be.

Aorist, perfect, future, present. A saint is not someone who has mastered all this grammar. A saint is not someone who has never sinned. A saint (and here I ask forgiveness of my Wesleyan friends), a saint might not even be perfect now. A saint is someone who knows, in her bones, that the powers of this age have already been broken, that the new Jerusalem is coming soon and very soon, and that Jesus is present, even now. A saint is someone whose life tells us what time it is, like a living clock.

The Time of Revelation

I think of Saint Oscar Romero, acting in the confidence that the powers of the Salvadoran government had already been broken, knowing that he was not yet in the future when there are no more sniper's bullets, and still breaking the bread to share the presence of Christ who is present even now.

I think of Saint Fannie Lou Hamer, registering people to vote in defiance of a Jim Crow power that was already defeated, knowing full well she was not yet in the promised time of no more beatings, no more cancer, and still testifying that—right now, in the present—God kept her sane.

I think of Saint Betty Kirkland, whom I knew when I was a pastor in rural New York State. Betty lived in a trailer, in part because she gave away what the world called "too much." She gave too much to missionaries, too much to needy neighbors who then spent too much on cigarettes and beer. She gave too much to a church whose pastor didn't even stick around. None of this bothered Betty. She was so joyful I sometimes wondered whether she was grounded in reality. But she wasn't crazy. She wasn't naive. She just knew what time it was.

Alleluia! Amen.

Bibliography

Ajer, Peter Claver. *The Death of Jesus and the Politics of Place in the Gospel of John*. Eugene, OR: Pickwick, 2016.
Alter, Robert. *The Pleasures of Reading in an Ideological Age*. New York: Simon & Schuster, 1989.
Anatolios, Khaled. *Retrieving Nicaea: The Development and Meaning of Trinitarian Doctrine*. Grand Rapids: Baker Academic, 2011.
Ashton, John. *The Gospel of John and Christian Origins*. Minneapolis: Fortress, 2014.
———. *Understanding the Fourth Gospel*. Oxford: Clarendon, 1991.
Attridge, Harold W. " 'Don't Be Touching Me': Recent Feminist Scholarship on Mary Magdalene." Pages 140–66 in vol. 2 of *A Feminist Companion to John*. Edited by Amy-Jill Levine with Marianne Blickenstaff. Cleveland: Pilgrim, 2003.
Augustine. *City of God*. Translated by Henry Bettenson. London: Penguin, 1972.
Aune, David E. *Revelation 1–5*. WBC 52A. Dallas: Word, 1997.
Ayres, Lewis. *Nicaea and Its Legacy: An Approach to Fourth-Century Trinitarian Theology*. Oxford: Oxford University Press, 2004.
Barrett, C. K. *The Gospel according to St. John: An Introduction with Commentary and Notes on the Greek Text*. London: SPCK, 1962.
———. *The Gospel according to St. John: An Introduction with Commentary and Notes on the Greek Text*. 2nd ed. Philadelphia: Westminster, 1978.
Barron, Robert. *Exploring Catholic Theology: Essays on God, Liturgy, and Evangelization*. Grand Rapids: Baker Academic, 2015.
———. *The Priority of Christ: Toward a Postliberal Catholicism*. Grand Rapids: Brazos, 2007.
Bauckham, Richard. *The Climax of Prophecy: Studies on the Book of Revelation*. Edinburgh: T&T Clark, 1993.
Baur, Chrysostomus, O.S.B. *John Chrysostom and His Time*. 2 vols. Translated by Sr. M. Gonzaga, R.S.M. Westminster, Newman, 1959.

Beale, Gregory K. *The Book of Revelation: A Commentary on the Greek Text*. NIGTC. Grand Rapids: Eerdmans, 1999.

Bennema, Cornelis. *Encountering Jesus: Character Studies in the Gospel of John*. 2nd ed. Minneapolis: Fortress, 2014.

Beutler, Johannes. *A Commentary on the Gospel of John*. Translated by Michael Tait. Grand Rapids: Eerdmans, 2017.

Biguzzi, Giancarlo. "A Figurative and Narrative Language Grammar of Revelation." *NovT* 45 (2003): 382–402.

Blount, Brian K. *Revelation: A Commentary*. NTL. Louisville: Westminster John Knox, 2009.

Boer, Martinus C. de. "The Narrative Function of Pilate in John." Pages 141–58 in *Narrativity in Biblical and Related Texts*. Edited by G. J. Brook and J.-D. Kaestli. BETL 149. Leuven: Leuven University Press, 2000.

Boersma, Hans. *Scripture as Real Presence: Sacramental Exegesis in the Early Church*. Grand Rapids: Baker Academic, 2017.

Bond, Helen K. *Pontius Pilate in History and Interpretation*. SNTSMS 100. Cambridge: Cambridge University Press, 1998.

Boring, M. Eugene. *Revelation*. IBC. Louisville: John Knox, 1989.

Brown, Raymond E. *The Community of the Beloved Disciple: The Life, Loves, and Hates of an Individual Church in New Testament Times*. New York: Paulist, 1979.

———. *The Death of the Messiah: From Gethsemane to the Grave; A Commentary on the Passion Narratives in the Four Gospels*. 2 vols. ABRL. New York: Doubleday, 1994.

———. *The Gospel according to John*. 2 vols. AB 29–29A. New York: Doubleday, 1966–1970.

Brown, Sherri. "What Is Truth? Jesus, Pilate, and the Staging of the Dialogue of the Cross in John 18:28–19:16a." *CBQ* 77 (2015): 69–86.

Bultmann, Rudolf. *The Gospel of John: A Commentary*. Translated by G. R. Beasley-Murray, R. W. N. Hoare, and J. K. Riches. Philadelphia: Westminster, 1971.

———. "New Testament and Mythology." Pages 1–44 in *Kerygma and Myth: A Theological Debate*. Edited by Hans Werner Bartsch. Translated by Reginald H. Fuller. London: SPCK, 1957.

———. *Theology of the New Testament*. 2 vols. New York: Scribner, 1955.

Caird, G. B. *The Revelation of Saint John*. Peabody, MA: Hendrickson, 1966.

Carey, Greg. "The Apocalypse and Its Ambiguous Ethos." Pages 163–80 in *Studies in the Book of Revelation*. Edited by Steve Moyise. Edinburgh: T&T Clark, 2001.
Carter, Warren. *John and Empire: Initial Explorations*. New York: T&T Clark, 2008.
———. *Pontius Pilate: Portraits of a Roman Governor*. Interfaces. Collegeville, MN: Liturgical Press, 2003.
Cassidy, Richard J. *John's Gospel in New Perspective: Christology and the Realities of Roman Power*. Maryknoll, NY: Orbis Books, 1992.
Charles, R. H. *A Critical and Exegetical Commentary on the Revelation of St. John*. 2 vols. ICC. Edinburgh: T&T Clark, 1920.
Childers, Jana, ed. *Purposes of Preaching*. St. Louis: Chalice, 2004.
Conway, Colleen M. *Men and Women in the Fourth Gospel: Gender and Johannine Characterization*. SBLDS 167. Atlanta: Society of Biblical Literature, 1999.
Counet, Patrick Chatelion. *John, a Postmodern Gospel: Introduction to Deconstructive Exegesis Applied to the Fourth Gospel*. Leiden: Brill, 2000.
Culpepper, R. Alan. *Anatomy of the Fourth Gospel: A Study in Literary Design*. Philadelphia: Fortress, 1983.
———. "Nicodemus: The Travail of New Birth." Pages 249–59 in *Character Studies in the Fourth Gospel: Narrative Approaches to Seventy Figures in John*. Edited by Steven A. Hunt, Francois Tolmie, and Ruben Zimmermann. Grand Rapids: Eerdmans, 2016.
Culpepper, R. Alan, and Paul N. Anderson. *John and Judaism: A Contested Relationship in Context*. Atlanta: SBL Press, 2017.
D'Angelo, Mary Rose. "A Critical Note: John 20:17 and Apocalypse of Moses 31." *JTS* 41 (1990): 529–36.
Dewailly, Louis-Marie. "'D'où es-tu?' (Jean 19,9)." *RB* 92 (1985): 481–96.
Dimitrova, Nora. "Inscriptions and Iconography in the Monuments of the Thracian Rider." *Hesperia* 71 (2002): 209–29.
Dodd, C. H. *Historical Tradition in the Fourth Gospel*. Cambridge: Cambridge University Press, 1963.
Donahue, John R., ed. *Life in Abundance: Studies of John's Gospel in Tribute to Raymond E. Brown*. Collegeville, MN: Liturgical Press, 2005.
duBois, Page. *Out of Athens: The New Ancient Greeks*. Cambridge: Harvard University Press, 2010.
Duke, Paul D. *Irony in the Fourth Gospel*. Atlanta: John Knox, 1985.

Empson, William. *Seven Types of Ambiguity*. 2nd ed. New York: New Directions, 1947.
Engberg-Pedersen, Troels. *John and Philosophy: A New Reading of the Fourth Gospel*. Oxford: Oxford University Press, 2017.
Fauconnier, Gilles. *Mappings in Thought and Language*. Cambridge: Cambridge University Press, 1997.
Fauconnier, Gilles, and Mark Turner. *The Way We Think: Conceptual Blending and the Mind's Hidden Complexities*. New York: Basic Books, 2002.
Fiorenza, Elisabeth Schüssler. *The Book of Revelation: Justice and Judgment*. 2nd ed. Minneapolis: Fortress, 1998.
Fleer, David, and David Bland, eds. *Preaching John's Gospel: The World It Imagines*. St. Louis: Chalice, 2008.
Fortna, Robert T. *The Gospel of Signs: A Reconstruction of the Narrative Source Underlying the Fourth Gospel*. SNTSMS 11. Cambridge: Cambridge University Press, 1970.
Frey, Jörg. *The Glory of the Crucified One: Christology and Theology in the Gospel of John*. Translated by Wayne Coppins and Christoph Heilig. Waco, TX: Baylor University Press, 2018.
Gaventa, Beverly Roberts. "The Archive of Excess: John 21 and the Problem of Narrative Closure." Pages 240–52 in *Exploring the Gospel of John: In Honor of D. Moody Smith*. Edited by R. Alan Culpepper and C. Clifton Black. Louisville: Westminster John Knox, 1996.
Giblin, Charles Homer. "John's Narration of the Hearing before Pilate (John 18,28–19,16a)." *Bib* 67 (1986): 221–39.
Glancy, Jennifer A. "Torture: Flesh, Truth, and the Fourth Gospel." *BibInt* 13 (2005): 107–36.
Gombrich, E. H. *Art and Illusion: A Study in the Psychology of Pictorial Representation*. New York: Pantheon, 1960.
Haenchen, Ernst. *John*. 2 vols. Edited by Robert W. Funk and Ulrich Busse. Translated by Robert W. Funk. Hermeneia. Philadelphia: Fortress, 1984.
Hasitschka, Martin. "The Significance of the Resurrection Appearance in John 21." Pages 311–28 in *The Resurrection of Jesus in the Gospel of John*. Edited by Craig Koester and Reimund Bieringer. Tübingen: Mohr Siebeck, 2008.
Haws, Molly. " 'Put Your Finger Here': Resurrection and the Construction of the Body." *Theology & Sexuality* 13 (2007): 181–94.

Hill, Robert. "Chrysostom's Terminology for the Inspired Word." *EstBib* 41 (1973): 367–73.

———. "The Incarnation of the Word in Scripture." *Compass Theology Review* 14 (1980): 34–38.

———. "Introduction." Pages 13–19 in John Chrysostom. *Homilies on Genesis 1–17*. FC 74. Washington, DC: Catholic University of America Press, 1986.

———. "On Looking Again at *Sunkatabasis*." *Prudentia* 13 (1981): 3–11.

———. "St. John Chrysostom's Teaching on Inspiration in 'Six Homilies on Isaiah.'" *VC* 22 (1968): 19–37.

Hoskyns, Edwyn Clement. *The Fourth Gospel*. Edited by F. N. Davey. London: Faber & Faber, 1947.

Huber, Lynn R. *Like a Bride Adorned: Reading Metaphor in John's Apocalypse*. Emory Studies in Early Christianity. New York: T&T Clark, 2007.

———. *Thinking and Seeing with Women in Revelation*. LNTS. London: Bloomsbury, 2013.

Hylen, Susan E. *Allusion and Meaning in John 6*. BZNW 137. Berlin: de Gruyter, 2005.

———. *Imperfect Believers: Ambiguous Characters in the Gospel of John*. Louisville: Westminster John Knox, 2009.

———. "Metaphor Matters: Violence and Ethics in Revelation." *CBQ* 73 (2011): 777–96.

John Chrysostom. *Commentary on Saint John the Apostle and Evangelist: Homilies 1–47*. Translated by Sister Thomas Aquinas Goggin, S.C.H. FC 33. Washington, DC: Catholic University of America Press, 1957.

———. *Commentary on Saint John the Apostle and Evangelist: Homilies 48–88*. Translated by Sister Thomas Aquinas Goggin, S.C.H. FC 41. Washington, DC: Catholic University of America Press, 1959.

———. *Homilies on Genesis 1–17*. Translated by Robert C. Hill. FC 74. Washington, DC: Catholic University of America Press, 1986.

———. *On the Incomprehensible Nature of God*. Translated by Paul W. Harkins. FC 72. Washington, DC: Catholic University of America Press, 1982.

Johns, Loren L. *The Lamb Christology of the Apocalypse of John: An Investigation into Its Origins and Rhetorical Force*. WUNT 2.167. Tübingen: Mohr Siebeck, 2003.

Juel, Donald H. "The Strange Silence of the Bible." *Int* 51 (1997): 5–19.

Käsemann, Ernst. *The Testament of Jesus: A Study of the Gospel of John in the Light of Chapter 17*. London: SCM, 1968.

Keener, Craig S. *The Gospel of John: A Commentary*. 2 vols. Peabody, MA: Hendrickson, 2003.

Kelly, J. N. D. *Golden Mouth: The Story of John Chrysostom—Ascetic, Preacher, Bishop*. Ithaca, NY: Cornell University Press, 1995.

Klauck, Hans-Josef. "Community, History, and Text(s): A Response to Robert Kysar." Pages 82–90 in *Life in Abundance: Studies of John's Gospel in Tribute to Raymond E. Brown*. Edited by John R. Donahue. Collegeville, MN: Liturgical Press, 2005.

Koester, Craig R. *Revelation*. Anchor Yale Bible 38A. New Haven: Yale University Press, 2014.

———. *Symbolism in the Fourth Gospel: Meaning, Mystery, Community*. 2nd ed. Minneapolis: Fortress, 2003.

Kovacs, Judith, and Christopher Rowland. *Revelation*. Blackwell Bible Commentaries. Oxford: Blackwell, 2004.

Kysar, Robert. *Preaching John*. Minneapolis: Fortress, 2002.

———. "The Whence and Whither of the Johannine Community." Pages 65–81 in *Life in Abundance: Studies of John's Gospel in Tribute to Raymond E. Brown*. Edited by John R. Donahue. Collegeville, MN: Liturgical Press, 2005.

La Potterie, Ignace de. *The Hour of Jesus: The Passion and the Resurrection of Jesus according to John; Text and Spirit*. Translated by Dom Gregory Murray. Slough, UK: Saint Paul, 1989.

———. "Jésus Roi et Juge d'Après Jn 19,13: Ἐκάθισεν ἐπὶ βήματος." *Bib* 41 (1960): 217–47.

Lanham, Richard A. *A Handlist of Rhetorical Terms: A Guide for Students of English Literature*. Berkeley: University of California Press, 1968.

Laws, Sophie. *In the Light of the Lamb: Image, Parody, and Theology in the Apocalypse of John*. Good News Studies 31. Wilmington, DE: Glazier, 1988.

Lewis, C. S. *An Experiment in Criticism*. Cambridge: Cambridge University Press, 1961.

Lewis, Karoline M. *Rereading the "Shepherd Discourse": Restoring the Integrity of John 9:39–10:21*. Edited by Hemchand Gossai. StBibLit 113. New York: Lang, 2008.

Liew, Tat-siong Benny. "The Word of Bare Life: Working of Death and Dream in the Fourth Gospel." Pages 167–93 in *Anatomies of Narrative Criticism: The Past, Present, and Futures of the Fourth Gospel as Litera-*

ture. Edited by Tom Thatcher and Stephen D. Moore. RBS 55. Atlanta: Society of Biblical Literature, 2008.

Lindars, Barnabas. *The Gospel of John*. NCB. London: Oliphants, 1972.

Long, Thomas G. *The Witness of Preaching*. 3rd ed. Louisville: Westminster John Knox, 2016.

Lunceford, J. E. *Parody and Counterimagery in the Apocalypse*. Eugene, OR: Wipf & Stock, 2009.

Maier, Harry O. *Apocalypse Recalled: The Book of Revelation after Christendom*. Minneapolis: Fortress, 2002.

Margerie, Bertrand de, S.J. *The Greek Fathers*. Vol. 1 of *An Introduction to the History of Exegesis*. Translated by Leonard Maluf. Petersham, MA: Saint Bede's, 1993.

Marriner, K. T. *Following the Lamb: The Theme of Discipleship in the Book of Revelation*. Eugene, OR: Wipf & Stock, 2016.

Martin, Clarice J. "Womanist Interpretations of the New Testament: The Quest for Holistic and Inclusive Translation and Interpretation." *JFSR* 6 (1990): 41–61.

Martyn, J. Louis. *History and Theology in the Fourth Gospel*. 3rd ed. NTL. Louisville: Westminster John Knox, 2003.

Mayer, Wendy, and Pauline Allen. *John Chrysostom*. London: Routledge, 2000.

McDonnell, Myles. *Roman Manliness: "Virtus" and the Roman Republic*. Cambridge: Cambridge University Press, 2006.

McGing, Brian C. "Pontius Pilate and the Sources." *CBQ* 53 (1991): 416–38.

Meeks, Wayne A. "The Man from Heaven in Johannine Sectarianism." *JBL* 91 (1972): 44–72.

Merton, Thomas. *Conjectures of a Guilty Bystander*. Garden City, NY: Doubleday, 1966.

Moloney, Francis J. "'For As Yet They Did Not Know the Scripture' (John 20:9): A Study in Narrative Time." *ITQ* 79 (2014): 97–111.

———. *The Gospel of John*. SP 4. Collegeville, MN: Liturgical Press, 1998.

———. *The Gospel of John: Text and Context*. BibInt 72. Boston: Brill, 2005.

———. "John 21 and the Johannine Story." Pages 237–51 in *Anatomies of Narrative Criticism: The Past, Present, and Futures of the Fourth Gospel as Literature*. Edited by Tom Thatcher and Stephen D. Moore. RBS 55. Atlanta: Scholars Press, 2008.

Moore, Stephen D. *Empire and Apocalypse: Postcolonialism and the New Testament*. Bible in the Modern World 12. Sheffield: Sheffield Phoenix, 2006.

———. "Ruminations on Revelation's Ruminant, Quadrupedal Christ; or, the Even-Toed Ungulate That Therefore I Am." Pages 301–26 in *The Bible and Posthumanism*. Edited by Jennifer L. Koosed. Atlanta: SBL Press, 2014.

Neyrey, Jerome H., S.J. *The Gospel of John*. NCBC. Cambridge: Cambridge University Press, 2007.

Oakley, John Howard, and Rebecca H. Sinos. *The Wedding in Ancient Athens*. Madison: University of Wisconsin Press, 1993.

O'Day, Gail R. "The Gospel of John: Introduction, Commentary, and Reflections." *NIB* 9:491–865.

———. "Jesus as Friend in the Gospel of John." *Int* 58 (2004): 144–57.

———. "John 6:15–21: Jesus Walking on Water as Narrative Embodiment of Johannine Christology." Pages 149–59 in *Critical Readings of John 6*. Edited by R. Alan Culpepper. BibInt 22. Leiden: Brill, 1997.

———. "Narrative Mode and Theological Claim: A Study in the Fourth Gospel." *JBL* 105 (1986): 657–68.

———. "Revelation." Pages 471–79 in *Theological Bible Commentary*. Edited by Gail R. O'Day and David L. Petersen. Louisville: Westminster John Knox, 2009.

———. *Revelation in the Fourth Gospel: Narrative Mode and Theological Claim*. Philadelphia: Fortress, 1986.

———. "'Show Us the Father and We Will Be Satisfied' (John 14:8)." *Semeia* 85 (1999): 11–17.

———. "The Word Become Flesh: Story and Theology in the Gospel of John." Pages 67–78 in *Literary and Social Readings of the Fourth Gospel*. Vol. 2 of *What Is John?* Edited by Fernando F. Segovia. SymS 7. Atlanta: Scholars Press, 1998.

———. *The Word Disclosed: Preaching the Gospel of John*. St. Louis: Chalice, 2002.

O'Day, Gail R., and Susan E. Hylen. *John*. Westminster Bible Companion. Louisville: Westminster John Knox, 2006.

Origen. *Homilies on Jeremiah; Homily on 1 Kings 28*. Translated by John Clark Smith. FC 97. Washington, DC: Catholic University of America Press, 1998.

Pate, C. M. *Interpreting Revelation and Other Apocalyptic Literature: An Exegetical Handbook*. Grand Rapids: Kregel Academic, 2016.

Petterson, Christina. *From Tomb to Text: The Body of Jesus in the Book of John*. London: Bloomsbury T&T Clark, 2017.

Philostratus. *The Life of Apollonius of Tyana, Books 1–4*. Edited and translated by Christopher P. Jones. LCL. Cambridge: Harvard University Press, 2005.

Pliny. *Letters: Books VIII–X; Panegyricus*. Translated by Betty Radice. LCL. Cambridge: Harvard University Press, 1969.

Quasten, Johannes. *The Golden Age of Greek Patristic Literature from the Council of Nicaea to the Council of Chalcedon*. Vol. 3 of *Patrology*. Westminster: Newman, 1960.

Reinhartz, Adele. "John and Judaism: A Response to Burton Visotzky." Pages 108–16 in *Life in Abundance: Studies of John's Gospel in Tribute to Raymond E. Brown*. Edited by John R. Donahue. Collegeville, MN: Liturgical Press, 2005.

Rensberger, David. *Johannine Faith and Liberating Community*. Philadelphia: Westminster, 1988.

———. "The Politics of John: The Trial of Jesus in the Fourth Gospel." *JBL* 103 (1984): 395–411.

Reynolds, Benjamin E. "Apocalyptic Revelation in the Gospel of John: Revealed Cosmology, the Vision of God, and Visionary Showing." Pages 109–28 in *The Jewish Apocalyptic Tradition and the Shaping of New Testament Thought*. Edited by Benjamin E. Reynolds and Loren T. Stuckenbruck. Minneapolis: Augsburg Fortress, 2016.

Rhoads, David M., Joanna Dewey, and Donald Michie. *Mark as Story: An Introduction to the Narrative of a Gospel*. 2nd ed. Minneapolis: Fortress, 1999.

Richey, Lance Byron. *Roman Imperial Ideology and the Gospel of John*. CBQMS 43. Washington, DC: Catholic Biblical Association of America, 2007.

Ridderbos, Herman N. *The Gospel of John: A Theological Commentary*. Translated by John Vriend. Grand Rapids: Eerdmans, 1997.

Robbins, Vernon K. "Kinetic Divine Concepts, the Baptist, and the Enfleshed Logos in the Prologue and Precreation Storyline of the Fourth Gospel." Pages 281–99 in *Seeing the God: Image, Space, Performance, and Vision in the Religion of the Roman Empire*. Edited by Marlis Arnhold, Harry O. Maier, and Jörg Rüpke. Culture, Religion, and Politics in the Greco-Roman World. Tübingen: Mohr Siebeck, 2018.

Rylaardsdam, David. *John Chrysostom on Divine Pedagogy: The Coherence of His Theology and Preaching*. New York: Oxford University Press, 2014.

Sandys-Wunsch, John, and Laurence Eldredge. "J. P. Gabler and the Distinction between Biblical and Dogmatic Theology: Translation, Commentary, and Discussion of his Originality." *SJT* 33 (1980): 133–58.

Schnackenburg, Rudolf. *The Gospel according to St. John.* Translated by Kevin Smyth et al. 3 vols. New York: Seabury/Crossroad, 1968–1982.

Schneiders, Sandra M. "The Resurrection (of the Body) in the Fourth Gospel: A Key to Johannine Spirituality." Pages 168–98 in *Life in Abundance: Studies of John's Gospel in Tribute to Raymond E. Brown.* Edited by John R. Donahue. Collegeville, MN: Liturgical Press, 2005.

Schnelle, Udo. "Cross and Resurrection in the Gospel of John." Pages 127–51 in *The Resurrection of Jesus in the Gospel of John.* Edited by Craig R. Koester and Reimund Bieringer. WUNT 222. Tübingen: Mohr Siebeck, 2008.

Segovia, Fernando F. "The Final Farewell of Jesus: A Reading of John 20:30–21:25." *Semeia* 53 (1991): 167–90.

———. "Johannine Studies and the Geopolitical: Reflections upon Absence and Irruption." Pages 281–306 in *What We Have Heard from the Beginning: The Past, Present, and Future of Johannine Studies.* Edited by Tom Thatcher. Waco, TX: Baylor University Press, 2007.

Slater, Thomas. *Christ and Community: A Socio-Historical Study of the Christology of Revelation.* LNTS 178. London: Bloomsbury, 1999.

Smith, D. Moody. *John.* ANTC. Nashville: Abingdon, 1999.

Sokolowski, Robert. *Christian Faith and Human Understanding: Studies on the Eucharist, Trinity, and the Human Person.* Washington, DC: Catholic University of America Press, 2006.

———. *Eucharistic Presence: A Study in the Theology of Disclosure.* Washington, DC: Catholic University of America Press, 1993.

———. *The God of Faith and Reason: Foundations of Christian Theology.* Notre Dame: University of Notre Dame Press, 1982.

Stibbe, Mark W. G. *John as Storyteller: Narrative Criticism and the Fourth Gospel.* SNTSMS 73. Cambridge: Cambridge University Press, 1992.

Stone, Michael E., and Matthias Henze. *4 Ezra and 2 Baruch: Translations, Introductions, and Notes.* Minneapolis: Fortress, 2013.

Stovell, Beth M. *Mapping Metaphorical Discourse in the Fourth Gospel: John's Eternal King.* Linguistic Biblical Studies 5. Leiden: Brill, 2012.

Talbert, Charles. *Reading John: A Literary and Theological Commentary on the Fourth Gospel and the Johannine Epistles.* New York: Crossroad, 1994.

Thatcher, Tom. *Greater Than Caesar: Christology and Empire in the Fourth Gospel*. Minneapolis: Fortress, 2009.
Thomas, R. L. *Magical Motifs in the Book of Revelation*. London: T&T Clark, 2010.
Thompson, Marianne Meye. *John: A Commentary*. NTL. Louisville: Westminster John Knox, 2015.
Tolmie, D. Francois. "Pontius Pilate: Failing in More Ways Than One." Pages 578–97 in *Character Studies in the Fourth Gospel: Narrative Approaches to Seventy Figures in John*. Edited by Steven A. Hunt, D. Francois Tolmie, and Ruben Zimmerman. WUNT 314. Tübingen: Mohr Siebeck, 2013. Repr., Grand Rapids: Eerdmans, 2016.
Tuckett, Christopher M. "Pilate in John 18–19: A Narrative Critical Approach." Pages 131–40 in *Narrativity in Biblical and Related Texts*. Edited by G. J. Brook and J.-D. Kaestli. BETL 149. Leuven: Leuven University Press, 2000.
Varebeke, A. Janssens de. "La Structure des Scènes du Récit de la Passion en Joh., xviii–xix." *ETL* 38 (1962): 504–22.
Visotzky, Burton L. "Methodological Considerations in the Study of John's Interaction with First-Century Judaism." Pages 91–107 in *Life in Abundance: Studies of John's Gospel in Tribute to Raymond E. Brown*. Edited by John R. Donahue. Collegeville, MN: Liturgical Press, 2005.
Webster, Jane S. *Ingesting Jesus: Eating and Drinking in the Gospel of John*. Atlanta: Society of Biblical Literature, 2003.
Westcott, B. F. *The Gospel according to Saint John: The Authorised Version with Introduction and Notes*. London: John Murray, 1882.
Whitaker, Robyn J. *Ekphrasis, Vision, and Persuasion in the Book of Revelation*. WUNT 2/410. Tübingen: Mohr Siebeck, 2015.
Wilken, Robert Louis. *John Chrysostom and the Jews: Rhetoric and Reality in the Late Fourth Century*. Berkeley: University of California Press, 1983.
Wittgenstein, Ludwig. *Philosophical Investigations*. Translated by G. E. M. Anscombe. Oxford: Blackwell, 1958.
Wrede, William. "The Task and Methods of 'New Testament Theology.'" Pages 68–116 in *The Nature of New Testament Theology*. Edited by Robert Morgan. London: SCM, 1973.
Wright, William M., IV. "Inspired Scripture as a Sacramental Vehicle of Divine Presence in the Gospel of John and Dei Verbum." *Nova et Vetera* [English edition] 13 (2015): 155–80.

Zimmerman, Ruben. "The Narrative Hermeneutics of John 11: Learning with Lazarus How to Understand Death, Life, and Resurrection." Pages 75–101 in *The Resurrection of Jesus in the Gospel of John*. Edited by Craig R. Koester and Reimund Bieringer. WUNT 222. Tübingen: Mohr Siebeck, 2008.

Contributors

Yoshimi Azuma, Associate Professor of New Testament, Kwansei Gakuin University

Teresa Fry Brown, Bandy Professor of Preaching, Candler School of Theology, Emory University

Patrick Gray, Professor of Religious Studies, Rhodes College

Lynn R. Huber, Maude Sharpe Powell Professor of Religion, Elon University

Susan E. Hylen, Associate Professor of New Testament, Candler School of Theology, Emory University

Karoline M. Lewis, Marbury E. Anderson Chair of Biblical Preaching, Luther Seminary

Thomas G. Long, Bandy Professor Emeritus of Preaching, Candler School of Theology, Emory University

Veronice Miles, Associate Professor of Preaching, Wesley Theological Seminary

Vernon K. Robbins, Professor Emeritus of New Testament and Comparative Sacred Texts, Emory University

Gilberto A. Ruiz, Associate Professor of New Testament, Anselm College

Ted A. Smith, Professor of Preaching and Ethics, Almar H. Shatford Professor of Preaching and Ethics

William M. Wright IV, Professor of Catholic Studies and Theology, Duquesne University

Scripture Index

Hebrew Bible/ Old Testament

Genesis
  49:9–11   103

Exodus
  13:3–10   163–68

Psalms
  2   90, 106
  36:5–10   141–45
  45:3–4   106
  76:1–2   90

Isaiah
  6:2   115
  62:1–5   141–45

Daniel
  10:5–9   116

Pseudepigrapha

4 Ezra
  11:37–46   103
  13:9–10   107

New Testament

Matthew
  1:1   103
  27:19   60–61

Luke
  2:4   103
  3:31   103

John
  1:1–3   55
  1:3   79
  1:3–4   26
  1:10   26
  1:14   26, 128
  1:16   136
  1:18   55
  1:40–49   31
  2   27
  2:1–11   28, 141–45
  2:4   53
  2:13–19   32
  2:22   32, 76
  2:23   32
  3   119, 123–24
  3:1   119
  3:1–2   32
  3:1–15   120–25
  3:1–21   33
  3:3   27, 122
  3:4   122–23
  3:6–8   124
  3:7   27
  3:9   124
  3:10   124
  3:11   32
  3:31–36   33
  3:34   55
  4   2, 27, 138
  4–5   27
  4:4–42   20, 57, 104
  4:8   8

Scripture Index

John (cont.)

Reference	Page
4:9	97
4:10	104
4:27	2
4:27–38	3
4:31–38	8
4:38	10
4:39	33
4:42	33, 37
4:50	34
4:53	34
5:1	34
5:1–14	147–62
5:3	148
5:5	148, 151
5:6	151
5:7	153
5:16–18	34
5:18	45, 58
5:19	28
5:21	28
5:21–44	35
6	27, 66, 79–80
6:1	79
6:1–21	138
6:11	80
6:20	80
6:23	79
6:25–35	47
6:33	55
6:35	137
6:56–58	63
7	119
7–8	138
7:28–29	55
7:30	53
7:45–52	119, 125–26
7:48	125–26
7:48–49	125
7:51	125
7:53–8:11	126
8:12	126
8:20	53
9	138, 165
9:22	8–9
10	136
10:3	54
10:7	137
10:11	137
10:14	137
10:16	54
10:27	45
10:33	45, 58
10:40	22
11	21
11–12	21
11:1–3	22, 27
11:1–52	36
11:3	19
11:4	22, 26
11:7–16	27, 30
11:8	19
11:9	28
11:9–10	26
11:11	30
11:12	19, 30
11:14–15	30
11:16	30, 35
11:19	27
11:21–27	27
11:22	28
11:28	30
11:29	30
11:31	27, 30
11:33	21, 30
11:33–45	31
11:36	19, 30
11:37	30
11:40	27
11:43–44	28
11:45	30
11:47–48	36
11:50	36
11:52	10
12	21
12:1–2	36
12:2–4	36
12:4–7	37
12:11–19	37
12:13	166

12:23	53	18:38	42–43, 53, 97
12:28–30	25	18:39	38, 42
12:31–32	165	19:1	42, 45, 50
12:42	38	19:1–3	51
12:42–43	119, 120–21	19:3	49
12:48–50	38	19:4	42–43
13:1–17	163–68	19:4–5	51–52
13:3	165	19:6	42–43, 46
13:12	168	19:7	45–46, 53, 58
13:34–35	163–68	19:7–8	40
14	13	19:8	41, 45, 50, 60, 63
14:1–12	60	19:8–9	55
14:2	13	19:9	59
14:6	54, 97	19:9–10	58
14:6–7	13	19:9–11	41, 51, 53
14:12	71	19:10	56
14:16	71	19:11	53, 56
14:31	12	19:12	42–43
15–16	13	19:12–16	61
15–17	12	19:14	43
15:1	137	19:15	43
15:1–10	63	19:15–16	43
15:5	137	19:16	53
15:6	63	19:16–17	52
16:2	9	19:19–22	38
16:27–28	55	19:38–42	119, 126–27
17:1	53	19:41–42	69
17:1–5	68	19:42	69
17:6	79	20	74, 77
18	136	20–21	66–68, 75, 81
18:1	12	20:1	69, 79
18:1–21:25	68	20:1–18	68, 73
18:6	50	20:2	69
18:12	48, 137	20:3–4	70
18:13	49	20:4	69
18:24	49	20:4–5	70
18:28	49	20:5	69
18:28–19:16	39, 41, 47–48, 50, 53	20:6–7	69
18:33	54	20:7	70
18:33–38	41, 59	20:8	70, 75
18:34	51	20:8–9	76
18:35	48, 54	20:9	75–76
18:36	51, 53–54, 56	20:11	70, 79
18:36–37	58	20:11–18	71–72
18:37	51, 54, 56	20:12	70

John (cont.)		1:10–12	99
20:13	70	1:12–20	99
20:14	70–71, 79	1:14	102
20:15	70–71	1:16	135
20:17	72, 77	2–3	99, 103
20:18	71, 75, 81	2:1–11	106, 135
20:19	71–72, 74–75, 81	2:7	103
20:19–20	75	2:10	99
20:19–23	69, 73, 74	2:11	103
20:19–29	68, 71–73	2:17	103
20:20	73	2:26	103
20:21	74	2:26–27	90
20:22	77	3:3	132
20:24–29	69	3:5	103
20:25	73	3:12	103
20:27	73	3:14	105
20:28	74	3:16	132
20:30	77	3:21	103
20:30–31	46, 65, 68, 75–76, 78	4–5	102
20:31	77	4:1	99, 101
21	79, 81	4:1–5:14	87
21:1–23	68–69, 74–75	4:2	101
21:1–25	79	4:46–54	106
21:7	79	5	135
21:7–8	79	5:1	102
21:13	80	5:1–6	104
21:21	79	5:1–46	106, 136
21:24	8	5:2	102
21:24–25	75, 78	5:5	101–3
21:25	78	5:5–6	93
		5:6	88, 103, 107
1 Corinthians		5:6–10	91
1:23–24	94	5:8–10	91
15	21	5:9–14	102
		5:11–14	106
Hebrews		6:1–14	135
9:14	90	6:1–8:5	87
12:22–24	90	6:2	101
		6:5	101
Revelation		6:8	101
1:1	94, 98	6:14	90
1:3	101	6:15–17	90
1:5	104, 106–7	6:15–21	135
1:9	101	6:17	89
1:10	135	6:22–71	135

7:1	89	15:3	91
7:9	89, 101	15:3–4	91, 102
7:10–12	102	15:38	135
7:11–12	91	16:16	90
7:14	93	16:20	91
7:17	106	17	91, 104
8:6–11:19	87	17:1–2	100
8:8–9	90	17:7–8	100
9:1–10:21	135	17:9	91
9:13–15	100	17:14	104
9:32	136	19	105
10:10	135	19:1–8	102
11:1–44	135–36	19:2	106
11:17–18	102	19:7	105
12	135	19:9–10	100
12:1–6	84	19:11	101, 105
12:1–17	87	19:11–21	105
12:3	101	19:13	107
12:5	106	19:15	106
12:6	84	19:16	106
12:18–13:18	87	19:19	106
13	89	19:21	106
13:3	88	21	136
13:6–7	89	21:1–6	169–73
13:8	88		
13:11	88		
13:14	88		
13:16–17	89		
13:17	92		
13:18	89		
14	91		
14:1	88, 90, 101		
14:1–5	86–87, 89, 91–92		
14:2	91		
14:3	91		
14:4	103		
14:5	90		
14:6–16:21	87		
14:7	90		
14:9–11	92		
14:14	101		
14:16	131		
14:19–20	106		
15–16	91		
15:2	91		

Modern Authors Index

Ajer, Peter Claver	62	Conway, Colleen M.	54–55, 58–59, 61
Allen, Pauline	120	Counet, Patrick Chatelion	78
Alter, Robert	94	Culpepper, R. Alan	6, 67, 119, 129, 131, 139
Anatolios, Khaled	115		
Anderson, Paul N.	131	D'Angelo, Mary Rose	72
Ashton, John	20, 25, 33, 65	Dewailly, Louis-Marie	56
Attridge, Harold W.	72	Dewey, Joanna	97
Aune, David E.	84–85	Dimitrova, Nora	105
Ayres, Lewis	114	Dodd, C. H.	59
Barrett, C. K.	3, 33, 41, 55, 80	Donahue, John R.	61, 74
Barron, Robert	115	Duke, Paul D.	53, 59
Bauckham, Richard	85, 91	Eldredge, Laurence	11
Baur, Chrysostomus	120	Empson, William	86
Beale, Gregory K.	98	Engberg-Pedersen, Troels	20–21, 24, 28, 35
Bennema, Cornelis	44–45, 54, 59		
Beutler, Johannes	42–43, 55, 59	Fauconnier, Gilles	23
Biguzzi, Giancarlo	100	Fiorenza, Elisabeth Schüssler	85
Bland, David	132	Fleer, David	132
Blount, Brian	107	Fortna, Robert T.	2
Boer, Martinus C. de	46, 53	Frey, Jörg	3–5, 7
Boersma, Hans	112	Gaventa, Beverly Roberts	67
Bond, Helen K.	42–44, 50, 54–55, 58–59	Giblin, Charles Homer	49, 55
		Glancy, Jennifer A.	45, 51, 53
Boring, M. Eugene	84, 107	Gombrich, E.H.	93
Brown, Raymond E.	3, 41–43, 48–49, 53–55, 58–59, 61, 67, 77	Haenchen, Ernst	41, 43, 55, 56
		Hasitschka, Martin	78–79
Brown, Sherri	42	Haws, Molly	73
Bultmann, Rudolf	1, 3, 41, 48, 67, 73, 96	Hill, Robert	112, 116
Caird, G. B.	84	Hoskyns, Edwyn Clement	3
Carey, Greg	85, 92	Huber, Lynn R.	6, 98, 100
Carter, Warren	43–44, 46, 49–50, 58–59, 62–63	Hylen, Susan E.	6, 20, 30, 32–33, 80, 84, 107–8, 119
Cassidy, Richard J.	45, 62	Johns, Loren L.	99, 101
Charles, R. H.	89	Juel, Donald H.	140
Childers, Jana	133	Käsemann, Ernst	1

Keener, Craig S.	59	Richey, Lance Byron	40, 61–62
Kelly, J. N. D.	114, 121	Ridderbos, Herman N.	42
Klauck, Hans-Josef	61	Robbins, Vernon K.	23, 27
Koester, Craig R.	6, 89, 103, 105, 107	Rowland, Christopher	89
Kovacs, Judith	89	Rylaarsdam, David	112–14, 116–17, 120–21, 124
Kysar, Robert D.	61, 133	Sandys-Wunsch, John	11
La Potterie, Ignace de	48–49	Schnackenburg, Rudolf	41–42, 54–56, 58–59, 67
Lanham, Richard A.	9	Schneiders, Sandra M.	74
Laws, Sophie	86	Schnelle, Udo	71
Lewis, C. S.	92	Segovia, Fernando F.	62, 68
Lewis, Karoline M.	6	Sinos, Rebecca H.	98
Liew, Tat-siong Benny	80	Slater, Thomas	101
Lindars, Barnabas	55	Smith, D. Moody	33, 42
Long, Thomas G.	136	Sokolowski, Robert	115
Lunceford, J. E.	88	Stibbe, Mark W. G.	42
Maier, Harry O.	85	Stovell, Beth M.	46, 50, 54, 60
Margerie, Bertrand de	112, 114, 116–17, 120	Talbert, Charles	67
Marriner, K. T.	84	Thatcher, Tom	41, 44, 46, 53, 60, 62–63
Martin, Clarice J.	100	Thomas, R.L.	85
Martyn, J. Louis	61	Thompson, Marianne Meye	42, 45, 53, 55, 60
Mayer, Wendy	120	Tolmie, D. Francois	41, 54, 55, 58
McDonnell, Myles	105	Tuckett, Christopher M.	42, 44, 54
McGing, Brian C.	44	Turner, Mark	23
Meeks, Wayne A.	61	Varebeke, A. Janssens de	49
Merton, Thomas	144	Visotzky, Burton L.	62
Michie, Donald	97	Webster, Jane S.	80
Moloney, Francis J.	3, 49, 53–54, 56, 67, 76	Westcott, B. F.	49
Moore, Stephen D.	40, 44–46, 50, 62, 103	Whitaker, Robyn J.	101
Neyrey, Jerome H.	19, 33	Wilken, Robert Louis	120–21
Oakley, John Howard	98	Wittgenstein, Ludwig	93
O'Day, Gail R.	1–3, 5, 10, 13, 15, 19–20, 33, 39–40, 44, 51, 55–57, 59, 65–66, 68, 70, 74, 77, 79–81, 94–97, 99, 101, 104, 108, 111–12, 129, 134	Wrede, William	11
		Wright, William M., IV	128
Pate, C. M.	85	Zimmerman, Ruben	28
Petterson, Christina	65, 76–79		
Quasten, Johannes	118, 120		
Reinhartz, Adele	62		
Rensberger, David	40, 42–43, 46, 53, 55, 60–62		
Reynolds, Benjamin E.	23		
Rhodes, David M.	97		

Subject Index

abundance, 80, 135–36, 143
ambiguity, 20, 25, 35, 70, 83–94, 119–20
apocalyptic, 18, 20, 23, 24–25, 27, 28, 34, 35–36
ascension, 66, 69, 71–75, 78, 80, 81
belief, 12, 19, 29, 31, 32, 33, 34, 36, 37, 38, 63, 126
Beloved Disciple, 69–70, 75–76
Caiaphas, 36
characters, characterization, 22, 40–43, 45, 60, 103, 119
conceptual blending, 21
creation 22–24, 28–30, 32–34, 38, 74, 114, 117, 141
death, 5, 9, 11, 20–22, 26, 30, 35, 37, 119
dialogue, 138–39
disciples 2–3, 8, 16, 19–20, 27, 29–32, 37, 72
divine accommodation, 112–20, 122, 125
dualism, 5
ellipsis, 69–75, 81
eschatology, 15, 28, 32, 99, 141
Eucharist, 80
fear, 40–47, 50, 53–63, 119–21, 125–27, 170–72
figurative language. *See* metaphor
glory, 22, 26–30
historical criticism, 1–3, 7–8, 11–12, 61
and history, 7–10
incarnation, 111–12, 117–20, 127–28
irony, 2, 4–6, 14, 19, 36, 39, 58, 65, 95–99, 102, 105–6, 108, 128, 134
Jesus
coming from above, 23, 25, 38

Jews, the, 42, 46–48, 51, 58, 61. *See also* Judeans
Johannine community, 9, 61
John and Judaism, 8, 14, 131. *See also* Jews, the
John the Baptist, 22, 26, 31, 33, 37, 60
Judas, 36–37, 167
Judeans, 14, 19, 27, 29–34, 36–38. *See also* Jews, the
king, 31, 55, 58–59
Lamb, 87–92, 98, 101–8
Lazarus, 19, 21–22, 26–30, 36–38, 136
life, 21–23, 26, 28–29, 35, 40, 99
light, 21, 22, 26, 29, 137
literary criticism, 2–3, 10, 12
and history, 4–7, 9–10, 13
and preaching, 15
literary unity of John, 2, 14, 67
logos, 20–23, 25–26, 28–30, 32–33, 37–38, 58, 96, 107, 118, 128
Mary Magdalene, 68–76
Mary of Bethany, 19, 22, 27–28, 30–31, 36
Martha, 19, 22, 27–28, 30, 36
metaphor, 2, 6, 20, 100, 106, 108
misunderstanding, 36, 127, 139
multiple meanings, 2, 6, 10, 12, 14–16, 129, 147
narrative
asides, 75–79, 81
as shaping meaning, 2, 65
and reader's experience/participation, 2, 14, 39, 95, 100–101, 104, 108, 111, 128

Nicodemus, 15, 32–33, 112, 119–27
Passover, 6, 21, 32, 36, 48, 104, 164–65
Peter, 69, 76
Pharisees, 37
Pilate, 14, 39–63
pneuma. *See* Spirit
preaching, 13, 14–16, 130–40
precreation, 26
repetition, 134–37
resurrection, 14, 21, 65–66, 69–71, 75, 77, 80–81
revelation, 1, 14, 16, 19, 25, 28–29, 32, 63, 65, 79, 95–98, 100–101, 108, 111–12
rhetorical criticism. *See* literary criticism
Rome, 40, 43, 53, 57, 105
Sabbath, 34
Samaritan woman 2, 8, 19–20, 33–34, 37, 97, 104, 138
signs, 12, 66, 74, 76–77, 139
Son of God, 46, 56, 58–59
source criticism, 2, 8–9, 67
Spirit, 21–22, 35, 72, 74, 124
Stoic philosophy, 21
temple, 32
testimony. *See* witness
theological claim, 11–13, 15–16, 65–66, 81
Thomas, 29–30, 73–74
witness, 25, 31, 37–38
Word of God. *See logos*

www.ingramcontent.com/pod-product-compliance
Lightning Source LLC
Chambersburg PA
CBHW030826230426
43667CB00008B/1401